THE
APPALACHIAN
TRAIL

A BIOGRAPHY

PHILIP
D'ANIERI

"Philip D'Anieri has found a new and inspiring way to tell the story of one of the American environmental movement's crowning achievements... This book throws new light on a cherished institution and enlarges our sense of what the American environmental movement can accomplish."

"In this engrossing debut, urban planning professor D'Anieri takes a breezy trek through the century-long history of the Appalachian Trail... In genial prose, D'Anieri captures the trail's majesty and its power to inspire those who ramble on it. Hikers will be captivated by the rich history, as will those in need of inspiration for their next escape."

"Written in a voice somehow both erudite and brisk, this history deepens our understanding of this most beloved belt of wild land. Every hiker of the Appalachian Mountains—or any mountains at all, really—will be fascinated by this book."

"Philip D'Anieri's tour de force fills a gap in Appalachian Trail literature that we didn't even know was there. By stringing together historical narratives so as to explore the trail's family tree, he constructs the AT as a living entity worthy of its own biography. This book should appeal as much to history buffs as it does to trail crew, thru-hikers, and other AT devotees."

"Superbly rendered biographies of the adventurers who were instrumental in conceiving, building, popularizing, and sustaining the storied Appalachian Trail... [D'Anieri's] character studies are uniformly fascinating, as readers learn far more than expected about these obsessive, sometimes cranky creators... An incisive take on an American treasure that shines with illuminating detail and insight."

The

APPALACHIAN TRAIL

A Biography

PHILIP D'ANIERI

MARINER BOOKS

Boston   New York

Select excerpts from the Myron Haliburton Avery Memorial Volume and
General Correspondence, and the Jean Stephenson Correspondence, used
by kind permission of the Appalachian Trail Conservancy Archives.

HarperCollins books may be purchased for educational, business, or
sales promotional use. For information, please email the Special Markets
Department at SPsales@harpercollins.com.

A hardcover edition of this book was published in 2021 by Houghton Mifflin
Harcourt.

FIRST MARINER BOOKS PAPERBACK EDITION PUBLISHED 2022

Designed by Chris Granniss

Library of Congress Cataloging-in-Publication Data has been applied for.
ISBN 978-0-358-69740-4

22 23 24 25 26 LSC 10 9 8 7 6 5 4 3 2 1

To Alicia

CONTENTS

THE APPALACHIAN TRAIL

INTRODUCTION

Environment is the influence upon *each* inner mind of the thing shared by *every* inner mind: it is the common layer of air which we all breathe — the filament which binds our separate lives.

— Benton MacKaye

Beginning nearly five hundred million years ago, North America and Africa collided. Like two cars meeting head-on, both continents crumpled at the point of contact. Today's Appalachian highlands — the mountain ranges, foothills, ridges, and valleys stretching from Atlantic Canada to the middle of Alabama — are, in the simplest possible explanation, the result of that collision. The two land masses collided repeatedly, in successive mountain-building events that geologists call orogenies. Before humans, or dinosaurs, or any land animal of any kind existed on Earth, these collisions and others brought together the supercontinent Pangea, connecting what are now North America, South America, Africa, and parts of Europe.

It was not in any way a simple process. Millions of years of mountain building were followed by millions of years of erosion, in successive cycles, as the continents crunched together in repeated orogenic pulses — the Taconic, the Acadian, the Alleghenian — until, one day, the tide reversed. The same roiling liquid innards of Earth that had brought the continents together split them apart again. Beginning about 250 million years ago, a rift opened and widened, creating the basin of the Atlantic Ocean, pushing North America west in a process that continues to this day. No longer on the colliding, mountain-building side of the continent (the younger, western mountains have taken over that role), the Appalachians continue their evolution in slightly less dramatic fashion.

This development of the Appalachians over eons demands of our faculties a timescale we can barely make sense of. "If geologic time could somehow be seen in the perspective of human time," John McPhee writes,

> sea level would be rising and falling hundreds of feet, ice would come pouring over continents and as quickly go away. Yucatans and Floridas would be under the sun one moment and underwater the next, oceans would swing open like doors, mountains would grow like clouds and come down like melting sherbet, continents would crawl like amoebae, rivers would arrive and disappear like rainstreaks down an umbrella, lakes would go away like puddles after rain, and volcanoes would light the earth as if it were a garden full of fireflies.

It's hard not to sense at some level this vastness of nature's story, the smallness of our lives in the context of its massive sweep, when we go hiking in the mountains. The feeling can be both inspiring and intimidating, a fact that was clearly brought home to me one late summer day during a hike on the Appalachian Trail in western Massachusetts. My destination was that state's highest point, Mt. Greylock, which, at just 3,500 feet, does not exactly rate in the pantheon of mountaineering. But then neither do I. More comfortable spending time in a library archive than a backcountry tent, I am a day-hiker only — five or six hours at a stretch, out and back from the comfort of a car.

This particular trip would combine town, country, and mountain, starting from the nearby community of Cheshire, one of the places where the AT jogs down a Main Street before resuming its ridgeline march from Maine to Georgia. Getting underway in the early afternoon, such that running late would mean running out of light to see with, I estimated what time the sun would set, and hoped to reach the peak with at least half my time remaining.

The trail led out of town past the local elementary school, through a cornfield, into the woods, and up a moderately steep ascent. As I walked, a pleasant sense of separation from the world settled in, the subtly altered mental state that is in my mind the main reason to go for a hike. It's not just the physical change of scenery, or even the literal change in perspective that is sometimes afforded from a lookout. It's a more figurative change in viewpoint, the hiker reduced to a world with basically two directions, forward and back. It's the adjustment of our sense of time and distance to walking scale, and the knowledge that only physical effort, rather than a press on the accelerator or a click on the screen, can change the view.

Physical effort, indeed. This trail was accomplishing a fair bit of vertical in the space of not very much horizontal. Only an hour or so into the hike, I was winded, sweating a fair bit, mildly alarmed by the first sensations of queasiness. It occurred to me, with the 20-20 hindsight that not only clarifies but embarrasses, that the total height of a mountain has very little to do with the distance and change in elevation of any particular hike. Sure, Greylock is shorter than other mountains I'd stood on top of. But how high were those starting trailheads? And how gradual was the ascent?

The situation was made worse by the fact that I had no water to drink. It was August, after all, and the moisture that was soaking through my shirt seemed to come directly from my increasingly dry mouth. This was an inexcusable oversight, an overreaction to my years of suburban fatherhood, in which every activity a kid engaged in seemed to be shadowed by a parent waving a disposable water bottle in the young one's direction. Sometimes it seemed a wonder that I had survived my own youth without a parental water source at my elbow. Those serious hikers who overnight on the trail, for days or weeks or months, they needed to think seriously about water. Schlubby old me, out for an afternoon excursion? Shrug.

Mistake.

I pressed on up the trail, my discomfort growing and confidence waning. The internal conversation cycled rapidly between "Pull yourself together, this is Massachusetts, not Tibet" and "I've made a terrible mistake." During frequent breaks I would consult the trail map and try to gauge the distance and time remaining. When there were about forty-five minutes to go before the halfway mark, the map indicated there was about that much time left to the summit. I was at the top of a lower, neighboring peak, Saddle Ball, presumably named for its position at the opposite end of a saddle shape from Greylock. Reaching the goal would mean walking the saddle down into the gap between the two summits and up to the top of Greylock. If my calculations were right, I'd barely make it in time, and have to immediately turn around to make it out of the woods before dark. A trip that was already closer to safety limits, in terms of exertion, time of day, and hydration, than was prudently advisable would be pushed even closer.

On the upside, pressing on would mean that I would get to the top, achieve the goal; I would not have to say that I failed to summit a mountain of utterly mediocre stature. Yet the remaining hike would also be just another down-and-up sequence, the kind I'd already enjoyed plenty of, the kind that AT thru-hikers endure thousands of, over and over and over again. This particular one promised to be special only because it would get me to the top of Greylock, a state's highest peak. Not world famous, but at least regionally known and frequently visited, with a touch more cachet than the chucklingly named Saddle Ball.

In the end, I decided that this was a pretty slim distinction. Only a straight line first drawn on a colonial map, separating Massachusetts from Vermont, distinguished this mountain from its higher neighbors a few miles to the north. In the context of the Taconic Range it is a part of, Greylock was really no different from Saddle Ball, one of many peaks that ascend eventually to an apex at Vermont's Mt. Equinox about 50 miles away. And the Taconics are only a part of the much larger complex of northern Appalachians, with their highest point at Mt. Washington in New Hampshire . . . which is not as tall as Mt. Mitchell, down in North Carolina. And so on. Treating these mountains like badges to acquire or experiences to own did not, at that point, seem to make a whole lot of sense. Labels, borders, lists—these are a human artifice laid on top of nature, not the thing itself. They have meaning only in the workaday world that a backwoods trail is meant to provide a break from.

I turned around and made a tired, halting descent to the trailhead, the slow, balanced lowering from one foothold to the next murder on the knees. At one point I stood up too quickly from a rest break, and the world swam. But as the trail leveled out at lower elevation, and the late-day sun broke through into hillside meadows, a sense of equanimity slowly emerged from the exhaustion. It was a physical kind of knowledge, as much as mental: the yin-yang sense that any trail or summit is, for all its specialness, at the same time meaningless. The meaning comes from outside—our heads, our society and culture. Mt. Greylock does not know or care whether I made it to its summit. One can read a lot of fiercely intelligent work on nature as a social construct, but nothing brings it home like feeling, in a visceral sense, the actual indifference of the natural world to one's own existence.

It was Henry David Thoreau who most famously proclaimed this indifference of nature to human affairs. In 1846, interrupting his two-year tenure on Walden Pond, Thoreau undertook an expedition to the top of Maine's highest peak, Mt. Katahdin. Today, Katahdin's summit is the northern terminus of the Appalachian Trail, at the center of a state park, a popular summer destination. Back then, it was deep in the wilderness, several days' upstream journey by canoe and portage.

On a blustery September morning, Thoreau separated from his small group of expedition companions and made the final ascent of Katahdin on his own. Being alone on the mountaintop, he found, was anything but comforting. Immersed in clouds, knocked around by the wind, stumbling amid rocks he could barely see, Thoreau was overwhelmed. In its purest form, he declared, nature "was vast, Titanic, and such as man never inhabits. Some part of the beholder, even some vital part, seems to escape through the loose grating of his ribs as he ascends. He is more lone than you can imagine. . . . Nature was here something savage and awful, though beautiful . . . not for him to tread on."

At some point in Thoreau's journey, he had crossed a threshold, from nature as a refreshing alternative to society, to nature as a dangerous and heartless master. For all his desire to separate from the world —first in a shack on Walden Pond, then farther away, in the remote Maine wilderness—Thoreau found there was something he did not want to leave behind: his sense of self, the realms of thought and feeling that established his humanity, which required safe surroundings and some community, however small, to share them with. Even the author of the phrase "in wildness is the preservation of the world" desired not only a pathway into nature, but a connection back to civilization as well.

It turns out this contradiction, and the search for a place that resolves it, is about as old as Western civilization. The scholar Leo Marx traced it all the way back to the first century BCE and Virgil's account of a shepherd, disenfranchised by the political powers that be, longing for a better home.

> It is a place where [the shepherd] is spared the deprivations and anxieties associated with both the city and the wilderness. Although he is free of the repressions entailed by a complex civilization, he is not prey to the violent uncertainties of nature. His mind is cultivated and his instincts are gratified. . . . He enjoys the best of both worlds — the sophisticated order of art and the simple spontaneity of nature.

Every year, the Appalachian Trail hosts hundreds of thousands of people seeking some kind of connection to nature, without abandoning their civilized selves. The vast majority of these visitors are, as I was on Greylock, out for an hour or a half-day, with a parking lot as the start and end point. For a much smaller group, multiday backpacking trips might cover the trail's extent in one national park, or one state. And a tiny percentage of Appalachian Trail users hike the entire thing in one trip, a months-long rite of passage. But even the hardest-core thru-hikers maintain ties to the wider world: they use lightweight, durable gear made of materials Thoreau could not have imagined, maintain precise locational awareness with sophisticated GPS, and take advantage of infrastructure, in town and on the trail, provided by the society around them.

To be perfectly clear: the person who nearly passed out trekking up Mt. Greylock, of all places, is not questioning the fortitude of those rare few who navigate months of mental and physical hardship to thru-hike the Appalachian Trail. The point is that even a journey of that scale and ambition is not a total separation from the modern world. It is one instance of something more universal in our retreats into nature: a productive tension between shelter and escape, freedom and abandonment.

Any place that aspires to provide such a retreat—a park, a recreational area, a 2,100-mile-long trail over the Appalachian Mountains —will reflect this tension. The places we choose, and the way we then develop and manage them, tell us a lot about what we are asking from nature, what exactly we think we are traveling toward and escaping from, where we want to strike the balance between maddening civilization on the one hand, and heartless nature on the other.

Telling the story of the Appalachian Trail, then, means telling a story of people. In each of the chapters that follow, I have tried to capture an important piece of the trail's history by profiling an individual (or two or three) whose own life made an important intersection with the development of the AT. My hope is that to the extent we can understand these individuals in the context of their own lives—their personalities, their successes and failures, the cultures they were a part of—we can gain some insight into the very human process of crafting a natural environment around ourselves.

It should be clear, therefore, what this book is not. It is not a comprehensive history of every aspect of the Appalachian Trail's development, and it is even less about the details of hiking on the trail. It is a biography: an attempt to render something essential about the life of this place by looking at how it developed over time.

Like any approach to telling an interesting story, this one has its limitations. Focusing on a handful of individuals could easily be misread as an oversimplification of the trail's history, which involves more people, events, and outside influences than this narrative tries to account for. And just as the trail's story is refracted through the separate lives of the individuals profiled, so is the accounting of their lives skewed to capture their interaction with the AT. But together, the individuals' stories and the trail's should form a useful symbiosis, and provide a unique perspective on a one-of-a-kind place. The chapter notes and bibliography will point the reader toward fuller treatment of many topics, including book-length biographies of five of the subjects profiled.

Ten out of the twelve people named in the chapter titles are men, and they are all white, which roughly captures the makeup of the broader cast of characters in the trail's development over the years. As the body of the text makes clear, the invention, construction, and protection of the AT was a project firmly grounded in America's white middle class, responsive to its needs and reflective of its worldview. In this respect, unfortunately, the AT is an accurate representative of much of American environmental history, full of the presumption that one privileged slice of society could make its own needs the nation's, and that its own version of nature was the only authentic one. My goal here is to describe the world of ideas that built the AT over the twentieth century, and in fact that was a very monochromatic world.

A final caveat: I am an outsider to the AT community, a proud and increasingly diverse collection of people who over a hundred years have made the trail into what it is. They are trail builders, donors, citizen scientists, and organizers who volunteer the thousands of hours each year to make this project work. And they are the serious hikers whose identity with the AT has been won through their dogged use of the trail on hikes of all manner and description. They would tell (and have told) their own stories in their own way. But I hope that bringing an outsider's perspective to the trail's history can make a welcome contribution to that body of understanding, and capture for a wider audience the special window onto American nature that the Appalachian Trail provides.

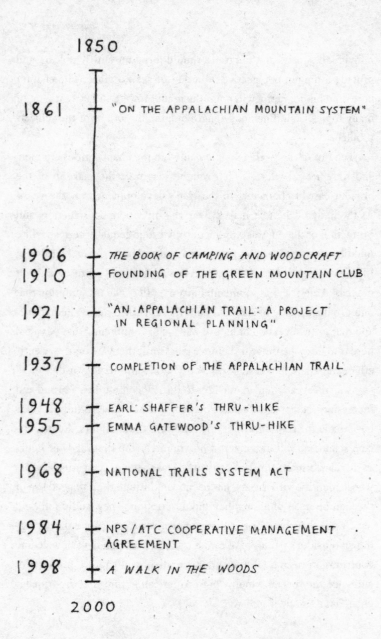

1850

1861 — "ON THE APPALACHIAN MOUNTAIN SYSTEM"

1906 — *THE BOOK OF CAMPING AND WOODCRAFT*
1910 — FOUNDING OF THE GREEN MOUNTAIN CLUB

1921 — "AN APPALACHIAN TRAIL: A PROJECT
        IN REGIONAL PLANNING"

1937 — COMPLETION OF THE APPALACHIAN TRAIL

1948 — EARL SHAFFER'S THRU-HIKE
1955 — EMMA GATEWOOD'S THRU-HIKE

1968 — NATIONAL TRAILS SYSTEM ACT

1984 — NPS/ATC COOPERATIVE MANAGEMENT
        AGREEMENT
1998 — *A WALK IN THE WOODS*

2000

Significant events from each chapter of this book.

1

The Appalachians: Arnold Guyot

//

The tree of Science, which bears the noblest fruits, is placed high up on precipitous rocks. It holds out to our view these precious fruits from afar. Happy is he who by his efforts may pluck one of them, even were it the humblest.

—Arnold Guyot

The Appalachian Mountains are, in a sense, less than two hundred years old. Geologically, of course, their age is measured in millennia. But as a place that registers in the European-American consciousness as a singular feature, with one name encompassing its full extent, the Appalachians are largely a product of the nineteenth century. More than any other single person, it was an immigrant Swiss scientist, Arnold Guyot, who literally put the Appalachians on the map.

The key to his accomplishment was a new worldview, just emerging in the rarefied air of Europe's intellectual elites, that imagined the whole of Creation as a vast, interwoven tapestry. With this new perspective, and the ambition of a tireless Guyot, a scattered collection of

11

unexplored mountain wastelands coalesced into the defining natural feature of the eastern half of the United States.

At the heart of Guyot's work were two ambitions: scientific rigor and spiritual appreciation. To him the mountains were both structures to be measured and gifts to be revered, the two approaches blended together in what seemed to be a near-perfect symbiosis. As the science developed over Guyot's lifetime, however, it produced inconvenient truths that disrupted this deeply longed-for harmony.

For Guyot, as for those who would later build and hike a trail along the Appalachians he so deeply appreciated, making the mountains the home of an imagined idyll would prove as problematic as it was inspiring.

Guyot was born in Switzerland's Jura Mountains in 1807, near the small lakeside city of Neuchatel. From his home the young Guyot could stand with his back to the Juras, look across Lake Neuchatel over the Swiss Plateau on the other side, and see the massive Swiss Alps rising in the distance. The young boy developed a keen interest in nature, exploring the woods when he could, collecting plants and insects, but only after attending to his formal studies in subjects such as theology and Latin. An intense young man, from a proudly Protestant family, Guyot looked forward to life as a minister.

When he was eighteen, Guyot spent a summer at the home of some wealthy family friends in Germany. Karl Braun, the head of the household, was an avid student of nature, and his son, twenty-year-old Alexander, was already a published scientist. That summer the Braun mansion played host to Alexander and his friends from university, and they welcomed Guyot into their circle.

Together they pored over the elder Braun's specimen collections, made expeditions into the surrounding forest, and "discussed at length with youthful ardor and audacity the theories suggested by the facts

A late-nineteenth-century postcard shows the city of Neuchatel and the Alps across the lake beyond.

observed," Guyot later recalled. "My remembrances of these few months of alternate work and play, attended by so much real progress, are among the most delightful of my younger days."

Still, the young man felt committed to a life in the pulpit. He headed to the University of Berlin in 1829, at the age of twenty-two, to study theology, and immediately fell into his childhood routine: serious commitment to his formal course of study, but with every free minute devoted to natural science. Only now, instead of wandering on his own through the woods, he had access to some of the leading scientists in the world.

The greatest of them all was Alexander von Humboldt—global explorer, philosopher of nature, intellectual celebrity, and founder of the field we now call ecology. Humboldt's fame rested on the incredible journey he had made to the New World in the first years of the 1800s. Making stops in South, Central, and North America over the course of five years, Humboldt built an encyclopedic account of virtually everything he encountered — plants, animals, mountains, the weather. And then he boldly created some of the first theories about how all of these phenomena fit together. Essential concepts that we now take for granted — changes in elevation yield predictable changes in plant and animal life; ocean currents and land features influence weather patterns — were first articulated by Humboldt.

In Berlin, Guyot met with Humboldt, the two of them strolling through the great man's collections at the botanical garden, and the pious young man was introduced to a story of Creation infinitely richer than the one he had grown up with. In the conventional understanding, God had made everything under the sun and arranged it all in its proper order; the task of the scientist was simply to record His work. But Humboldt saw a far more dynamic process at work, a drama of larger forces interacting over time — weather, water, topography. God was still in charge, but His plan was fantastically more complex. Nature was not a list, it was a story.

Guyot committed himself to learning and telling that story. He would study to be a scientist, not a theologian, but to him this was only a shift in the emphasis and style of his studies, a different approach to the same overall ambition of understanding, and therefore revering, God's great works. He began studying under a colleague of Humboldt's, Carl Ritter, in a new field that promised to unify all of the Humboldtian bits of knowledge from around the world into a single, definitive understanding of Earth as a whole. Geography would provide an intellectual home to Guyot for the rest of his life. Five years after arriving in Berlin, he completed a dissertation on the classification of lakes, and began looking for work.

In this era long before research universities paid the bills for scientists, the freshly minted doctor of philosophy found work where he could: as a live-in tutor to the children of a French nobleman. He was left to pursue his research on the side, but still managed to be quite productive. On a trip to Italy with his employers, he went to the top of the Leaning Tower of Pisa to make his first-ever measurement of elevation with a barometer.

Guyot's scientific career took a critical turn when he was visited in Paris, in 1838, by an old friend. Louis Agassiz was one of the aspiring naturalists with whom Guyot had shared his eye-opening summer at the Braun mansion in Germany more than ten years earlier. The same age as Guyot, thirty-one, and from the same region in Switzerland, the fiercely ambitious Agassiz was by far the more prominent of the two young scientists. Agassiz had begun his university studies at an earlier age and published his first book while Guyot was still thinking about the ministry. While Guyot had enjoyed his time as a student under Humboldt in Berlin, Agassiz had over time established himself as the great man's protégé, supported by him not just intellectually but financially.

When he came to visit Guyot, Agassiz was establishing his reputation as the discoverer of an ice age that had once covered wide swaths of the planet in glaciers. Agassiz was adept at attracting other young scientists into his orbit, and after the two met, Guyot immediately began investigating the behavior of glaciers. The following year he moved back to Neuchatel, where a new university was taking shape under Agassiz's direction.

Guyot taught geography and history at the Neuchatel Academy during the school year. In the summers, he tried to unlock the mystery of long-ago glacial activity by investigating the "erratic" boulders he found strewn between the Juras of Neuchatel and the distant Alps. These boulders were erratic because they did not match up with the other rocks around them. In their makeup, they were consistent with rock formations in the Alps, yet they were deposited dozens of miles away. Could they have made the journey on a glacier? Answering that question would require methodically piecing together a picture of the erratics' distribution, and matching that up with the behavior of glaciers that Agassiz and his colleagues were deciphering in the high Alps.

Anticipating his later work in the Appalachians, Guyot's research demanded both hard labor and keen scientific insight, played out over a period of several years. While Agassiz worked at the center of a collegial group each summer in an encampment on the Aar Glacier, Guyot worked alone. "I devoted, absolutely single handed, seven laborious summers, from 1840 to 1847, only giving myself, at the end of my working season, the pleasure of a visit of a few days to the lively band of friends, established on the glacier of the Aar, in order to learn the results of their doings and to communicate mine to them."

At the conclusion of all this, Guyot recalled, Agassiz was going to publish a three-volume work on glaciation, with Agassiz, Guyot, and a third scientist each authoring one of the volumes. But after Agassiz's section was published in 1847, the project stalled. In fact, by then Agassiz had sailed for the United States. His own work on glaciers was complete, and with the help of his mentor, Humboldt, Agassiz had secured funding to begin a new project, investigating the wildlife of North America. Guyot would have to find another means of publishing the results of his nearly decade-long investigation of the erratic boulders of Switzerland.

He never got the chance to do that, though. While Guyot, Agassiz, and their colleagues had been studying the Switzerland of millennia ago, its present-day residents were building a political revolution. Neuchatel at the time was a possession of the German Empire, an arrangement that the locals found intolerable amidst the democratic reforms sweeping through Europe. They were especially suspicious of the university, funded from Berlin, as an outpost of imperial rule.

In the summer of 1848, Neuchatel Academy was abruptly shut down, leaving Guyot without a professional home.

He was torn about what to do next. At forty-one years old, Guyot was responsible for a household that included his mother and two sisters, and he had no desire to leave the comforts of his hometown. Yet it was clear that he could not be a productive scientist if he stayed. Agassiz had written from America, urging Guyot to join him there. In the end, it was Guyot's mother who gave him the confidence to go, with the understanding that the family would follow once he was established. "Her last sob as I took my leave went straight to my heart," Guyot recalled. "Oh! May God allow me to see her again and make her happy in her old age," he wished, as he sailed for New York in the late summer of 1848.

Guyot moved in with Agassiz in Cambridge, Massachusetts, rejoining the entourage of admirers, assistants, and rivals that Agassiz enjoyed cultivating around himself. Guyot had always maintained a healthy distance from the drama of Agassiz's innermost circle—working all those summers alone among the erratics—but presumably at this point he welcomed the sense of home that the group provided.

Just days after Guyot arrived, he and Agassiz traveled to Philadelphia to attend the inaugural meeting of what would become one of the most prestigious scientific institutions in the world, the American Association for the Advancement of Science. The two Europeans had a certain celebrity among their American colleagues, because the state of the scientific art was far more advanced across the Atlantic; the Philadelphia meeting was the start of an attempt to grow America's fledgling scientific community into a more robust, European-style profession. Guyot became a founding member of the AAAS, two weeks after first setting foot on American soil.

After the conference, he headed west, to the mountains of Pennsylvania. Two hundred miles inland from Philadelphia, he got his first glimpse of the landscape on which he would build his American reputation. Stretching from the northeast corner of the continent almost to the Gulf of Mexico, the mountains we now call the Appalachians would provide him with the ideal scientific opportunity. In an America that barely saw beyond the edges of its farm fields, the mountains buried deep in the forest were like the surface of the moon: plainly visible, but impossibly distant. Guyot aimed to travel that distance and, as he had in the Alps, tell the mountains' story from the inside.

Entering the wilderness was not just an unusual thing to do in early America—economically useless, physically dangerous—it was morally suspect as well. Popular thinking held that the farther away people traveled from Christian civilization, the more they opened their inner selves to the heathen nature of the dark woods. It made no sense at all to plunge into the wild on its own terms; there was nothing to gain, and everything to lose.

Guyot, of course, had a very different story to tell. For the theological scientist, there was no contradiction between the civilized world and the natural one. The two were simply higher and lower tiers in a layered universe of God's design. Guyot could find the deity in the boulders on a mountain as readily as in the stones of a cathedral, and for years in Neuchatel he had been regaling his students with an account of natural history that was equal parts science and Christianity.

Returning to Cambridge after his brief investigation of the mountains, Guyot prepared to tell this story to a new audience. He was invited to give a series of public lectures in Boston by the prestigious Lowell Institute, and the result was a cultural sensation. Over several days, Guyot provided a tour de force of knowledge and insight, ex-

plaining the entirety of the world's physical form and its human set-
tlements in a way that was both confidently scientific and reassuringly
Christian.

"Geography ought to be something different from a mere description," Guyot told the audience that first wintry night in Boston.
"It should not only describe, it should compare, it should interpret,
it should rise to the how and wherefore of the phenomena which it
describes. . . . It must endeavor to seize those incessant mutual actions
of the different portions of physical nature upon each other . . . the
perpetual play of which constitutes what might be called the life of
the globe."

Guyot took the worldview that had been emerging in the work of
Humboldt, Ritter, and others—the ecological idea, for lack of a better
term—and masterfully described it for a general audience. "Science
thus comprehends the whole of created things," Guyot argued, "as a
vast harmony, all the parts of which are closely connected together," in
a plan of divine providence. "Inorganic nature is made for organized
nature, and the whole globe for man, as both are made for God, the
origin and end of all things."

Published as *The Earth and Man,* Guyot's work was an immediate
bestseller. It was translated into several languages and remained in
print a full fifty years after the original lectures.

Having established his reputation so prominently just a few
months after his arrival in America, Guyot quickly secured the work
that would allow him to pay his bills and move out of Agassiz's orbit.
He created for the newly established Smithsonian Institution a set of
procedures for weather observers around the country; he established
a first-of-its-kind network of weather stations in New York State, with
data reported by telegraph; he wrote a new geography curriculum,
with accompanying wall maps, for use in the nation's schools. And he
continued to give lectures on science and religion. His industriousness

THE

EARTH AND MAN

LECTURES ON

COMPARATIVE PHYSICAL GEOGRAPHY,

IN ITS

RELATION TO THE HISTORY OF MANKIND.

BY

ARNOLD GUYOT,

LATE PROF. OF PHYSICAL GEOGRAPHY AND HISTORY, AT NEUCHATEL, SWITZERLAND

TRANSLATED FROM THE FRENCH, BY

C. C. FELTON,

PROFESSOR IN HARVARD UNIVERSITY.

Our Earth is a star among the stars; and should not we, who are on it, prepare
ourselves by it for the contemplation of the Universe and its Author? — CARL RITTER.

ELEVENTH THOUSAND.

BOSTON:
GOULD AND LINCOLN.
NEW YORK: SHELDON, LAMPORT, AND BLAKEMAN.
CINCINNATI: GEORGE S. BLANCHARD.
1855.

The title page of Guyot's bestseller The Earth and Man

allowed Guyot to send for his mother and sisters, who joined him in Cambridge just a year after their tearful goodbye in Neuchatel.

Well situated in middle age, Guyot might reasonably have settled into a comfortable academic career at this point. But pure science—the face-to-face discovery of nature's order—was his calling and ambition. The chain of mountains stretching from New England to the Deep South loomed before him, an obvious and irresistible challenge; he had resolved, likely before even setting foot in America, to make them his next project. At that time, America's eastern highlands did not even have a name recognized by everyone. There were plentiful local names for the Smokies, and the Cumberlands, and the Catskills, but the entire complex was rarely referred to. Sometimes the whole range was the Alleghenies, or the Appalachians, but until there was an understanding and appreciation of them as a singular feature, a label was not really necessary.

"One of my first labors, on arriving in America, in 1848, was to collect all the measurements of the Appalachian system which had then been published," Guyot later wrote. These early measurements were incomplete and inaccurate, but most troubling from Guyot's perspective, they concerned only the valleys and passes where railways and roads could be built. The internal shape and structure of the mountain range on its own terms was terra incognita. To tell this story, he would need the elevations of hundreds of peaks, nearly all of them deep in the wilderness, stretching over hundreds of miles.

The challenge of acquiring that data was clearly what attracted him to the project. True to the traditions of severe Protestantism, Guyot was fiercely driven to prove himself with more work, always setting a just-out-of-reach standard for himself. According to his biographer Leonard Jones, "the lamentations which his letters contain on the smallness of his accomplishment and his waste of time . . . produce a curious effect. One wonders just how much activity he would have found necessary to satisfy his ideal." In mapping and measuring the Appalachians, Guyot would advance the state of the scientific art; he would capture the story of a major mountain chain; and he would exert himself terrifically to do so.

Determining the height of a mountain in Guyot's time was based on the concept of atmospheric pressure. The atmosphere is the miles-high sea of gases that surrounds the planet, pulled toward the surface by the same gravity that grounds our feet to the earth. All of that gas exerts a downward pressure, like water on a tub basin. The higher one travels, the less gas there is above and the less pressure the atmosphere will exert. Other things being equal, if you can quantify the change in atmospheric pressure between two points, you can calculate their difference in height.

The concept is simple; the execution, however, was far more complicated, for the very reason that Guyot was siting all of those meteorological stations. Atmospheric pressure builds and recedes and moves around the planet; the difference in pressure between two points could well be due to a difference in the weather, not a difference in elevation. Accurate calculations required that measurements be taken at multiple points simultaneously, not just of pressure but of temperature, in order to parse out the difference in pressure for which change in elevation was the cause.

The work demanded both a deep understanding of the science involved and a hands-on mastery of the necessary tools. And that was just to measure the Leaning Tower of Pisa. To measure mountains, Guyot would have the additional requirement of executing intensely demanding hiking and climbing. There were no trails or established routes, only dead reckoning through miles of forest and underbrush.

On a typical expedition in New Hampshire's White Mountains in 1857, Guyot invited an acquaintance, a New Yorker named Hastings Grant, to join him, and Grant recorded his experience. On a Monday,

Arnold Guyot.

they hiked up the highest mountain in New England, Mt. Washington, "in a drenching rain," camped out overnight in freezing temperatures, and hiked back down on Tuesday, with the "wind blowing a hurricane." The next day they summited the smaller Mt. Willard before beginning an ascent of 4,500-foot Mt. Carrigain. After what Grant called "six hours of about the hardest tramping in the woods I was ever associated with," bushwhacking amidst swarming black flies with the help of a local guide, the party spent the night partway up the mountain. Thursday morning at six o'clock they began the final ascent. During a break, Grant wrote,

> As many as twenty-five or thirty peaks can be seen from my sitting place. We have still fourteen or fifteen hundred feet to climb and no pathway at all. Over fallen trees, through thick undergrowth we pass, and all the time climbing, climbing. But the weather is so beautiful we enjoy it much, and were it not for these awful flies, which will not allow me to write one word in peace, I should be quite happy.

They reached the peak at midday, took their measurements, descended, and emerged from the woods at six o'clock in the evening; a three-hour wagon ride later, they reached the comfort of an inn. Restored by "glorious tea," Grant wrote of the climb up Carrigain,

"Now that the expedition is all over I can look back upon it with plea-sure as a great feat accomplished; but so far as my memory serves me, I never went through more, in two days, of toil and exertion."

What was for Grant a once-in-a-lifetime trial was routine for Guyot. In the decade after his arrival in the United States, he climbed scores of mountains up and down the Appalachians, many of them more de-manding than Carrigain. In just one expedition to North Carolina in the summer of 1859, he camped out twenty nights on the highest peaks of the Smokies. It was in these southern mountains that the going was tough-est, thanks to the dense undergrowth of rhododendron shrubs, "which form a second forest growth under the large trees, ... where their tough and interwoven stems form thickets almost absolutely impenetrable.... The only resource in such cases is the bear trail, which almost always exists along the top of each ridge, and allows a kind of narrow passage, provided the traveler consents to move along on his hands and feet."

Guyot was small and wiry, renowned for his stamina and endur-ance well into old age. Though he frequently had help in his fieldwork —from his nephew and mapmaker, Ernest Sandoz, or Agassiz's son Alexander—the one constant on every climb was the indefatigable Guyot himself. There can be no doubt it was dangerous work; the tall-est peak in the Appalachians, North Carolina's Mt. Mitchell, is named for a scientist who died in 1857 when he fell into a waterfall on the mountain during an expedition to measure its elevation.

Occasionally, Guyot had to fight to keep his spirits up amid the incessant demands. "My trip in the Smoky was a long and laborious one. Much rain, great distances," he wrote to a friend in 1859. "I wish I could once in my life travel without haste and be free to stop where I have more to learn, more to see, and see with reflection and repose. Will such a pleasure be granted to me before I die? I do not know, but I hope it will."

When Guyot reported the results of his decade-long fieldwork, he was at pains to make sure readers understood his work as a scientific accomplishment, not simply a surveying exercise. "When studying a group of mountains, my attention is far from being confined to the measurement of the elevation of the highest points," he wrote. More important to him was the geological character of the mountain range: "the physical structure, the proportion of all parts and the relative situation of the various chains composing it." His 1861 article "On the Appalachian Mountain System" revealed the mountains in three complementary ways: a written description, a table of 346 elevation measurements, and a richly detailed map.

The map, drawn by Guyot's nephew Sandoz, evokes a vivid three-dimensional reality. Typical maps of that time simply filled in the mountainous area with a uniform pattern of peaked marks, but Guyot's shows a fine-grained complex of individual summits, ridges, and valleys. It suggests the ordered irregularity of a leaf's edge, or a forest's treetops. These are the mountains as nature, fascinating and knowable, rather than vague and mysterious. Perhaps most important,

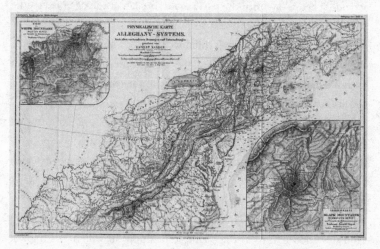

Guyot and Sandoz's map of the Appalachians

the map represents the mountain chain as the dominant feature of the eastern American landscape. In place of the familiar borders of states, the lines of railroads, or the points of cities, one sees the improbably long Appalachians rising above the land, giving shape and function to the great rivers flowing away to either side. The negative space on the map had become positive.

Guyot was fifty-four years old when his Appalachian masterwork was published, and he stood at the forefront of American science. No longer dependent on one-off projects to support his family, he had secured an endowed professorship in geography at Princeton, funded by a benefactor who admired Guyot's marriage of scientific expertise "with a winning manner and an impeccable but gentle Christianity." *The Earth and Man* was widely read and he was in high demand for public lectures. He was even called on to help the Union cause in the Civil War. The southern Appalachians were considered crucial military territory, and no one knew them as well as Guyot. He secretly prepared a report and map for the United States government that stayed locked away until the early 1900s. In 1867, at the age of sixty, he got married.

But just as Guyot's Appalachian work was coming to a conclusion, the worldview that had given it shape and meaning was coming under assault. Charles Darwin had turned up a troublesome truth that would haunt Guyot for the remainder of his days.

Both Darwin and Guyot, disciples of the great Humboldt, started from the same understanding of nature as a fantastically complex interaction of matter and energy over time, a single system in which each piece was a reflection of the larger whole. But what was the driving force behind this unitary natural history? To the Guyot of *The Earth and Man*, the answer was simple and profound: an all-knowing God designed nature as the stable foundation on which His highest creature, the human species, would thrive.

But just as Guyot had discerned glacial processes from the boulders of the Alps, Darwin observed in the finches of the Galápagos Islands a very different understanding of Earth's creatures. Competition—naked, ugly, remorseless—was the natural world's defining feature in Darwin's telling. The niches that every plant and animal filled in their respective environments were the product not of divine design but of a fight—for food, for safety, for reproductive success. Individuals lucky enough to have a small advantage over their peers would succeed, at their fellows' expense, and pass on that advantage to their offspring. Over thousands of generations of such natural selection, the world built (and was still building) its cornucopia of living things. There was no more logic or plan to their arrangement than the random opportunism of genetic mutation over time.

This was a deeply troubling challenge to Guyot's understanding of himself and the world. The same science that had provided him a path to appreciation of the divine was now pointing toward a vulgar reality, with barely any room for the Christian God. As a scientist, Guyot could not help but appreciate Darwin's work, but neither could he accept the assault it made on his theological understanding.

Guyot responded as he had throughout his career, exploring the theological heights at the same time as the terrestrial ones. With his students, he explored and mapped New York's Catskill Mountains. On his own, he worked on a Christian natural history that, he hoped, would reconcile Darwin's theory with his own theology.

The aging man was returned to the central conflict of his youth, between science and religion. For his entire adult life in the mountains, Guyot had, he thought, successfully brought them together in his work and worldview. But faced with Darwin's existential quicksand, Guyot felt his only recourse was to divide them again into different realms.

"Let us not ... ask from science the knowledge which it can never give; nor seek from the Bible the science which it does not intend to teach. Let us receive from the Bible, on trust, the fundamental truths to which human science cannot attain," he wrote. Guyot conceded the explanatory value of evolution, but he insisted it could not provide the whole story. Any process that took place on Earth required an initiating event and a trajectory that science could never fully deduce.

"The *invisible* is father of the *visible* and not the reverse," he insisted to a friend.

As he worked out these thoughts to share with the wider world, Guyot's aging body steadily declined. His last piece of work on the mountains was a map of the Catskills, presented in 1880 to a recently formed group devoted to the new pastime of hiking, the Appalachian Mountain Club. Late in 1883, he wrote to a friend, "even last year I could have told you of my seventy-six years and my ability still to climb our mountains, but unhappily it is not so now."

In early 1884, Guyot put the finishing touches on *Creation, or the Biblical Cosmogony in the Light of Modern Science.* "The marvelous unity of plan which we observe is in the mind of the Creator," he wrote, "and not a single great unconscious whole developing by itself."

A few days after sending off the final manuscript, Arnold Guyot died in Princeton, New Jersey, at the age of seventy-seven.

2

Back to Nature: Horace Kephart

I love the wilderness because there are no shams in it.

— Horace Kephart

Horace Kephart was, at various times in his life, a child of the prairies, an urbane East Coast scholar, a quiet St. Louis librarian, a drunken ne'er-do-well, and from a perch in the foothills of North Carolina's Smoky Mountains, a sage of the American outdoors.

It was in this final guise, as the "Dean of American Campers," that Kephart came to widespread public acclaim. In an early-twentieth-century America increasingly suspicious of the comforts of urban life, his guidance on campfire building and fish cleaning promised a kind of authenticity that only the backwoods could provide. Together with other writers in the back-to-nature movement, Kephart conjured an outdoor stage where those equipped with the right gear and the right expertise could establish a rugged new identity for themselves, distinct from the more banal aspects of the workaday world.

His own personal journey out of the urban wilderness to a better life in the Appalachian foothills was at the center of Kephart's identity as a writer, and he parlayed that carefully curated story into a popularity that give him considerable influence over the surrounding landscape. He was instrumental in the effort to establish Great Smoky Mountains National Park, where the Appalachian Trail would reach its greatest heights, and he played a central role in determining the route of the southernmost AT.

But if Kephart was a hero, he was almost certainly a tragic one. The personal story that he packaged for an outside audience was considerably more complicated than the mythology of going back to nature allowed for. No matter how much he wished for it, the world would not separate itself neatly into urban ills on the one hand and woodsy virtues on the other. As he understood perhaps as well as anyone, the popular image of Horace Kephart said as much about his audience as it did about him.

Kephart was born in 1862 in central Pennsylvania, not far from where Arnold Guyot made his first foray into the Appalachian system in 1848. When Horace was five, he moved with his family to a tiny town on the Iowa prairie where his father would work as a minister and teacher.

"I had no playmates," he recalled, living in a home "with little to be seen from our front door but a sea of grass waving to the horizon." He played by himself in a backyard grove, his only companion a copy of the book *Robinson Crusoe*. "I read it through and through, I don't know how many times."

As his father's career advanced, the family moved twice more, first to a small college near Cedar Rapids, Iowa, where the young Horace sat in on his father's classes, then back to Pennsylvania. As Horace entered his teen years, he wasted no time putting his parents' parochial life behind him. He graduated from a small church college when he was seventeen, "not without misgivings on the part of the faculty as to my orthodoxy," and enrolled as a senior at Boston University. He was officially pursuing studies in natural history, his father's subject, but actually "enjoying the blessed privilege of studying whatever I pleased in the Boston Public Library. The absolute academic freedom of the Library was such a relief to one who had suffered from set curriculums that I resolved to help others find it: I chose librarianship for a career."

Kephart headed to the recently founded Cornell University to study under Willard Fiske, the university's first librarian. Fiske was in many ways the opposite of Kephart's father: a scholar of languages and history, a world traveler, and an innovator in his field. At a time when most libraries were open just a few hours per day with limited access to their collections, Fiske employed assistants such as Kephart to keep the facility open for longer hours, allowing even undergraduates to make use of the materials. Kephart's life would effectively be hitched to his mentor's for the next five years.

Fiske's tenure at Cornell, however, was quickly embroiled in controversy. He sued to win half the estate of his wealthy late wife, the vast majority of which had been willed to Cornell. Fiske argued that by law, husbands and wives were entitled to no less than half of their spouse's estate. In a case that rose to the United States Supreme Court, he won. Not surprisingly, Fiske's position at Cornell became quite uncomfortable, so in 1883 he decamped to Italy, where he would spend his time and newfound riches building scholarly collections of rare books. He invited his protégé Kephart to join him in Florence. (In the end, Fiske and Cornell made peace; he donated his impressive collections and the remainder of the estate to Cornell when he died.)

Kephart spent a year in Italy, living in Fiske's Florentine villa. His job was to catalog Fiske's growing collection of the works of Petrarch, the fourteenth-century Italian poet who helped launch the Renaissance. But Kephart wasn't just squirreled away among old volumes. He learned Italian and studied anthropology in Florence, conducted research in Munich, and hiked in the Austrian Alps.

In 1886, when he was twenty-four years old, Kephart's youthful explorations came to an end. He returned to America to undertake a conventional professional life. Before leaving Ithaca, he had become engaged to Laura Mack, a young woman from a prominent local family, and they got married shortly after his return. They moved to New Haven for his new job as an assistant librarian at Yale; the couple's first child was born a year later.

Almost from the start, Kephart showed signs of restlessness with his newly domesticated circumstances. The scholarly universe that was so attractive to the young man from the hinterland apparently lost some of its luster when it became the stuff of 9-to-5 drudgery. He wrote a humorous essay for *Harper's Weekly* magazine in which he portrayed his job as being more a gatekeeper of trivia than an organizer of the world's knowledge.

> A bell rings, and in comes a troop of students. All talk at once.
> "Have you got any of Cardan's formulas?"
> "I'd like to get the latest Canadian tariff list."
> "Where can I get a traverse table?"
> "Can you give me Lord Bacon's 'New Atlantis'? I think it's a magazine article."
> "I must work up something on 'Byronism on the Continent' for tomorrow morning. Can you give a fellow a lift?"

In his spare time, Kephart began researching the history of the American frontier, and he took up shooting as a hobby. He proudly wrote to Fiske that shooting "gives me what my master's degree does not—the consciousness that I would be good for something in a crisis." After four years in New Haven, Kephart landed what would have appeared to be the perfect job, as director of one of the nation's major libraries, the St. Louis Mercantile. Organized by the business commu-

nity in the burgeoning midwestern metropolis, the library had aspirations to house the foremost research collection on the American West.
Kephart became the leader of an institution with more volumes and
more staff than the Yale library he was leaving behind, with research
interests right up his alley.

At first Kephart thrived, at least professionally, in St. Louis. He
revamped the library's staff and procedures. He grew the collection of
western Americana, publishing articles on history and library science.
"Each month he was buying as much of the material relating to the
West as the library's budget would permit," remembered his assistant,
Clarence Miller. "With all the loving labor of an artist creating a mo-
saic he added a few volumes a week in his chosen field."

But whatever restlessness had been nagging Kephart back in New
Haven did not go away with the new job. While he excelled as a cu-
rator, he quickly grew tired of his director's duties. And it wasn't only
professional life that troubled him. As his household grew to six children under the age of ten, Kephart showed steadily less interest in
family life. Regarding the chaos of a home filled with youngsters, his
daughter later wrote, "My father was not a normal man and he could
not stand it as most men do. So my mother in St. Louis became just a
buffer between husband and babies. He began to stay away from home
more or less, and to drink."

In place of both his professional and husbandly duties, Kephart
increasingly gave his attention to the outdoors: camping, hunting, and
tramping through the woods. He joined a shooting club, where Sunday
outings evolved into multiday excursions in the nearby Ozark Mountains. He read up on the best practices of roughing it, and made his
den at home into a workshop for guns and gear, strictly off-limits to
the children.

The man had come full circle. Having escaped his parents' rugged
and unadorned life, he was now trying to build a connection back to

it, or at least an idealized, weekend-getaway version of it. And he was far from alone. The path Kephart had traveled, from the rustic rural to the more comfortable urban, and his nostalgic response were things that he shared with a huge segment of the American population at the end of the nineteenth century. Even his parents were living in Dayton, Ohio, at this point.

America's discomfort with its newly urban reality was most famously captured by the historian Frederick Jackson Turner in 1893, a few years after Kephart arrived in St. Louis. In a widely discussed article, Turner decreed the closing of the American frontier, a turning point in the life of the nation. He argued that an always present "meeting point between savagery and civilization" had been the defining element in United States history. "This perennial rebirth, this fluidity of American life, this expansion westward with its new opportunities, its continuous touch with the simplicity of primitive society, furnish the forces dominating American character," he said. And it was disappearing forever.

Turner's lament was, in retrospect, just one version of a story as old as Virgil: the location of a lost ideal just over the historical horizon in a more perfect, less refined past. And as the historian William Cronon points out, it masked a pretty serious contradiction: "Frontier nostalgia became an important vehicle for expressing a peculiarly bourgeois form of anti-modernism. The very men who most benefited from urban-industrial capitalism were among those who believed they must escape its debilitating effect." Kephart's comfortable employment in a library, funded by the commercial wealth of St. Louis, put him squarely in the center of this phenomenon.

Contradictions notwithstanding, "Back to Nature" became the rallying cry of middle-class America, stoking demand for anything that provided entree to the old, rustic life. "Surrogate adventurers sought distant places with brush and camera, sending back trophy words and images for city people," according to historian Peter Schmitt. More and more, these city dwellers ventured out to try their own hand at a spell in the woods.

Kephart aspired not only to be one of these weekend campers, but to be their correspondent, learning the requirements of outdoor life and sharing them with the wider world. In the summer of 1895, he published a series of articles in *Forest and Stream*, "Notes from Camp Nessmuk," describing his experiences establishing a summer encampment for himself in the Ozarks. (Nessmuk was the pen name of an older authority on the outdoors, George Washington Sears, whose expertise Kephart depended on.) The essays gave readers both tangible advice for their own adventures, and a standard of rugged living that they could imagine themselves a part of. For example, he introduced a section on campfires with the story of two college graduates who had built a textbook fire on a cold night—but too far away from their tent to keep them warm. "The fire was all right, but somehow those campers nearly froze. So it may not be out of place to give a few details, for every season a swarm of city boys makes for the woods who never spent a night in camp." He managed to be informative and haughty at the same time, folksy but demanding.

The Nessmuk articles were a significant accomplishment for a man who had long harbored literary ambitions. They did not, though, make him any happier in his day-to-day life. He continued to distance himself from the career and family that he had seemed committed to just a few years earlier. Increasingly, the respites of camp life and alcohol—frequently overlapping with one another—crowded out his more traditional duties.

"Kephart's aura of loneliness deepened in the years 1902 and 1903," his loyal assistant Clarence Miller wrote. "His trips to the Ozarks became more frequent, and these absences soon began to alienate the library's directors." In the fall of 1903, the board of the library demanded and received Kephart's resignation. Just before Christmas, Laura took the six children permanently back to Ithaca, and began a new life raising them on her own. Before leaving, she helped settle Kephart in a rooming house in St. Louis.

On a hunting trip the following March, Kephart began to have paranoid delusions, shooting at imagined enemies through the walls of a cabin where he was staying with friends. The friends got him back to the city, but his breakdown continued. Later that week, he wrote out a suicide note while sitting at a bar, and walked toward the architectural pride of the city, the Eads Bridge over the Mississippi River, to throw himself off. The bartender notified the police, who intercepted Kephart and had him committed to a mental hospital. The attempted suicide of the former library director became front-page news in St. Louis.

Hearing of the dire straits in which her husband found himself, Laura traveled back to St. Louis, as did Kephart's parents. Together they wrapped up the sick man's affairs, Laura returned east, and the elder Kepharts brought Horace to recuperate at their home.

A few weeks later, sobered up and mentally stable in Dayton, Horace Kephart found himself at forty-one years old completely without the structures that had defined his adulthood. He had no job or means of income; he had no standing in his profession; he had no wife to take responsibility for his household. To be sure, Kephart had long resented much of what constituted his former life and was glad to be done with it. But with virtually every aspect of his adult self tossed aside, what would he do with himself?

In the retelling, Kephart would describe this process as almost accidental: he sought an unpopulated place on the map, and went there with no more plan than to live simply and rebuild his health. That is at best an incomplete account; there is plenty of evidence to indicate that he had more of a plan in mind than he later allowed.

Kephart had long aspired to be a popular writer, and in between the storms of his gradual breakdown in St. Louis, he had established a foothold in the literary marketplace. The question must have presented itself to him: If short trips to the woods yielded enough paying material for an occasional correspondent, might a full immersion in the outdoor life provide enough for a full-time writer? At this point, Kephart had nothing to lose in finding out. And for several years he had had his eye on a particular place that would serve his purposes.

"In default of any other name we shall call it Appalachian America," wrote William Goodell Frost, the president of Kentucky's Berea College, in a widely read *Atlantic Monthly* article in 1899. "In this vast inland and upland realm may be found a contemporary survival of that pioneer life which has been such a striking feature in American history." Because early settlers in the deep hollows and faraway coves were essentially cut off from progress, Frost said, Appalachia was the one-hundred-year-old past smack in the midst of the present. "It is a longer journey from northern Ohio to Kentucky than from America to Europe," he wrote, "for one day's ride brings us into the eighteenth century."

Kephart had long been intrigued by the southern mountains. Whether because of Frost's article or his own investigations, Kephart began to see in this region the long-lost American idyll. When his assistant Clarence Miller had to quit the library and travel to the mountains of eastern Tennessee on a personal matter in 1900, Kephart asked for a full report upon Miller's return (and promptly rehired him). "He was much interested in my experiences among the hill people and for the first time I felt really close to my old employer," Miller said. "[He] remarked that I had visited what was perhaps our permanent frontier."

Horace Kephart at Camp Toco.

And so in Dayton in the summer of 1904, Horace Kephart planned a new project, at once a clean break from his past and a continuation of it. He would travel to the mountains of western North Carolina, live the rustic life for a period of time, and report his findings to a paying audience. He immediately began curating his experience for outside consumption. He asked *Library Journal* to report that the traumatic, years-long dissolution of his life in St. Louis was merely a "recent illness ... much exaggerated" by the newspapers, and that he was now "entirely recovered ..., in good health and engaged in literary work."

Roughly four months after being hospitalized, Kephart arrived by train in the small riverside town of Dillsboro, North Carolina, nestled in the foothills of the Great Smoky Mountains. After a few days making arrangements, he made camp about a mile west of town, where Dick's Creek came tumbling down from the mountains and joined the Tuckasegee River.

Camp Toco, which Kephart named after a giant fish of Cherokee legend, was much the same as his Camp Nessmuk in the Ozarks of ten years earlier: a fenced-in enclosure, a walk-in tent, a cot, and even a desk. He used this initial encampment for two purposes: bolstering his collection of backwoods tidbits for a forthcoming book on camping, and scouting a more permanent location embedded among the mountain people on whom he hoped to report.

Kephart approached his work in the woods as the library scientist he was, precisely cataloging information for future reference. Instead of the works of Petrarch or settlers' accounts of western migration, he was now dealing in the physical realities of outdoor life: tent configurations, camp food, axe technique. No matter of relevance to the camper escaped his attention. The chapter he eventually wrote on clothing included sections on every item the outdoorsman would wear, from head to toe.

> DRAWERS must fit snugly in the crotch, and be not too thick, or they will chafe the wearer. They should be loose in the leg, to permit free knee action. Full-length drawers are best because they protect the knees against dirt and bruises, and safety-pins can be used to hold up the socks (garters impede circulation).

After three months gathering material from his solo encampment outside Dillsboro, Kephart made arrangements to move into a community deeper in the woods and higher in the mountains. Camping, and the practical knowledge to succeed at it, was for Kephart only a means to an end. The larger goal was finding the nebulous ideal of frontier life, where human affairs were seemingly unsullied by city ways. To get there, Kephart arranged to stay in an abandoned cabin near an idle copper mine, part of a tiny creekside settlement called Medlin.

Medlin was not a town or village, but a collection of homesteads strung along a section of Hazel Creek and the stream forks that joined it, well up in the Smokies. "A mountain settlement consists of all who get their mail at the same place," Kephart later wrote.

> Ours was made up of forty-two households (about two hun-
> dred souls) scattered over an area eight miles long by two
> wide.... All about us was the forest primeval, where roamed
> some sparse herds of cattle, razorback hogs, and the wild
> beasts.... Our settlement was a mere slash in the vast wood-
> land that encompassed it.

Still, Kephart here was living in a community, not a camp. He and
his neighbors would gather at the store for the daily (horseback) mail
delivery. Roads wide enough for wagons connected most of the inhab-
itants to one another and to the railroad. Kephart became especially
close friends with the caretaker of the mining company's property, Bob
Barnett, and his wife, Sarah. For all that he valued being alone on his
own terms, he also clearly required company. He eventually left his
cabin and moved in with the Barnetts.

At Medlin, Kephart turned his cataloger's eye to the people, the
language, and the lifeways around him. He hiked through the woods,
introduced himself to wary neighbors, and joined in the life of the
community.

In the cold of winter, he joined a party of five locals and their pack
of hunting dogs on a multiday bear hunt. Bunking in a bare-bones
mountaintop cabin as a storm howled outside, the dogs snapping at
each other while cook-fire smoke clouded the room, Kephart perhaps
wondered just what he had gotten himself into.

> "Any danger of this roost being blown off the mountain?" I
> inquired.
> "Hit's stood hyur twenty year through all the storms; I
> reckon it can stand one more night of it."
> "A man couldn't walk upright, outside the cabin," I asserted,

thinking of the St. Louis tornado, in which I had lain flat on my belly clinging to an iron post.

Notwithstanding whatever social and physical discomforts were involved, the aspiring writer persisted, and after a year's immersion in mountain life, he returned to his parents' home in Dayton with a trove of publishable material.

Over six months there in the winter of 1905–06, Kephart produced two works that would firmly establish his reputation as a writer: *The Book of Camping and Woodcraft,* a comprehensive guide built from material collected over years of study and research, and "The Mountain Moonshiner," a five-part series of articles for *Forest and Stream* magazine, based on his Smoky Mountain explorations.

Camping and Woodcraft, with its encyclopedic treatment of backwoods technique, portrayed outdoor life as a kind of spiritual practice, the pursuit of a Platonic ideal.

> A camper should know for himself how to outfit, how to select and make a camp, how to wield an axe and make proper fires, how to cook, wash, mend, how to travel without losing his course, or what to do when he has lost it; how to trail, hunt, shoot, fish, dress game, manage boat or canoe, and how to extemporize such makeshifts as may be needed in wilderness faring. And he should know these things as he does the way to his mouth. Then is he truly a woodsman, sure to do promptly the right thing at the right time, whatever befalls.

The moonshining series, meanwhile, conjured an Appalachia of peculiar people and exotic terrain intertwined in a realm of rugged authenticity. The Kephart at the center of both works was something of a renaissance man: literate and worldly, humble and competent, equally at home narrating Scottish history and chopping firewood.

The time in North Carolina, from a writing perspective, had gone as well as could have been hoped. But Kephart did not settle immediately into his new literary life. Though he would make no mention of this period in future accounts of his life, he spent four years moving from place to place. He returned to the Smokies for a spell, lived with the Barnetts in Georgia, spent time tending to his ailing father in Dayton, sought out a new library position, and even attempted a reconciliation with his family in Ithaca. But "at the first sign of the old trouble," Laura wrote, she sent him on his way.

In 1910, Kephart landed again on the southern flank of the Smokies, this time in Bryson City, North Carolina, about 20 miles down the Tuckasegee from his first stop six years earlier. In one sense, not much had changed. He was re-estranged from his family, without steady work, once more dependent on the kindness of the Barnetts.

But *Camping and Woodcraft* was finding its niche among the reading public. The material Kephart had collected in 1904–05 was selling well, and he came back for more. This time, his base of operation with the Barnetts was far up Deep Creek, which originated among the highest peaks of the Smokies and drained into the Tuckasegee near Bryson City. He returned to the same two projects, adding original material to build the *Camping and Woodcraft* compendium into two separate volumes, and gathering fresh anecdotes to turn the moonshining series into a book.

That book, *Our Southern Highlanders,* was published in 1913. Two volumes of *Camping and Woodcraft* followed in 1916 and '17. Kephart, for the first time since St. Louis, settled into a permanent life in Bryson City. He moved into a rooming house, worked out of an office overlooking the river, and continued to trek into the mountains, always gathering fresh material for articles and revisions to his two enormously popular books.

By this time, the back-to-nature movement was a dominating force in American culture. It made bestsellers of Jack London's wilderness novels and John Muir's nature essays. It sparked new consumer markets in camping gear, travel, and tourism. It launched the Boy Scouts of America, a movement so popular that for years in the early 1900s, the *Boy Scout Handbook* trailed only the Bible in annual sales. And it spawned the national park movement in the United States, dedicated to putting Americans in closer touch with their natural heritage. Congress created the National Park Service in 1916, as the widening availability of automobiles vastly increased the demand for protected, scenic land.

In this rush to embrace the outdoors, the middle-aged Kephart became a fully fledged literary giant. Revised and expanded editions of his masterworks were issued in 1921 and '22. A monthly "Roving with Kephart" column in *All Outdoors* dispensed regular pearls of wisdom, while feature articles on topics such as the history of firearms, the Cherokee Indians of North Carolina, and automotive camping showed up in a variety of national magazines. Correspondents from around the world sought his counsel and offered him praise.

From Grand Rapids, Michigan:

> Yesterday, after dipping into "Camping and Woodcraft" as I do occasionally when dead tired of all things citified, I began to wonder if you had any idea of the pleasure a city dweller, who has no opportunities for wilderness wandering, can get out of your camping books. . . . It does not take much in the way of imagination to have a perfectly splendid time.

From Birmingham, England:

> As a delighted reader of your book, "Camping and Woodcraft" may I venture to ask for help? It is not possible to obtain

"smoke tanned caribou moccasins" in this country, can you put
me in touch with a firm who can supply?

At the heart of Kephart's popularity was the legend of his own redemption. It was not just that he possessed great knowledge, or that he
presented it with a tone of spiritual reverence, but the fact that his authority stemmed from his own personal experience: escaping from the
oppressions of city life to the freedoms of the backwoods, he became
his true, best self.

> In the summer of 1904, finding that I must abandon profes-
> sional work and city life, I came to western North Carolina,
> looking for a big primitive forest where I could build up
> strength anew and indulge my lifelong fondness for hunting,
> fishing and exploring new ground. Knowing nobody who had
> ever been here, I took a topographic map and picked out on it,
> by means of the contour lines and the blank spaces showing no
> settlement, what seemed to be the wildest part of this region;
> and there I went. . . . The first three years I lived most of the
> time alone in a little log cabin . . . deep in the virgin woods.

But as Kephart's biographers George Ellison and Janet McCue
discovered in carefully reconstructing his life, Kephart embellished
considerably in constructing his own legend. His tale of arriving in
a virtually unknown corner of Appalachia seriously overstated how
much of a mystery the region was to the outside world, left out the fact
that he came as a writer hunting for material, and characterized his life
as far more solitary than it actually was.

Perhaps the most glaring omission from Kephart's story of himself
was the fact that his "health"—his euphemism for sobriety—was not,
in fact, restored. He was, by all accounts, prone to the same multiday

alcoholic binges in North Carolina as he had been in St. Louis. A close friend in his later years wrote that

> Kep was his own worst enemy. Many persons never knew when he was so low spirited whether he was drinking or doping too much — or whether the man was actually very sick and in want. A proud and talented man whose personal life problems were almost beyond solution. . . . Bryson City had little patience with the man even while they acknowledged his literary genius, and they "patronized" Kep for his erratic living while they were jealous of his literary success.

Kephart was an expert, then, not only in the backwoods life, but in the limits of its magic. His ability to conjure the backwoods ideal came not from actually living it in any complete way, but in devoting himself to its elusive possibility.

That possibility resided in a very specific place for him — the Smoky Mountains — and he began committing his fame to preserving them as a national park. Amid the political leaders from North Carolina and Tennessee, the tourism boosters from Asheville and Knoxville, and the national figures devoted to expanding the park system eastward, Kephart played a unique role in the campaign to preserve the Smokies. None of those actors had the intimate, authoritative knowledge of the mountains, especially the Carolina side, as Kephart did after twenty years of exploration. Nor did they have his literary profile, his oracle-like status as the "Dean of American Campers."

The founding of Great Smoky Mountains National Park proceeded in several stages through the 1920s, with success far from assured at each one. The National Park Service had to agree, and then convince Congress, to make the Smokies one of the first national parks in the eastern half of the country. And the funds had to be raised—

President Franklin Roosevelt dedicates Great Smoky Mountains National Park at New-found Gap, 1940. The AT passes into the forest, toward Mt. Kephart, in the upper right.

from local residents and businesses, from the two states' legislatures, and from national philanthropists—to acquire the land from its private owners, mostly lumber companies.

At the heart of the campaign was a 20-page booklet, "A National Park in the Great Smokies," written by Kephart. A national park would provide a much-needed destination for urban vacationers, he argued. It would preserve a unique feature of the American landscape; it would be a boon to North Carolina's economy. In places, he spoke of it as a pristine nature preserve, providing the spiritual blessings of the forest primeval; in others, he welcomed the prospect of busy group camps, large dining halls, and new roads crisscrossing the park. If he noticed the inherent contradictions, he made no attempt to resolve them. The goal was to save the Smokies from the lumbermen's saws, and Kephart's writing was a finely tuned, strategically minded means to that end. By 1928, the work of securing the park was essentially done. "It was a big undertaking, and beset with discouragements of all sorts; but we've won! And now congratulations are coming in from all over the U.S.," he wrote.

For Kephart, those congratulations took a rare and precious form: the naming of a mountain in the park after him. The secretary of the United States Geographic Board informed Kephart of the honor in early 1929, not quite twenty-five years after the day he had first arrived in North Carolina. "The Board seldom approves naming features for living men—for very obvious reasons—unless in unusual cases which merit the honor. In this case the Board felt the name was fully merited, due to your distinguished services to the public in connection with this peak." Kephart's response, in keeping with his humble persona, was one of quiet gratitude. But almost nothing involving Kephart was simple or straightforward, and this crowning achievement of his life would prove no different.

In fact, the board in Washington had not acted on its own initiative in the naming of Mt. Kephart. It had been lobbied to make the name change by Irving "I. K." Stearns, Kephart's close friend, admirer, and business partner in a plan to sell Kephart-branded camping gear. The request had come at a fortuitous time. The Smokies in the 1920s were still a mysterious realm, notwithstanding Arnold Guyot's earlier work. While Guyot had done his best to adopt whatever local names he could find and invent others when necessary, fifty years after his seminal article there were many features unnamed or with conflicting local names. That would have to change with the coming of the national park, and both states appointed committees—Kephart served on North Carolina's—to assign definitive names.

The appeal to name Mt. Kephart, however, happened outside of this process, and quickly sparked controversy. The peak chosen was already called Mt. Collins by many, especially on the Tennessee side of the mountains, and they loudly objected, asking the United States Geographic Board to reverse its decision. Kephart's boosters in North Carolina vowed to fight back. The board in Washington, frustrated that a decision presented to them as noncontroversial was in fact anything but, demanded that the locals sort it out. Kephart claimed to be embarrassed by the dustup, never having sought the honor in the first place, and agnostic about how it should be resolved.

He was not being honest. In an 11-page historical monograph based on his always fastidious research, Kephart fiercely defended the appropriateness of having this particular peak named for him. In addition to tracing the history of previous efforts to name the mountains, including Guyot's, he relied on personal experience. When he had returned to the Smokies to take up full-time residence in 1910, he wrote, he had stayed with his friends the Barnetts far up Deep Creek on the mountain's side. The Bryson Place, as the cabin there was known, would serve as a base camp and writing retreat for Kephart for years. In all that time, he argued, he had never heard anyone refer to the mountain by a specific name. Based on history and convention, he argued, the Mt. Kephart name should stick.

His friends and allies were torn between their desire to honor the great man and their sense that he was overreaching. In the end, they devised a solution and got his approval to name a different peak, in some respects more significant but lacking Kephart's personal connection to it, after him. That mountain, not far from the center of the national park, is visited today by thousands of day-hikers per year, who take a short excursion along a path that constituted the last significant project of Kephart's life: the Appalachian Trail.

The AT effort had been underway for several years when it came to Kephart's attention in the late 1920s. Needing southern participa-

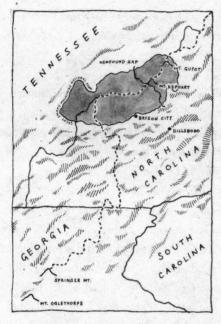

The southern Appalachian Trail.

tion, the Appalachian Trail Conference invited Kephart to serve on its national board of directors, and his close friend George Masa to organize a Carolina Appalachian Trail Club. Masa, like his mentor Kephart, was something of an exile in the region. A lone immigrant from Japan, with no family of any kind in his life, he owned a photography studio in Asheville. The two bachelors bonded on frequent camping trips together and quickly became partners in both the national park campaign and the plan for the Appalachian Trail.

Masa was tireless in his trail work, painstakingly scouting and blazing sections of trail, and leading hiking trips for Asheville enthusiasts. Kephart acted more in the role of elder statesman, but it was from that position that he helped solve one of the trail project's toughest questions in the early days: Where would it end? There were multiple plausible options for routing the trail's terminal section south of the Smokies, and in an all-volunteer effort with shaky coordination, the question of the southern route was rapidly brewing into a controversy. Kephart brought his expertise and authority to bear, lending his support to the plan that ultimately directed the trail roughly due south of the national park to its terminus on

Georgia's Mt. Oglethorpe. (Development on Oglethorpe forced a move of the southern terminus to Springer Mountain, a bit farther north, in 1958.)

In its April 1931 issue, *National Sportsman* magazine proudly introduced the first contribution from its new camping columnist. "His writing in the camping field is the most widely quoted of all authors," the editors said. "We feel that no more able man for the task is procurable."

Shortly after submitting his first column to the magazine, Kephart and a friend visiting from Georgia, the author Fiswoode Tarleton, hired a car to drive them to a moonshiner up in the hills. On the way back to Bryson City late at night, perhaps after the driver himself had sampled the liquor, their car swerved off the road, hit a low bridge abutment, and flipped. Tarleton was pinned beneath the car and Kephart was thrown 40 feet. Both were dead by the time a passing motorist discovered the wreck. Three days later, the crowd for Kephart's memorial service overflowed Bryson City's high school auditorium, and hundreds of mourners stood outside. He was sixty-eight years old.

The piece Kephart had submitted to *National Sportsman,* called "Then and Now," serves as a kind of self-eulogy. In it, he traced the explosion of interest in the outdoors that took place over the course of his lifetime. And he sang the praises of the just-emerging Appalachian Trail as the culmination of that movement.

> When I was a boy, in the old West, we often camped out, as a matter of course. But cooking in the open and sleeping under the stars were only incidental to the main business in hand, which was hunting or fishing or moving from place to place. Camping for its own sake, as a recreation or a means of rejuvenation, was a thing unheard of.

That changed, Kephart said, as an industrializing America drew more and more of its residents to the cities. In a story he knew all too well,

> The urban population was feeling the nerve-strain and bodily exhaustions that are the penalties of a hurrying, high-tensioned civilization. To ease it there came an urge to break away from it all, now and then, and get back to Mother Earth —"back to Nature," as we were fond of phrasing it. City folk were finding out that the best of all restoratives is to cruise the woods and waters, fend for ourselves, and camp out.

The beauty of the new Appalachian Trail, he said, was the fact that it would bring this opportunity of a genuine backwoods experience within the reach of millions. For only the cost of "their lunches and the shoe leather they wear out," people could leave the city for a short time, drive to the nearby AT, and reconnect themselves with the wilderness.

Concluding the piece, Kephart wondered whether he had perhaps been too enthusiastic about the AT, and promptly dismissed the notion.

> Well, why should not one be an enthusiast who, at sixty-eight, is still climbing the highest hills of the Trail Country, and sleeping out o' nights, just for the sheer enjoyment of it, although twenty-five years ago that same man could not have climbed Bunker Hill Monument without halting now and then to regain his breath? What the mountains and forests did for me they can do for other run-down folks—and then they, too, will be enthusiasts; for one just can't be stolid or despondent when his lungs are full of mountain air and his blood is coursing free.

3

The Long Trail: James P. Taylor

///

> If patriotism is love of country, it is a fair inquiry how far one can love country which he has not studied intimately, over which he has not frequently walked, upon which he has not joyously built camp fires.
>
> —James P. Taylor

When James P. Taylor arrived in Vermont as a mid-career schoolteacher in 1908, he heard about the state's long, slow decline, the farms and mill towns of colonial America growing obsolete in the Industrial Age. To many longtime locals, the decline seemed inevitable; nature had placed an irreducible burden on the state in the form of the Green Mountains. The mountain chain ran right down the center of the state, taking up land that could otherwise be profitably cultivated, and dividing the state's people in two.

Taylor had a different view of the situation, and with overpowering sincerity, he shared it with anyone who would listen. An avid hiker and skier, Taylor saw in the Green Mountains opportunities rather than limitations, an almost limitless source of economic and civic renewal. The key to it all was a trail, running over the mountains from Massachusetts to Canada, tying the mountains together into a single natural feature, open for exploration. Side trails would branch off either side, connecting the towns below to nature on high. Local clubs would each maintain their section. Shelters would provide warm and safe accommodation to visitors in all seasons. Outdoor recreation would connect the people to the landscape, and attract nature-seeking visitors from the outside world. The mountains that had been the bane of the nineteenth century would become a priceless asset to the twentieth.

His vision was a curious mix of the romantic and the commercial, yet it proved remarkably accurate; Vermont has wrangled with the paradox of these twin identities ever since. At its heart lay Taylor's Long Trail, a hiking path linking the Green Mountains together for the first time, opening them up to public appreciation and enjoyment. The trail was completed just a few years after the newly arrived outsider first proposed it; it would provide a model for—and a lengthy section of—the Appalachian Trail that would follow about a decade later.

But like its successor, the Long Trail would also excite conflicting passions about just what, and whom, the outdoors were for. To Taylor, the wonders of the mountains deserved to be experienced by as many people as possible; the people, and the society they were a part of, would be better for it. That catholic mindset did not sit well with many of his peers. Old-time Vermonters, raised according to the virtues of Yankee self-reliance, were suspicious of a strategy based on something as frivolous as "outdoor sports." And their seeming opposites in the urbane community of hikers were similarly resistant, worried that the specialness of the outdoors might be ruined by popularity. Taylor's fervent sense of possibility, which at first placed him at the forefront of the life of his adopted state, increasingly left him out of step with the times.

• • •

Taylor arrived in Vermont at the age of thirty-five, with a background that gave no inkling of the outsized role he would come to play in the life of his new home. He had lived nearly all his life in the small town of Hamilton, New York, the home of Colgate University, where his father was a math professor. James was born there in 1872, and the tiny but growing college campus, nestled in the rolling hills of central New York State, dominated the young man's life. As a child, he took private lessons from his father's colleagues, before becoming a student at Colgate's boarding school, and then enrolling at the college itself. Outside the classroom, young Jamie proofread the math texts his father authored, and worked on the campus grounds.

After college, Taylor attempted a new life away from Colgate multiple times, but he always returned. He pursued graduate studies at both Columbia and Harvard but left both programs without a degree, and returned to Colgate to become a teacher at the boarding school. For a while Taylor was apparently content, and he was well regarded as a teacher, a "most valuable man to the school," according to his principal. "His influence among the students, especially among the younger boys," was "most wholesome." But after seven years, for no reason that survives in the historical record, Taylor left his hometown for good, and without any definite plans. He talked about going back to graduate school, and secured a letter of introduction to a New York publisher, but it is not clear what he did for the year after he left Colgate.

When Taylor returned to teaching, he made a fresh start, landing the job of assistant headmaster at Vermont Academy, a boarding school in the village of Saxtons River, Vermont. He now had some administrative responsibilities, and was no longer working in the shadow of his more accomplished father. But perhaps the biggest change was in his physical surroundings. In place of the gently rolling terrain of central New York, Taylor now lived in the foothills of the Green Mountains, the lush heights looming to one side, and spilling down toward the

Connecticut River Valley on the other. From the start, he made the mountains a part of his curriculum.

Taylor viewed himself as more of a coach to his students than a teacher, charged with making them feel capable in the world around them. To that end, he took his young charges to the mountains, and urged them to go on their own. He led hikes and overnight trips, and organized a system of "degrees" to reward different accomplishments in the outdoors:

A. Making three ascents in one year, two of Ascutney and one of Monadnock, or vice-versa . . .

D. Writing accounts of trips to mountains, the accounts to consist of five thousand words . . .

X. (1st cooking degree.) Knowing how to cook flap-jacks, coffee, bacon, and hasty pudding.

Taylor described this world of outdoor exploration as being particularly beneficial to young men who weren't interested in the team sports of baseball and football that were increasingly defining the transition to manhood for a certain class of American male. "A nonathletic boy is the boy who lacks the physique, or the interest, or the desire, or the taste, or the temperament or all of these that would attract him to the games," Taylor wrote, presumably speaking from experience. Outdoor sports, on the other hand,

are by nature adapted to him and his needs

Simple

Natural

Useful

No overdoing or overdevelopment

Not competition but comradeship

Strife with nature, not with fellows

By-products are most valuable

Motives are enjoyment of the thing itself and cultural interests

In particular, Taylor liked to take his students to Mt. Ascutney, about 15 miles north of his school, where a local group of volunteers had made the peak accessible to outdoor enthusiasts. There were "a Fifth Avenue of a trail up the mountain, well-marked springs, a steel-roofed, granite-walled shelter hut on the summit," the sort of improve-ments that together made the mountain an accessible destination, and invited appreciation of its natural wonders. Ascutney, though, was an exception. Most of the Green Mountains, Taylor discovered, had very little in the way of accommodation for hikers. The trails were poorly marked, if present at all; there was no shelter from the elements. And there was nothing linking the mountains together. He and his students were frustrated after an excursion to the top of Killington Peak, the state's second highest, to discover there was no direct route to the neighboring Pico, which they could see clearly but could not reach.

Vermont had collectively turned its back on its mountains, Taylor determined, an unacceptable state of affairs. He was certain that more was possible. Just where this knowledge came from, he never explic-itly said, but it was apparently Germany's Black Forest, which he may have visited during his sabbatical year. Taylor only ever spoke ellipti-cally about his past, but friends and family remembered his traveling to Germany as a young man, and he used that country's Black Forest Association as a model for his Vermont efforts right from the start.

In the Germany of the late 1800s and early 1900s, the sense of *Hei-mat*—roughly translated as "homeland"—dominated the cultural conversation. It was an idea that took physical form in the countryside: at its most simple, access to nature was meant to provide a reminder of people's sense of belonging, a stable identity in a rapidly chang-

James P. Taylor.

ing world. The unification of Germany, in 1871, had created a new state on paper, but with little history or mythology tying itself together. At the same time—and in this regard Germany was hardly unique—old agrarian ways were being upended by the steamroller of industrial capitalism. The logic of the faraway, faceless market was erasing the contours of community life. As people struggled to understand their place in this new and different world, *Heimat* emerged as a response. Based largely on the work of a writer named Wilhelm Heinrich Riehl, *Heimat* put forward the German landscape, especially its forests, as the source of a unique and reassuring national identity. In the *Heimat* woods, Riehl said, there was an irreducible German essence, a wellspring of the nation's special virtues.

For a large number of turn-of-the-century Germans, in the middle class especially, *Heimat* became a kind of civic religion. Local beautification societies came together across the country, dedicated to forging closer connections between the community and the surrounding landscape. In the cities and towns, they built new parks and planted trees; outside of town, they cut trails through the woods and erected mountaintop observation towers. By opening up the forest for people to enjoy, Germans felt they were doing something fundamentally patriotic, providing access to the nation's natural identity. And in providing a venue for outsiders to experience and celebrate *Heimat*, they were also cultivating a welcome tourist trade. By the early 1900s, Germans were embracing enjoyment of the outdoors as a virtuous circle of naturalism, nationalism, and commerce.

James Taylor's introduction to this world apparently came on a trail, now known as the *Westweg,* that stretched more than 150 miles from town to town through the Black Forest of southwestern Germany. Then known as the *Höheweg* ("High Trail"), the path came together in pieces over the latter years of the 1800s, as small clubs in individual villages each cleared and maintained a nearby section, then joined sections together into a single long-distance trail. *Heimat* proved to be a scalable idea, stoking pride in individual communities for their nearby woods, drawing them together under the banner of the Black Forest as a whole, and encompassing the whole thing in a nation-spanning German identity.

This belief in the culturally authenticating power of place—as a people, we are as unique and steadfast as the natural landscape around us—was popping up in various places across the Western world; the Black Forest Association was hardly alone in the kind of work it was doing. But Europe, further along the path of industrialization than North America, was also further along in developing the social and physical infrastructure of nature as a counterweight to all of that industry. And so when Taylor arrived in Vermont in 1908, he had in some sense seen the future, and he would be its tireless representative in his new home.

The Vermont that Taylor encountered was a worn-out backwater of America's manifestly destined march across the continent. With the settlement of rich agricultural lands in the Midwest, and the knitting together of the country with railroads, Vermont's small Yankee farms had become increasingly obsolete. Younger generations decided their future was in the cities, and Vermont, like much of New England, was becoming a shell of its former self. Scenic tourism was beginning to emerge as an economic alternative for some places, especially in New Hampshire's majestic White Mountains, but Vermont's mountains were lower and their distance from Boston greater. The Appalachian Mountain Club, for example, founded by Massachusetts Institute of Technology faculty members in 1876, had for years been climbing in the White Mountains, while paying scant attention to the less imposing Greens.

Taylor had been a resident of Vermont for only a year when, seemingly out of nowhere, he conceived the idea to open up the Green Mountains for the public to experience, and in so doing redefine the state's sense of itself. A Green Mountain Club would pull together local clubs up and down the length of Vermont into a partnership that would blaze a trail and build adequate accommodations for hikers, making "the Vermont mountains play a larger part in the life of the people." He imagined the kind of social and political embrace of the backwoods that the Black Forest had.

Taylor's passion for the idea apparently outweighed whatever hesitation he may have felt as an outsider, and he promptly began trying to build an organization to carry forward his idea. An opportunity presented itself in his required attendance, in place of his school's headmaster, at a statewide education conference in Burlington. Encouraged by the positive reception his idea received there, Taylor began writing letters, asking sympathetic individuals to find like-minded others, and in the spring of 1910 convened the first meeting of the Green Mountain Club in Burlington.

"The Green Mountains have not been humanized," he argued in a speech drumming up support for his idea.

> Unclimbed, they have made a commonwealth of valley-dwellers, complacent and provincial. Undeveloped, they have fostered local conservatism and narrowness of interest. Unrevered, they have cultivated in us all an excess of individuality.

But a new day was at hand, and the Green Mountain Club would lead the way to a renaissance of Vermont's Revolutionary-era fighting spirit.

> The purpose of the Club is to help transform mountain curse into mountain blessing, to make the citizens of the state literally Green Mountain Boys in feeling and action.... We shall make trails, erect shelters, publish leaflets which describe and map the most important mountains.

In the future, Taylor imagined,

> Whatever else they may be, the Vermonters are mountaineers. The fastnesses of the mountains are known to boy and man, to child and grandsire, in peace and in war, in work and in play. The visitor finds every mountain hospitality: guide-book and map, road and trail, shelter and hotel. The mountains are the companions of the people, supreme blessings vouchsafed by a generous Providence.

Taylor's Vermontian *Heimat* immediately struck a chord. Political and economic leaders in the state endorsed his work and volunteers signed on to help. At first, though, Taylor got a decidedly cool reception from the leading outdoors group in New England, Boston's Appalachian Mountain Club. The AMC, composed largely of professionals and academics, modeled itself not on any Teutonic notion of homeland, but to a great extent on England's somewhat aristocratic Alpine Club, where the focus was on the social distinctions of having accomplished various ascents. Taylor, with his gushing rhetoric of civic ambition, must have seemed alien to the more exclusively climbing-oriented members of the AMC; the less daunting, more lush

Green Mountains not up to the standards of the craggy Whites. In time the two groups would find plenty of common ground, but at first the Green Mountain Club would have to be a homegrown effort.

Taylor threw himself into the work. The first summer after the GMC was formed, he traveled to Mt. Mansfield, the state's highest peak, and cut trail for two weeks. He was looking a bit worse for wear when he headed into nearby Burlington at the end of his work trip. "A little sensitive about being arrested on the streets for destitution and vagrancy," Taylor hastened to a volunteer's house to report on his progress, where he was greeted with the words "Young man, there is a bathtub upstairs."

But Taylor was a visionary much more than he was a trail worker, and his goal was to foster a movement in the people of Vermont, not simply clear a path. Leaving the backwoods labor to others, he put the bulk of his time and energy into giving speeches, attending the meetings of whatever fraternal organizations, garden clubs, and chambers of commerce he could get an audience with. His audiences were regularly enthusiastic, but polite applause did not translate into viable, local clubs as directly as he had hoped. After the first couple of years of work by Taylor and a handful of others devoting serious time to the GMC, only about 30 miles of the Long Trail had been built, all of it in the mountains closest to Burlington, out of a total of 250 miles to reach from Canada to Massachusetts. As the initial blush of enthusiasm wore off, it looked like the result of Taylor's work would in fact be a not very long trail.

In the battle between inspiring idea and everyday inertia, though, the idea eventually won out. The clinching event was Taylor's securing an agreement with Vermont's state forestry department to cut 100 miles of trail, down the heart of the state, if the GMC could raise the funds to pay the workers. Taylor cobbled together the money (including some from the AMC), and in the summer of 1913 the Long Trail was completed from Mt. Mansfield in the north, where the volunteers' work had petered out, to Killington Peak in the center of the state. The project at that point reached a critical mass; there was now a physical path in the woods to go along with the soaring rhetoric, proof that Taylor's idea wasn't just a dream.

Ironically, the state forestry section that clinched the Long Trail's viability was almost immediately abandoned. What it provided in length, it utterly lacked in scenic appeal. With an eye toward fighting forest fires and limiting the exertion required to traverse it, the state had built its trail fairly low on the mountainsides, rather than along the ridgeline. It was a right-of-way for a slog through the forest, but not the pathway to Green Mountain glory that Taylor had been giving speeches about.

Another outsider to the state, this time from New Jersey, took it upon himself to remake that portion of the trail. Will Monroe, a botanist and professor at New Jersey's teachers college in Montclair, began spending his summers at the University of Vermont just as the Long Trail effort was kicking off. With a potent mixture of passion for the outdoors and mountainous ego, Monroe organized and directed the building of an entirely new, scenically outstanding trail, over the same general territory as the uninspired forestry trail. Laura and Guy Waterman, in their definitive history of hiking in the Northeast, describe Monroe as a trail-making genius.

He painstakingly combed the ridges for spots of exceptional interest or beauty, then linked them together for his trail, so that the miles roll by in a dazzling succession of rock outcrops, mossy glades, secluded hollows, airy ledges, arching hogbacks, boulder heaps and caves with mysterious openings leading to unfathomed recesses, or exposed rock slabs commanding sweeping views of rugged mountainsides. Trail makers had found forest nooks before and climbed high ridges before, but Monroe may have been the first to combine such meticulous attention to detail with an overall skyline sweep.

Taylor's idea was now taking off under its own power. In southern Vermont, volunteers built the trail more or less on the model of the state forestry section, at first tying together whatever existing paths and logging roads they could, then once the Long Trail was a reality, going back to find better, more appealing routes. It wasn't always pretty. A writer in the *New York Times* warned her readers,

> It is your job to keep your eye peeled for the red markers of the Green Mountain Club and to trail ahead, no matter how little evidence there may be of others having gone that way before you. Here there may be a stream to ford over the rocks; here a precarious-looking rotten log across another stream; here the trail follows the bed of a stream which is dried up in mid-Summer; and, here you sink in above your ankles in swamp.

Notwithstanding its many rough patches, by 1917 the Long Trail was essentially complete, just seven years after Taylor had convened the first meeting of the Green Mountain Club.

Already, though, Taylor had moved on to his next big idea. Earlier, while the Long Trail was only half built and its completion far from guaranteed, Taylor had expanded his ambitions to take in New England as a whole. For too many people, he worried, the attractions of American nature existed only in the much celebrated open expanses of the West, in places like Yellowstone and the Grand Canyon. There were no places as big and as untouched in the long-settled Northeast. The only way, Taylor figured, to compete in the public's mind with the scale of western nature was to knit together all of New

As she approached her high school graduation in the spring of 1927, Kathleen Norris (right) of Schenectady, New York, aspired to undertake a unique adventure: hike Vermont's Long Trail from the bottom of the state to the top. Her father, with whom she had initially planned to make the journey, had died during the school year, but her gym teacher, twenty-four-year-old Hilda Kurth (center), agreed to accompany Kathleen, and recruited an acquaintance, twenty-five-year-old Catherine Robbins, to join them. Never one to pass up an opportunity for publicity, Jim Taylor put the word out to his reporter friends, and before long the women's excursion was being covered in newspapers all over the Northeast. Dubbed "The Three Musketeers," the women left Williamstown, Massachusetts, on July 25, 1927, and arrived at the Canadian border exactly a month later. Norris wrote to Taylor a few days before the end of their journey, "It is very kind of you to be so interested in our trip. We received so much discouragement at first."

England's natural assets into one big playground. The key was linking up what already existed—especially the GMC's Vermont trails with the AMC trails in New Hampshire's White Mountains—and then expanding outward. The AMC, which had been building and linking together trails years before Taylor even arrived in Vermont, welcomed his organizational energy, and the New England Trail Conference was born.

The group held its first official meeting in Boston in late 1916, to begin thinking through the possibilities of a connected series of trails traversing the New England mountains, from New York to Quebec and Maine. A then-obscure forester named Benton MacKaye took note of and supported the group's work, and began to think even more ambitiously about the possibilities of linking up natural corridors. It would be another five years before MacKaye formally proposed an Appalachian Trail, but as he readily acknowledged, the seeds were initially sown by the NETC's work.

Organizing, Taylor realized, was his life's work. He abandoned the teaching profession that had defined his early adulthood, and devoted himself full-time to creating a better future for his adopted home. He moved to Burlington, where he worked as the sole staff member of Vermont's Chamber of Commerce. In the years that followed, Taylor created roadside beautification campaigns, and promoted winter sports and Vermont as their ideal home. He held meetings, traveled to meetings, wrote letters following up meetings, and set up more meetings. One newspaper noted that Taylor "pestered the life out of anyone whose soul needed saving for the cause of a better Vermont."

It was a life that, for all of its contact with others, could be quite lonesome. Taylor never married or had any female companionship in his life that survives in the historical record, though some correspondence hints at furtive intimacy with men, something that in that time and place would have had to be utterly concealed. As Horace Kephart was doing at the same time down in North Carolina, Taylor lived on his own in a rented room. Outdoor outings provided a significant source of fellowship, and he was a frequent guest at the family home of his friend Clarence Cowles, whose children fondly remembered their honorary uncle joining them for holidays, and singing along with their mother's piano playing.

Taylor thought of himself at least in part as a writer—in fact one friend urged him to quit wasting his talent on mere tourism promotion and instead devote himself to writing full-time. The closest he came was publishing a pamphlet of essays celebrating the Vermont winter.

> Summer evenings give no such vivid contrasts as the brilliant white of the winter foreground against the black mass of the foothills, black as ink in the moonlight; summer evenings give no such ethereal hues as the soft grey of the distant mountains, softer and softer as they recede, till at the horizon the grey mists melt into the blue.

Though Taylor fairly quickly left the day-to-day work of the GMC behind, he had not lost interest in the Long Trail or hiking in general. Quite the contrary. It was just that Taylor's notion of trail building concerned networks of people—organizations, events, initiatives—more than it did blazes, hatchets, and switchbacks. Laura and Guy Waterman characterize Taylor, with his fondness for promotion, as something of an impostor in the outdoors, the "supersalesman trailsman" who doesn't quite measure up to the men and women who spent more time roughing it. But Taylor was no less committed to the promise of hiking because his talents and interest lay in scheming ways to make it more popular and accessible. For those who thought of the mountains as an escape, Taylor's boosterism could be troublesome, a blurring of the line between shiny city life and the rustic virtues of nature. That was a distinction he did not wish to draw. To put the mountains at the center of Vermont's, and later New England's, life was not a despoiling of the mountains, in his mind, but an enriching of society as a whole. His approach was at its heart inclusive and expansive, rather than exclusive and distinctive.

Taylor carried on in this vein, from his perch at the Vermont Chamber of Commerce in Burlington, for the remainder of his adult life, certain that a progressive embrace of the land—good roads, good government, a seamless connection between town and country—would lead the way to a brighter future. His vision seemed on the cusp of its fullest realization when, in 1933, a prominent Vermonter put forward an idea as bold as the Long Trail had once been. William J. Wilgus, a civil engineer famous for designing New York's Grand Central Terminal, proposed a Green Mountain Parkway that would run the length of Vermont, opening up the mountains to tourists in cars the same way the Long Trail had opened it to them on foot. The parkway would form the spine of a national park, protecting from development a roughly 10-mile-wide corridor on either side of the ridgeline. (Virginia's Shenandoah National Park had just recently been established in roughly the same manner.)

The threat that roads posed to trails would soon become a flashpoint in the development of the Appalachian Trail (Chapters 4 and 5), but Taylor loved the parkway idea. The Green Mountains' beauty would be preserved and made accessible; tourist dollars and federal investment would boost the state's economy; and the destiny of Vermont and its mountains would be fully integrated in the way he had first imagined as a brash outsider some twenty-five years earlier. Wilgus, with his national reputation and connections, became something of a hero to Taylor, and the two men worked closely together to rally support for the plan.

The National Park Service was willing to build the road and establish a national park, provided Vermont could raise its share of the funds in a bond proposal. A large fraction of the state's political and business establishment supported the effort, but there was also significant resistance. In a Republican state proud of its reputation for independence, a major intrusion from Franklin Roosevelt's New Deal was, for many, simply unacceptable, the loss of a huge swath of state territory to federal control. And to a substantial portion of the outdoors community, including in the end the very Green Mountain Club that Taylor had founded, a roadway through the mountains intruded too much on the natural seclusion such a landscape was meant to provide. Unfortunately for the parkway's backers, making concessions to one of these groups would only strengthen the other. When Taylor's campaign played up the wide corridor that would be protected, it seemed to justify the fears of the conservative skeptics. If, however, supporters talked about it as simply a road project, then the preservationists would rightfully see only an invasion of cars, rather than the conservation of mountain land.

To Taylor's increasing frustration, the naysayers steadily weakened public support for the plan, and it was handily defeated in a statewide vote in 1936. He was mystified and angry, unable to come to terms with "the mysterious psychology of Vermont," his fellow citizens' refusal to embrace his vision "a pathological case" of ignorance and closed-mindedness.

Still, Taylor pressed on with his vision for a better Vermont. It was all that he knew. He became especially concerned with the state's waters and the need to clean them up. The streams and rivers that came tumbling down with crystal clarity from the Green Mountains were being soiled with the waste of its farms and the untreated sewage of its towns. Decades before the explosion of the American environmental movement, Taylor anticipated the importance of clean water, and

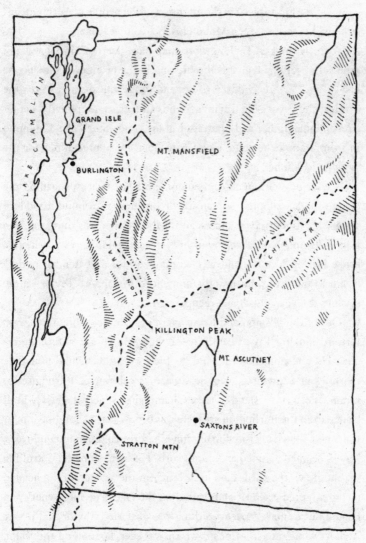

The Long Trail and Appalachian Trail in Vermont.

campaigned for its place in the attention of the people of Vermont, just as he had with the Green Mountains as a younger man.

As rewarding as Taylor's work may have been to him, it was not especially well paid, and as the lifelong bachelor entered old age, he had no nest egg or children to depend on. In the spring of 1945, the seventy-three-year-old Taylor's friends and associates pulled together a testimonial dinner and fundraiser in his honor. Small checks poured in from around the state, along with heartfelt appreciations for the work he had done.

Taylor never stopped campaigning; his last fight was leading the charge for his adopted hometown of Burlington to build a modern sewage treatment plant and clean up the mess it was dumping into Lake Champlain. He had to put his work on hold, however, when he broke his hip in a fall and was hospitalized for an extended period. Again a round of fundraising commenced to support Taylor, as the seventy-six-year-old slowly recuperated.

Out of the hospital and living again in his hotel room, the always forward-looking Taylor came face to face with an uncomfortable reality. He was alone and old, and his life's work was behind him. One morning in September 1949, he rode in a cab out of Burlington to Grand Isle, a rural island in Lake Champlain just across a newly built bridge from the Burlington area. He was dropped at a shoreline inn for tourists that he had visited many times before. To the inn's employees, Taylor seemed agitated and out of sorts. He spent some time strolling up and down the road, then after lunch in the restaurant, he headed out in a rented rowboat and drifted on the lake. The inn owner's son boated out to make sure everything was okay, and Taylor said it was. A short while later, Taylor's rowboat was seen floating on the water, empty, with his cane lying in it. A massive search ensued, without success. Five days later, James P. Taylor's body floated to the surface, his death presumed to be a suicide by drowning.

4

The Big Idea: Benton MacKaye

//

Our job in the new exploration is nothing short of making a uto-
pia of reconstruction—the remodeling of an unshapen and ca-
cophonous environment into a humanized and well-ordered one.

—Benton MacKaye

Benton MacKaye (the "Kaye" is pronounced with a long "i" sound) could be both inspiring and maddening; wise yet naïve. He was an ambitious thinker years ahead of his time, and a hopeless nostalgic out of touch with his contemporaries. This vision-ary who conceived of and founded the Appalachian Trail in 1921 was, by the time of its completion sixteen years later, almost completely estranged from the project.

At the heart of MacKaye's fraught relationship with the world was his peculiar way of understanding it. Where others saw objects and things, MacKaye saw relationships, processes, and flows. A street was not just a collection of people and shops, it was a branch in the network of commerce, a collision of social interests, a catalyst for a different to-morrow. The woods were neither cuttable timber nor enjoyable scen-ery, they were the foundation of a just society and an honest culture.

When MacKaye spoke of a particular place, he always meant something more, something fundamentally different, than did whomever he was speaking with, even as they used the same language.

It was a particular kind of brilliance, this piercing view of interconnectedness. It helped launch not only the AT, but the regional planning movement, the Wilderness Society, and the environmental activism of the 1960s and '70s. But only a few sympathetic souls could keep up with MacKaye's thinking—it frequently ran ahead of even his own ability to capture it in words—and in the workaday world where things got done, his musings frequently came across as more half-baked philosophy than actionable policy.

In the end, two things seem equally true. Were it not for MacKaye and his bold, clear vision, there would be no Appalachian Trail of the scale and prominence we know today. At the same time, the actual building of the trail happened mostly independently of, and sometimes in spite of, MacKaye's own work.

Benton MacKaye was born in 1879, to a family that was theatrical in every sense of the word. His father, Steele MacKaye, was a New York actor, writer, producer, and inventor who aspired to create entertainment that was both broadly popular and socially uplifting. Steele's dreams tended to run just ahead of the commercial realities, though, and while the family ran in some very exclusive social circles, its finances were wildly unpredictable. Benton grew up in a household where lofty inspiration went hand in hand with constant instability.

His mother, Mary MacKaye, was always devising new living arrangements for the family, to accommodate the ups and downs of Steele's career. Benton was born, the fifth of six children, near the end of a well-funded period of family life on an estate in Connecticut, but that was soon given up for more modest accommodations in New

York City. He would spend the majority of his youth, unhappily, in the clamor and chaos of the big city.

When Benton was nine years old, his twenty-year-old brother Will, a rising star of the New York stage, acquired for the family the only property they would ever own, an old house in the small community of Shirley Center, Massachusetts. Intended as a summer retreat, the Shirley Center property quickly became the MacKayes' home of last resort, the one place Mary and the younger children could live when other arrangements fell through. In the first of a series of tragedies that would define Benton's early life, Will died soon after the family celebrated its first Christmas together at the Shirley property.

Perhaps as a buffer against the uncertainties of his world, Benton at a young age became a serious student of science. He was fascinated by the classification of the world around him, whether it was the names of features on the landscape or the timetables of the trains that ran over it. When he was twelve, during a year spent in Washington so Mary and the younger children could live off his older brothers' government paychecks, Benton basically organized his own education, courtesy of the Smithsonian Institution. He attended explorers' lectures in the evenings and in the daytime helped out with the natural history collections. During summers in Shirley, he began mounting his own expeditions to the surrounding countryside, assiduously chronicling his findings in little notebooks.

Benton was particularly enthusiastic about railroads, and at the age of fourteen he got to travel with two of his brothers to Chicago, where Steele MacKaye had attempted his greatest project yet. For the Chicago World's Fair of 1893, Steele had conceived of a giant theater, the Spectatorium, that would present the story of the European discovery of the New World in a pageant of highbrow drama and state-of-the-art special effects. It was to be his crowning achievement and the key to the MacKaye family's lasting prosperity. But the financing collapsed, and construction of the massive structure was halted partway through. By the time Benton and his brothers met up with their father in Chicago, Steele was a shell of his former self, demoralized and unwell. Steele and his sons visited the World's Fair together, the boys taking turns pushing their father's wheelchair. After his children returned east, Steele headed west in an attempt to recover his health. He died soon thereafter, of what turned out to be cancer.

On the one hand, the teenaged Benton was accustomed to life without his father; Steele's frequent travels meant that for some time their primary connection had been through letters. But those absences had always carried with them the elusive prospect of success for the family — ambitions achieved and the future secured. With his father's death, the dramatic promise of MacKaye family life had been stripped away, and Benton was lonely and adrift. Increasingly, he turned to the little town in Massachusetts to find the stability that his father's citified striving had failed to provide.

Shirley Center was a classic New England village nestled, in Benton's eyes, perfectly in the world it was a part of. The distant wilderness gracefully gave way to farmers' woodlots, then their fields, and their homes, centered around a neatly ordered village: "a meeting house, a red brick schoolhouse, a store, farmhouses, wheelwright shop and town hall . . . the basic elements of civilization . . . arranged around the 'common.'" Compared with the loud and crowded city where MacKaye had spent the bulk of his school years, Shirley was a neat and tidy idyll, and MacKaye embraced it as his own. As he had at the Smithsonian, he found for himself an adult mentor, a neighbor named Melvin Longley, "from whom I received, on his big dairy farm (more than from the little red schoolhouse) my own basic education."

With Shirley as his home base, MacKaye spent his final two high school years in Cambridge, cramming to continue his brothers' legacy of attending Harvard. He succeeded, barely, and enrolled as a freshman in the fall of 1896. He was a mostly indifferent student, except in courses on geology and geography. Studying with the scholarly heirs of Louis Agassiz and Arnold Guyot, MacKaye found an intellectual home for his childhood fascination with an orderly world.

> I shall always recall how Professor Davis began his opening lecture in "Geography A" at Harvard University in 1898. He gave it in the Agassiz Museum and he held in his hand a six-inch globe. "Gentlemen," said he (I quote from memory), "here is the subject of our study—this planet, its lands, waters, atmosphere, and life; the abode of plant, animal, and man— *the earth as a habitable globe.*"

MacKaye found the greatest reward of his college years outside the classroom and away from campus, in travels all over New England. After his freshman year, he and a few friends mounted an excursion into the wilderness of New Hampshire's White Mountains, by then a well-mapped but still rigorously challenging environment. After graduation, in the summer of 1900, he and two others traveled up the length of Vermont's Green Mountains, nine years before James Taylor conceived of the Long Trail.

For the first few years after he finished his degree, MacKaye supported himself with tutoring jobs in New York during the school year, and work as a camp counselor in New Hampshire during the summers. But after three years of just paying the bills while he stewed over his future, MacKaye resolved to embark on a career. In the fall of 1903, he returned to Harvard to become the school's first-ever student in the field of forestry.

Forestry at that time was the leading edge of a conservation movement that promised to reinvent America for the new century. Rational, scientific management of the nation's resources would take the place of chaotic exploitation, and the long-term common good would win out over short-term profiteering. Conservation was a political philosophy and emerging science rolled into one, championed by then–president Theodore Roosevelt and the Progressive movement he was at the head of. It required highly educated, well-meaning individuals —who were usually of a certain social standing—to pilot the nation's affairs.

In 1905 Benton MacKaye became Harvard's first-ever forestry graduate, and went to work for both the recently founded United States Forest Service and for Harvard, where he taught classes and helped establish the university's research forest. "Forestry may be defined as the practice of growing woods instead of mining them," he would later write, and in that spirit the once directionless teen became, in his late twenties, a proud soldier in the conservation movement's battle to save America from itself.

Notwithstanding his success as a forester, however, MacKaye was restless, anxious to connect his work to a loftier ideal than the straightforward management of resources. He lived proudly in his family's tradition of proselytizing for a better world, imagining that a more harmonious future was just around the corner, waiting for the right mix of agitation and enlightenment to bring it into being. Benton's brother James, for example, was convinced he could discover the scientific laws that governed human welfare, no different than the ones that guided his everyday work as a chemist. When Benton wasn't teaching classes or doing fieldwork, he organized readings of James's *The Economy of Happiness,* and the two of them became active in Cambridge's socialist circles.

Perhaps the pinnacle of MacKaye's time as a forester came in the summer of 1912. Working full-time at this point out of the Forest Service's Washington headquarters, the thirty-three-year-old was tasked with one of the conservation movement's most critical assignments: building the scientific case that would justify the creation of New Hampshire's White Mountains National Forest.

The previous year, Congress had passed the Weeks Act, a law that for the first time authorized the federal government to create national forests in the eastern half of the country. In the West, forest reserves had been created by simply holding back from development land that the government already controlled. But in the East, the government would have to purchase land from private owners, often timber companies, if it hoped to bring forests under federal management. Conservationists had several reasons for wanting to do so—protecting some land for its scenic value, sustainably managing the timber harvest in other places. But one reason in particular gave them the legal justification to involve the federal government in land buying: the impact that logging had on the downstream behavior of rivers. Clear-cut mountainsides eroded soil into nearby waterways, complicating navigation, and they allowed rainfall that would have ordinarily been collected in the forest to instead rush downstream, causing disastrous flooding. Because rivers freely flowed among multiple states, their altered behavior had an impact on interstate commerce, and was therefore an appropriate matter for federal involvement.

With that reasoning built into the new law, the Forest Service could only acquire land for a national forest if it could document a particular land area's downstream impact. The United States Geological Survey, in MacKaye's telling, was able to do only half of the necessary science, measuring stream flows.

> The geologists, however, were not equipped to do the other half of the job, namely, to measure the amount of forest. So the Geological Survey borrowed a forester from the Forest Service. I was the forester and spent the autumn of 1912 in the wa-

tersheds, mapping the extent and density of their forest cover. When the two sets of measurements were put together they brought out the influence of forest cover on stream flow. So the area was acquired and became the White Mountains National Forest.

MacKaye's modesty does not capture the importance of his work. In fact, according to his biographer Larry Anderson, MacKaye had played a key role in an important episode.

> He had used his technical skills to achieve a specific social and political end. He had helped, in a modest way, to refine the discipline of scientific forestry in America, which had proceeded as much on faith and uplifting rhetoric as on empirically documented fact. His efforts had also buttressed the legal foundation of the Weeks Act, which withstood subsequent court challenges. And not least important, the eastern national forests that soon began to take shape (including the White Mountains National Forest) would later provide a protected environment for significant stretches of the Appalachian Trail.

Notwithstanding his professional success, MacKaye's relationship with the field of forestry was fraying, as his more radical aspirations sought a larger canvas. If the conservation movement asked how resources could best be managed on behalf of society, MacKaye wanted to know how they could be used to *remake* society. How could the order and logic that he admired so much in the natural world be brought to bear on the messy realities of the civilized one?

With the help of sympathetic patrons in the Forest Service and later the United States Labor Department, MacKaye took on a series of special projects that investigated the social economy of the forest, rather than just its productive capacity. He traveled to the Great Lakes states to examine the agricultural settlement of cutover land, and to Washington State to look into labor conflict in the timber industry. He came away from these investigations with a firm belief in the need for public ownership of the land. Only then could it be developed sensibly, according to a well-thought-out plan, in a way that reined in the typical excesses of America's exploitive economy.

In Minnesota and Wisconsin and Michigan, he saw the depressing results of a typical homesteading approach to land left bare by clear-cutting. Families with dreams of a prosperous farm life would borrow money to acquire a new "farm," only to find it riddled with stumps, in a location with poor soil and a short growing season. To MacKaye, the initial insult of denuding the forest was being repeated all over again with the exploitation of the settlers, and for the same reason: a blind pursuit of profit. The few with money made out great —the timber companies, the land brokers, the banks—at the expense of everyone and everything else. If, instead, the land could be publicly controlled for a period of time, experts like him could design a sensible, conservation-oriented settlement pattern. Built according to the possibilities and constraints of a given area's natural systems, the resulting communities would be sustainable over the long haul.

MacKaye's work on a new approach to "colonizing" the cutover lands of the Great Lakes is a great example of his tendency to solve problems by thinking systematically, always looking for solutions at a larger scale than the one at which the problem presented itself. In his mind, the problems of the individual farmer required an examination of the entire region—the terrain, the systems of nature and economy—of which the farm was a part. And a well-functioning region, in turn, depended on a national government that understood and supported it. Getting the regions right, he thought, would make the nation as a whole right; and a country devoted to the health of its individual regions would be on the path to a brighter future.

It was while trying to work out these ideas of regional planning and a populist approach to natural resources that MacKaye first came up with the idea for an Appalachian Trail. He wrote an article for a professional forestry journal in 1916 titled "The Recreational Possibilities of Public Forests," in which he argued that forests could do much more than provide timber production or watershed protection; the backcountry could give the American family more of the benefits of its own labor. The modern industrial economy, he said, had freed people from the incessant toil of agriculture, which would be a step toward a more civilized society only if it paid off for workers in improved quality of life. An industrial economy that simply replaced farm drudgery with factory drudgery had no point. But one that allowed people to spend leisure time in the woods, reestablishing their connection to the land, to him made much more sense. Cultivating the forests for recreational purposes, in MacKaye's eyes, had a perfect symmetry to it. The natural source of our economic success would also be the source of our cultural success, powering our modern lives and, in the form of outdoor recreation, feeding our modern souls.

Of course, productive and recreational uses couldn't occupy the exact same spaces, but nature had provided the obvious solution. Lower elevations, with their natural access to the outside world, served as the sensible location for productive activity, while the higher ground, on either side of the ridgeline connecting one peak to the next, was ideally suited to recreation. With this simple framework in mind, a vast, interconnected network of recreational land revealed itself to MacKaye.

"The mountain land . . . is the main recreation ground of the Nation," he wrote. "And the people will require, for a healthful and properly balanced life, all of this mountain land that is possible to place at their disposal." He approvingly took note of the early work of the "young and ambitious Green Mountain Club" to create a ridgeline trail the length of Vermont, and referenced the work of the Appalachian Mountain Club to link up trails with one another. If the AMC and GMC networks could be connected, "a good beginning would be made toward linking up and correlating the mountain camping grounds of New England," he wrote. And there would be no reason to stop there.

> The series of roads and trails already begun in the Adirondacks, and in New England, could be made to connect through the New Jersey and Pennsylvania highlands with the Blue Ridge of Virginia and thence quite readily throughout the Southern Appalachian Range.

Five years before he coined the term "Appalachian Trail," launching the effort to build it, MacKaye had the heart of the concept already worked out in his head: a recreational preserve to serve the people, anchored by a network of trails, running the length of the eastern mountains. In fact, he wrote, the same logic of recreational corridors could apply to high terrain across the country. And not only should the mountains be protected and opened up to recreation, so should the river systems at their base.

> Here, then, with the mountain lands and the navigable waters would be the skeleton on which to build a national recreation ground ... a thing to grow and be developed apart from our more hideous *commercial* development. It should be a network of "neutral zones" in which the clash of the ordinary life should be broken up—zones in which there would be "no

Betty MacKaye, left, with fellow campaigners for women's right to vote.

trespassing" by the exploiter. They would be zones of equal opportunity for real life.

What had begun as an assessment of recreational possibilities had turned out to be a bold and ambitious blueprint for national development. It was only an intellectual exercise at this point, an illustration of ideas more than an actual proposal. But it would remain in MacKaye's head over the next few years, as his life took a series of abrupt turns.

In 1915, MacKaye at the age of thirty-six married forty-year-old suffragist and social activist Jessie Hardy Stubbs, who went by the nickname Betty. She was far more prominent in her own field than MacKaye was in his, a leading organizer of efforts to grant women the right to vote. Betty MacKaye, like Benton, was devoted to social change on many fronts, and their marriage was as much a partnership in activism as it was a domestic arrangement. Washington was their base, and they shared communal living arrangements with like-minded friends in a place the group dubbed "Hell House" for the hell-raising sensibilities of its residents. Both of them spent long stretches of time traveling and apart from one another, she to organize campaign activity, he to conduct his research.

In early 1918, Betty had a nervous breakdown, in the parlance of the time, racked with anxiety to the point that she could not function. Betty and Benton struggled to find something that would make her better, including a hospital stay in Washington. But the prospect of confinement made Betty more upset, not less, so they made arrangements to travel to the country home of a friend, in the Hudson River Valley north of New York City. It worked; in the calm atmosphere of the countryside, Betty regained her equilibrium, and the two resumed life together. They resolved to follow the same program if she were to have any similar episodes in the future.

The next year, MacKaye's full-time employment with the federal government came to an end. He had written a major report outlining his proposal for planned settlement of forested land, "Employment and Natural Resources," and had for the most part left behind the profession of forestry. MacKaye was growing more radical as his maturing profession moved in the opposite direction.

He drummed up some consulting work in Washington, then moved with Betty and a friend of theirs to Milwaukee, where the friend, Herbert Brougham, would edit a socialist newspaper and MacKaye would write its editorials. For a period of time, MacKaye's mother and sister moved in as well. But just months after the MacKayes' arrival in Milwaukee, a dispute erupted over Betty's campaign for a women's sex strike to stop global militarism. When the paper refused to publicize it, Brougham quit, and he and Betty attempted to use the dispute to drum up publicity for her campaign. Benton seems to have remained on the sidelines of the dispute. Nevertheless, the three activists' joint undertaking was no longer viable, and they left Milwaukee for New York, where Benton looked for more work as a writer.

In the spring of 1921, MacKaye accepted the invitation of an old friend from Harvard, Rotus Eastman, to get away from the city and spend some time on Eastman's farm in Quebec. MacKaye planned to help out his friend on the farm and spend time working on "a special piece of writing," a return to the ideas in his "Recreational Possibilities" article. But a couple of weeks into his planned month-long stay in Quebec, MacKaye received a telegram urgently summoning him back to New York. Betty was in the throes of another breakdown—anxious, not sleeping, paranoid. Benton rushed back to the city and began to implement the plan they had agreed to three years earlier. Two days after his return, Benton and Betty and their friend Mabel Irwin went to Grand Central Station to catch the train to Irwin's country home north of the city. Betty's mood had improved with Benton's return, but she had become anxious again as they left home, frightened that she would be confined against her will. Benton remembered the same pattern of behavior from the earlier episode, and was confident that Betty would calm down if they could just get her to the countryside. At the station, he stood in line for tickets while Betty and Mabel went to the restroom. But as the women were heading back to meet him, Betty seemingly took a wrong turn and began walking toward the building exit. Mabel reminded her which way to go; Betty ran. Benton, wondering why the two women hadn't rejoined him, headed toward the restrooms and encountered a panicked Mabel, who told him what had happened. They notified the police and asked friends to join the search. Later that day, Betty's body was found floating in the East River.

In the weeks that followed, after newspapers around the country reported the passing of the noted suffragist, and after a small impromptu memorial service in the wilds of Staten Island, Benton retreated to his older brother's house in nearby Yonkers, and attended to the business of tying up his late wife's affairs. He wrote letters to her many friends, relatives, and acquaintances, recounting the story of her death, and acknowledging their condolences. He wrote to Betty's niece, "When we were married it seemed as if I could not love a woman more. But I found I could. I came to love her more and more as the years went by. We came to grow so near—in mind and soul—that her presence now seems at times even more vivid than when her body was here." He seemed to take some consolation from the fact that Betty had escaped the demons that had been haunting her for years. A friend comforted him that Betty's mental illness was bigger than anyone could manage, and the latest crisis was inevitable, "its threatened approach more or less clearly discernible to all who loved her."

When, after several weeks, there were no more tangible tasks to be dealt with in the wake of Betty's death, MacKaye accepted the invitation of his close friend Charles Whitaker to spend time at Whitaker's country retreat on an old farm in the hills of western New Jersey. "You would adore the spot," Whitaker wrote to the grieving MacKaye, "high in the mountains . . . and not a soul in sight." Whitaker was editor of the prestigious *Journal of the American Institute of Architects,* and like Mac-Kaye was deeply interested in reforming American life by designing and building an alternative. The two men had first become acquainted in Washington, running in the same circles of socialist reform, before Whitaker moved his office to New York. It was Whitaker, along with Betty's traveling companion Mabel Irwin, who had positively identified Betty's body.

At Whitaker's farmhouse, MacKaye returned to the project he had been working on in Quebec. He drafted a "Memorandum on Regional Planning" that laid out his ideas on land, economy, and society, concepts he had been mulling over and refining for the previous several years. The memo provided examples of the kind of projects that a regional planner—that is, MacKaye—could undertake to demonstrate the value of this approach. At some point, perhaps at Whitaker's urging, MacKaye set aside the larger concept and began to more fully develop one of these potential regional planning projects.

"Working out Appal. trail," he wrote in his diary on June 29. Five years after his "Recreational Possibilities" article, MacKaye was thinking of an Appalachian Trail not as simply an intellectual exercise, but as an actual project that he might undertake. As he drafted an article laying out his proposal, his host Whitaker got in touch with a friend, the New York architect Clarence Stein, whom Whitaker knew would see the potential in MacKaye's work. Stein was the chair of the American Institute of Architects' Committee on Community Planning, a group devoted to applying architecture's expertise not just to individual buildings but to the entire urban fabric. Stein came out to the New Jersey farm; together the three men talked, hiked, and came up with a plan to launch the Appalachian Trail. Whitaker would publish MacKaye's article in his magazine. Stein's committee would provide an administrative home for the effort. And MacKaye would reach out to and organize the various stakeholders around his project.

"An Appalachian Trail: A Project in Regional Planning" appeared in the October 1921 issue of the *Journal of the American Institute of Architects*. In it, MacKaye conjured a giant who strolled down the length of the Appalachian Mountains, viewing all of eastern America as a single landscape.

> Resting now on the top of Mt. Mitchell, highest point east of the Rockies, he counts up on his big long fingers the opportunities which yet await development along the skyline he has passed.
>
> First he notes the opportunities for recreation. Throughout the Southern Appalachians, throughout the Northwoods, and even through the Alleghenies that wind their way among

the smoky industrial towns of Pennsylvania, he recollects vast areas of secluded forests, pastoral lands, and water courses, which, with proper facilities and protection, could be made to serve as the breath of a real life for the toilers in the bee-hive cities along the Atlantic seaboard and elsewhere.

Second, he notes the possibilities for health and recuperation.

... Most sanitariums now established are perfectly useless to those afflicted with mental disease—the most terrible, usually, of any disease. Many of these sufferers could be cured. But not merely by "treatment." They need comprehensive provision made for them. They need acres not medicine.

... Next after the opportunities for recreation and recuperation our giant counts off, as a third big resource, the opportunities in the Appalachian belt for employment on the land. This brings up a need that is becoming urgent—the redistribution of our population, which grows more and more top heavy.

To MacKaye's giant, the Appalachian skyline provided a chance to craft a new alternative to the American way of life, grounded in the lessons that nature had to teach.

And this is the job that we propose: a project to develop the opportunities—for recreation, recuperation, and employment—in the region of the Appalachian skyline.

The project is one for a series of recreational communities through the Appalachian chain of mountains from New England to Georgia, these to be connected by a walking trail. Its purpose is to establish a base for a more extensive and systematic development of outdoor community life. It is a project in housing and community architecture.

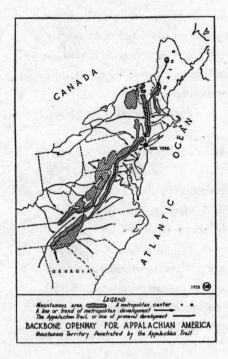

LEGEND
Mountainous area ~~~~~~ A metropolitan center • •
A line or trend of metropolitan development →
The Appalachian Trail, or line of primeval development ——
BACKBONE OPENWAY FOR APPALACHIAN AMERICA
Mountainous Territory Penetrated by the Appalachian Trail

From his book The New Exploration, *Benton MacKaye's map of the Appalachian Trail and surrounding protected land.*

The Appalachian Trail, in MacKaye's conception, was the backbone of a new geography; like the railroads he had loved as a child, it would do more than just connect places, it would transform them.

His idea immediately struck a chord with two audiences. To hiking enthusiasts, especially in the Northeast, a trail running the length of the Appalachians would realize an ambition that had been percolating in their community for years. MacKaye, as he always emphasized, had hardly originated the idea of long-distance trails or the possibilities of joining trail networks together. But to articulate an actual plan, and argue for it as part of a holistic vision of national renewal, went far beyond the incremental efforts that had come before. The second group to jump on board were the public intellectuals and social reformers who had never before considered the problems of urban life in MacKaye's broader, natural context. MacKaye was offering a vast new resource—the forested hinterlands—to the quest for a better modern life.

From the start, he was worried that the physical trail would overwhelm the larger project that it was a part of. Regional planning was the ultimate goal, not hiking for its own sake, and he wanted to think through that larger ambition before this one emblematic project, the Appalachian Trail, got too far ahead of him. This was a man, after all, who believed fervently in the necessity of careful planning, whose father's schemes so often came crashing down at the mercy of unreliable partners. MacKaye needed the participation of a broad cast of characters to make his vision a reality, but he also needed his philosophy, much of which still existed only in nebulous form in his own head, to stay front and center.

His collaborator, Stein, no slouch himself when it came to theorizing about American life, nevertheless was keen to get the project moving. MacKaye spent the winter of 1921–22, right after the article's publication, holed up at the Shirley Center homestead, developing his ideas, while Stein was trying to arrange meetings and get the ball rolling on the actual trail effort.

MacKaye to Stein:

> As a result of my work this winter and of the talks with my brother I am planning to write a book on this whole subject and to make of it a field for possible further writings.

Stein to MacKaye:

> I am immensely interested in your plan to bring your ideas together in book form; I feel sure that this is not going to interfere with our plans for the development of the Trail. I am however, strongly of the opinion that the time has come for us to get together and try to put our plans for development into more definite form. You have not as yet, as far as I know, been in direct touch with the New York crowd.

MacKaye agreed to travel to New York, a bit reluctantly. "Upon my return from seeing you, I want to get done a certain part of my writing. This is important to the whole development. I shall have to be alternately writer and organizer."

In New York, Stein connected MacKaye to the two people who would take up the organizational challenge of trail building about which MacKaye was so ambivalent: Raymond Torrey, who wrote a weekly outings column for the *New York Evening Post* and tirelessly organized the metropolitan region's hiking scene, and Major William Welch, head of the Palisades Interstate Park Commission, which encompassed state parks in New Jersey and New York protecting the Hudson Highlands north of New York City. Torrey and Welch had already been hard at work trying to organize a trail network across the Highlands and exploring the possibility of connecting New York–area trails to the expanding New England systems.

After their meetings, MacKaye moved on to Washington, where he built on his old contacts in government to drum up support for the trail. He continued the organizational work, in fits and starts, over the next several months. But for all of the attention that he drew to the trail idea, in part through his fastidiously prepared maps, MacKaye was resistant to focusing on it exclusively. He wanted the time and space to develop his thinking in book form, so that the whole AT project would be guided by a clear overall doctrine.

In a way that would at first perplex and later deeply frustrate the trail community that had been energized by his proposal, the founder of the Appalachian Trail was oddly ambivalent about the building of the trail itself. At times he would show great energy and interest, but more often he would stand aloof from it, determined to develop his larger program of regional planning. What likely saved the trail, before it had even been built, was the creation of a stand-alone organization that could carry the work forward. Though he had resisted it at first,

The Regional Planning Association of America was a short-lived but seminal group in the history of American urban planning. The RPAA advocated a careful deconcentration of overcrowded cities into new towns sensibly sited in the surrounding countryside. Rather than allow the metropolitan area to just ooze outward at lower densities, they argued for a carefully designed network of smaller Garden Cities, each contained by a ring of undeveloped area, well connected by parkways in a smoothly functioning, well-balanced region. The RPAA, with MacKaye at its center, saw the future of American urban sprawl, and offered an intriguing alternative. It was, in the end, far too radical a vision for an America committed to conventional real estate development, though a handful of communities, notably Greenbelt, Maryland (shown here), were built according to the RPAA's philosophy.

at a Washington meeting in 1925 MacKaye organized the Appalachian Trail Conference, with Major Welch as its chair, Stein and Torrey among those on the executive committee, and MacKaye as "field organizer."

At the same time, his larger ambitions were finding a new home in a loose confederation of writers, architects, and activists known as the Regional Planning Association of America. Thanks in large part to his RPAA colleague, the great urbanist writer Lewis Mumford, MacKaye was finally able to publish the book he had effectively been working on since he first went to Quebec in the weeks before Betty's suicide. Published in 1928, *The New Exploration: A Philosophy of Regional Planning* provided a critique of American society in the form of a blueprint for its physical renovation. MacKaye described an America that was entrenched in a struggle between two forces: the Indigenous, "the fundamental world of man's needs as a cultured being," and the Metropolitan, "a rootless, aimless, profoundly disharmonized environment." The Indigenous, in MacKaye's reckoning, was the deep and timeless culture of Shirley Center, or the pure wilderness of the mountaintop; the Metropolitan was the always expanding modern city, the subjugation of human culture to the faceless power of industry and wealth.

> First it occupies the lower valley, such as the locality of the Boston Basin, obliterating the original urban environment of "Boston Town." Next in finger-like projections it flows, glacier-wise, toward the outskirts, obliterating such rural villages and environment as comes within its wake. Then, its projections narrowing, it flows along the railways and motor roads back through the hinterland, starting little centers of provincial metropolitanism in the Main Street towns and around the numerous gasoline stations. Finally here and there it crawls up some mountain summit and obliterates a strategic particle of the primeval environment. It is mightiest in the valleys and weakest on the mountain ridges. The strategy of the indigenous world is just the other way. It is still mighty within the

primeval environment, as along the ridgeways of the Appalachian barrier.

The Appalachian Trail, in *The New Exploration*, was not simply some recreational opportunity. It was the backbone of a wilderness zone that would hold back the creeping industrial monotony of the modern world.

On paper, the AT was a shining example of a compelling vision. But in the real world, the work of building it was beginning to stall. MacKaye, who was supposed to have provided the day-to-day organizing of the trail effort, had neither relinquished that role nor given his full attention to it. Finally, with his blessing, new leadership took over the Appalachian Trail Conference in 1927. Arthur Perkins, a retired judge from Connecticut, had, simply by devoting his time and energy to the project, become its de facto leader, and then with MacKaye's encouragement the formal chairman of the trail conference. An acquaintance of Perkins's, a young lawyer in Washington, DC, named Myron Avery (Chapter 5), organized a Potomac Appalachian Trail Club, which quickly became the hub of all activity on the southern half of the trail. When Judge Perkins became ill a few years later, Avery became the ATC's tireless and pugnacious leader, while MacKaye was content, for a time, to stand aside, his only involvement making the occasional speech to encourage an effort he had mostly lost touch with.

MacKaye lived a proudly spartan life in Shirley Center, staying with his vast network of friends and allies when necessary, cobbling together various one-off writing and consulting projects that paid for his limited worldly needs. He was something of a monk in a church of his own invention. In 1934, now fifty-five years old, MacKaye returned to the full-time employment of the federal government. The nation was in the throes of the Great Depression, and President Franklin Delano Roosevelt was responding with the kind of massive role for the federal government in American life that MacKaye had been advocating for years. The time was ripe for regional planning, and MacKaye headed to Washington looking for work.

After a couple of false starts, he caught on with the Tennessee Valley Authority, which on the surface was an organization that embodied the ambitions of regional planning: an agency with broad federal power, defined by the natural boundaries of the massive Tennessee River watershed stretching across seven states and charged with converting the massive power potential of the river system into the social and economic development of the region. MacKaye moved to TVA headquarters in Knoxville, and assumed his by now well-practiced role of analyst, planner, and one-man think tank. At first energized by the possibilities of this new organization, he was soon disappointed that the TVA was interested primarily in becoming an electric utility, with little appetite for the more comprehensive ambitions of MacKaye's notion of regional planning.

It was from Knoxville that MacKaye had his final real involvement with the Appalachian Trail, a conflict that would leave him permanently alienated from the project. The National Park Service had, much to MacKaye's dismay, already begun construction of a scenic parkway, the Skyline Drive, over the ridgeline route of the AT in Shenandoah National Park, shunting the trail off to the side. The Park Service was keen to build more mountain parkways, opening up the mountaintops to a public that increasingly enjoyed outdoor scenery from behind the windshield of their automobiles.

The AT community was divided over how to respond. One faction, which included many longtime associates of MacKaye, including Raymond Torrey in New York, felt strongly that the ridgeline should belong to hikers alone. To essentially pave over the AT, while clearing

Benton MacKaye on the Appalachian Trail in the Great Smoky Mountains, 1933.

a new path a little ways off the road, they argued, was to make a wilderness trail into little more than a sidewalk. They reached out to MacKaye for support, and he needed little encouragement to vent his outrage at the prospect of an incursion by the dreaded Metropolitan into his sanctified Indigenous. He and his allies wanted the ATC to adopt a position opposing mountain parkways and put political weight behind it.

Myron Avery, though, rapidly consolidating his power at the top of the ATC, viewed the problem from what he saw as a more pragmatic perspective. The federal government was the ATC's essential partner in the trail effort, hosting hundreds of miles of trail in its national forests and parks. Rather than engage the ATC in an ideological battle with the Park Service, Avery argued for a more accommodating position, treating these mountain parkways on a case-by-case basis, but insisting regardless that the government always pay to relocate the AT away from the road.

To MacKaye, this was sacrilege. Wilderness was an inviolate principle that, once sullied by the automobile, was lost forever. "This clash of Trail vs. Highway on the mountain tops is something bigger than it seems," he wrote to a friend. "It is an early skirmish, perhaps the first significant skirmish, in the retention of a humanly balanced world."

What began as a relatively cordial disagreement among allies quickly devolved into a personal battle of wills. MacKaye accused

Avery of being a traitor to the cause they had been pursuing for years. Avery, who spent his days, nights, and weekends toiling in the trenches of trail building while MacKaye had not shown interest for years, had little patience for the older man's philosophizing. The two exchanged angry letters at the end of 1935, effectively ending MacKaye's involvement with the Appalachian Trail, though it had been only intermittent for some time.

The parkways controversy helped crystallize for MacKaye a new priority, simple and straightforward, a last-ditch attempt at holding off the metropolitan invasion. The government needed to create a new category of land—not a national forest or national park, both of which, he had learned, were as much invitations of the Metropolitan as rejections of it—that would maintain its natural state in perpetuity. It would be called Wilderness. As he had throughout his adult life, MacKaye joined together with a handful of like-minded individuals and formed an organization to advocate for their worldview. The Wilderness Society was founded on a Tennessee roadside by MacKaye and a handful of others in the fall of 1934.

MacKaye left Tennessee and the TVA in 1936, and though he would never stop drafting plans, maps, and proposals—a circuit of parkways around the Boston region; a plan for a Missouri Valley Authority to build on the unfulfilled promise of the TVA—MacKaye's time as an influential thinker and activist was mostly at an end. He served one final hitch in the federal government, for the Rural Electrification Administration, before effectively retiring in 1945 at the age of sixty-six.

In his later years, MacKaye attempted to put his lifetime of thought into a magnum opus, a philosophical-geographical-historical analysis of America. He seemed to believe throughout his life that the only thing standing in the way of the future he hoped to create was a deeper analysis, a more comprehensive philosophy, a better analogy. He proposed to a publisher a multivolume work that would not be completed until his one-hundredth birthday. It, not surprisingly, never came to pass.

MacKaye would never stop engaging with the issues that he cared so deeply about. He contributed thoughts, plans, and admonitions from afar as the Wilderness Society he helped found won passage of the Wilderness Act in 1964, placing vast swaths of federal land in a permanently protected primeval state. And four years later, after years of legislative machination that MacKaye closely tracked and never failed to offer his thoughts on, President Lyndon Johnson signed the National Trails System Act (Chapter 7), establishing the Appalachian National Scenic Trail as the responsibility of the federal government. MacKaye, now eighty-nine years old, did not attend the signing ceremony in Washington.

He lived on, his mind sharp, into the 1970s, as the nation awakened to the concepts of environmental protection for which he had been advocating for most of the twentieth century. When a writer for *Backpacker* magazine visited MacKaye to discuss the AT in 1975, she was astonished to find him with more questions than she had, eager for the latest news on the routing of the proposed Pacific Northwest Trail. The PNT would eventually join the network of national scenic trails — there are now eleven, in every corner of the country — that MacKaye first imagined in 1916.

Benton MacKaye died at his Shirley Center home on December 11, 1975. He was ninety-six years old.

5

The Organization: Myron Avery

A trail and its markings do not constitute any intrusion upon the naturalness of the forest wilderness. Trails should be marked and maintained in a manner to eliminate the necessity of labor and uncertainty in finding one's route. They should be an open course; a joy for travel.

—Myron Avery

I n the space of just a few years, the young Washington lawyer My-ron Avery went from being a local chapter volunteer in the na-scent Appalachian Trail movement to the unquestioned and in-creasingly resented leader of the entire effort. Benton MacKaye may have invented the Appalachian Trail, but Avery got it built, with a focus and commitment that were almost inexplicably intense. Avery was driven to arrange things as he was certain they should be, not out of ego or hubris, it seems, but from an almost desperate need to do things the right way, which happened to be his way, and why on earth couldn't others see that when it was so obvious?

There are no clues to how the Appalachian Mountains and the trail through them became the object of Avery's compulsive attention.

One could imagine his having an equally intense interest in, say, music, or engines. He had very little to say about the mountains' natural beauty, or their virtues as an escape from civilization, or their testing of athletic mettle. The building of the Appalachian Trail, for Myron Avery, seemed to achieve no broader purpose than the fact of its own completion: two ends connected; a trail blazed, cleared, and improved; shelters built; measurements made; and all of the associated data published in an appropriate format.

A big part of experiencing the outdoors for many people, perhaps ironically, is the cataloging of it—turning the unpredictability of wilderness into the order of lists: bird species spotted, peaks climbed, game animals hunted. Myron Avery found an opportunity to go one step further, to build the list itself, carving out of the woods the definitive path through the Appalachian Mountains that everyone else would use for their own accounting.

Avery was born in 1899 in the easternmost town in the United States, Lubec, Maine, where his father ran a fish-canning plant, part of the industry that defined the town. His high school had four classrooms, one for each grade of roughly thirty-five students; at sixteen, Avery graduated at the top of his small class. "Let us go forth with a purpose, a noble purpose," he urged in his valedictory speech, "and that inflexible determination that knows no failure."

He attended the elite Bowdoin College, south along the coast in Brunswick, and worked every summer in Maine's massive inland forests for the state forestry service. The service did demanding work —building fire towers in remote locations, stringing telephone lines to connect them—but Avery became fascinated with the deep woods setting, so different from the coastal world of canning factories he had grown up in. The rugged summer employment set Avery apart from many of his classmates, who were primarily the sons of New York and

New England's elite, people for whom summer was a season of leisure, not work. In school, the teenaged Avery did not make much of an impression on the Bowdoin scene, judging by the school newspaper; he was remembered by a classmate as a dogged striver, "plugging away to win a place on the cross-country team" and studying late at night to earn top grades.

The striving worked. He graduated from Bowdoin at twenty, and earned admission to Harvard Law School. But even as he undertook that significant challenge, the Maine backcountry—especially its pinnacle, Mt. Katahdin—occupied his attention. The highest peak in Maine, Katahdin was to many at that time something of a holy grail, the ultimate embodiment of the Maine wilderness. While managing the heavy workload of Harvard Law, Avery threw himself into understanding the history of Katahdin and its early exploration. From old books, journals, and newspaper clippings, and correspondence with people who had firsthand knowledge, he assiduously collected everything there was to know about the history of the mountain. Together with a geology graduate student studying the area for his dissertation, Avery published a bibliography of Katahdin. It set the pattern that he would follow for the rest of his adult life, spending virtually every waking moment engaged in one of two pursuits, the law or the mountains, with an intensity that few could match.

Avery graduated from law school in 1923 and took his degree to Hartford, Connecticut, where he worked for an insurance company and became active in the local branch of the Appalachian Mountain Club. He worked in Hartford for only about eighteen months, before moving on to a new job in Washington, DC, practicing maritime law for the federal agency overseeing the United States shipping industry. He soon married a young woman, originally from Wyoming, named Jeanette Leckie.

Leckie must have quickly wondered what she had gotten herself into. Avery almost immediately began disappearing for long stretches to take on major hiking expeditions. The year after his marriage, he secured for himself a place on the National Park Service's exploration of Virginia's Blue Ridge Mountains, in anticipation of establishing a national park there. Avery served as a scout, hiking ahead of the main group of visitors to identify places of interest and make arrangements. Upon his return he wrote to his old AMC friends in the Northeast that this foreign land was full of beautiful scenery and curious Appalachian residents. "Presenting a new country—a new topography —new trees (we had a small tree manual)—new types of people and living conditions—to say nothing of new kinds of cooking (Southern) the trip was remarkably profitable and pleasing. I hope to go back again with some of you people."

The following year, he took the first of what would be three trips in consecutive summers to Katahdin and the country surrounding it. As Maine's timber industry had reached deeper into the forests, and as automobiles made travel to faraway places easier, Katahdin was slowly coming within reach of outside visitors. Rising majestically from the surrounding forest, a towering rocky island in an ocean of trees, Katahdin took on a mythic status for the eastern hiking community. Avery was pleased to identify himself, from the research he had done, as the person who knew the most about Katahdin without ever actually visiting it, and he remedied that shortcoming with trips in the summers of 1927, '28, and '29. Not content to hike on the trails the AMC had been opening up, he explored the entire region, documenting his discoveries in articles he prepared and tried to get published in the AMC's *Appalachia* and other publications.

During this same period, Avery received a letter inviting him to help with the plans to build an Appalachian Trail, then proceeding very slowly under the intermittent stewardship of Benton MacKaye. With the enthusiastic buy-in of trail groups in New

York and New England, there was no shortage of support for the Appalachian Trail in the mid-1920s, but there was precious little leadership.

The man who first stepped into that vacuum was an acquaintance of Avery's from his time in Hartford, a retired judge named Arthur Perkins. Perkins had come to hiking relatively late in life, but in retirement he was keen to devote as much time as possible to it. The more Perkins learned about the AT effort, the more he discovered that MacKaye would welcome as much time as Perkins could give to it. The two men met frequently and became friends. "I sat with the Judge many an evening in his attractive home," MacKaye recalled years later, "discussing the fate of the Trail, section by section."

In the fall of 1926, Perkins wrote to his young and ambitious colleague in the nation's capital, Avery. "I know there are lots of good mountains in Virginia, not very far away from Washington, and it seems as if there ought to be some organization near you that would to some extent take the place of the A.M.C. Why do you not look up one, or else start one for yourself?"

Avery did just that. In the fall of 1927, just after he had completed his first Katahdin expedition, Avery and a handful of others organized the Potomac Appalachian Trail Club (PATC) to build and maintain the AT in Maryland and Virginia, and organize hiking opportunities for club members.

Partly by design—MacKaye had intended from the start that the AT organize itself organically, from the ground up—the handful of Washington enthusiasts had no directions from on high to follow in building a new path. The idea was enough. Learning as they went—about Virginia's Blue Ridge, how to clear trail, how to organize work trips—the small band of volunteers headed off to the woods virtually every weekend. "Our first real work trip," one of Avery's colleagues remembered,

Andy, Myron and I took a train to Harpers Ferry. We had to learn from sad experience how canteens are needed in the Blue Ridge, and we didn't have the kind of tools used today.... We learned our trail technique the hard way. We used, that day, mainly Boy Scout axes. We were all dying of thirst after getting to the top. It took us all day to get from south of Chimney Rock to a point about a half mile beyond. Our axes got so dull we couldn't cut with them. We just had to saw off the twigs.

Yet the small crew of enthusiasts, slowly recruiting new members, went back virtually every weekend. In its first year, the PATC cleared 42 miles of trail south from Harpers Ferry, West Virginia. Just as MacKaye had imagined, the new route allowed for relatively easy car or train trips from Washington out to one end and a return from the other.

Judge Perkins was soon able to report to MacKaye that the young Avery, in Washington, was doing great work not only to build his own section, but to organize other clubs outside the PATC's jurisdiction, in the southern half of the Appalachians where relatively little had been accomplished. Soon after founding the PATC, Avery lobbied Perkins to hold another full Appalachian Trail Conference in Washington. A small group attended—MacKaye did not—and Avery and Perkins began overhauling the tenuous organization that had been established at the first meeting less than three years earlier. A year later, in May of 1929, they organized the third Appalachian Trail Conference in Easton, Pennsylvania, and a new constitution drafted by Avery was adopted for the organization. MacKaye did attend this meeting, but his main contribution was an opening address titled "The Origin and Conception of the A.T." Avery would have been thrilled to have the philosophizing out of the way early, so that the meeting could focus on what he considered the real work—getting the trail built.

The new constitution divided the length of the proposed trail into five regional districts, each of which would have three representatives on the Appalachian Trail Conference's board of managers, including Horace Kephart for the southern district. The constitution bears all the hallmarks of Avery's organizational enthusiasm, though one of the elements of his draft—that the ATC be headquartered in his home city of Washington, and all of its meetings be held there, was edited out.

"The purpose of this organization shall be to promote, construct and maintain a connected trail," the document began, and stressed that the AT's overriding purpose was as a facility for backwoods recreation. But MacKaye's larger interests maintained a toehold in the statement of purpose, "for conserving and developing, within this region, the primeval environment as a natural resource."

"Primeval environment," to Avery, was just so much clutter. Trail mileage could be counted; trail clubs could be listed, and their activities itemized. "Primeval environment," with its allusion to some sort of social–spiritual harmony, had no acceptable format in a map or guidebook, and as such it was worse than useless to Avery. The entire AT project "had degenerated into a fireside philosophy," he would later write, and only the building of real, physical trail would get it on track.

Less than a year after the Easton meeting, Judge Perkins suffered the first of what would turn out to be a series of strokes, and he asked Avery to take on a greater share of the chairman's duties. In retrospect, Avery's drive and ambition were so intense that there was bound to be a clash between the two men at some point; Perkins's ill health spared them that showdown.

There were, for Avery, four basic steps in getting the AT built: (1) getting a trail club organized to take control of a certain section; (2) determining the best route for the trail through that section; (3) clearing, marking, and maintaining the trail; and (4) gathering and keeping up-to-date trail data and maps to publish in ATC guidebooks. It was a combination of finding others to take on local leadership, motivating and admonishing them to get the work done, and overseeing the work to ensure that it was up to Avery's standards for the trail as a whole. He accomplished this in part through voluminous letter writing, the letters dictated during evening meetings to women members of the PATC who, like Avery, participated in the trail effort not just with excursions and work trips, but in volunteering the considerable office work necessary to organize such a far-flung effort. And he spent virtually every free day that he had—weekends, vacations—getting out to scout, hike, and help clear new sections of trail. He was a tireless hiker, plunging deep into the unmarked forest to scout and mark new sections of trail and inspect and oversee the work of others.

In June of 1930, Avery hiked 70 miles through the Natural Bridge National Forest in Virginia, marking new trail and leaving behind a new local club to attend to that section. But even where there were established groups doing their own work, he inserted himself. The very first Appalachian Trail built for that purpose, before Avery had any involvement at all, was in the New York–New Jersey area, where the trail enthusiast and organizer Raymond Torrey tended to a vibrant local hiking scene through his weekly newspaper column. Still, in the fall of 1930, Avery hiked 155 miles of trail between the Hudson River and the Delaware Water Gap, noting deficiencies ("which we shall polish up straightaway," Torrey noted, most likely rolling his eyes) along the way. Over this same period, Avery wrote letters constantly—to Pennsylvania organizers to get their act together in determining the routing through their state, to the New England Trail Conference to open connections between existing sections of trail, to Horace Kephart and other southern leaders trying to determine the correct path from the Smokies down to Georgia. He even dictated the letters that he wanted his committee chairmen to send, presenting them for their signature. In 1931, he and the president of the Georgia AT club hiked 200 miles together to the AT's annual conference in Gatlinburg, Tennessee.

The relationship between Avery's centralized, coordinated effort and the grassroots, bottom-up ownership of the trail sections was bound to be a delicate one. Avery in his zeal did not have much patience for, or perhaps even comprehension of, tact. MacKaye, in his conception of the trail, was both philosophically and habitually inclined to let locals take the lead. He imagined that his vision would attract like-minded individuals to the cause, and that the trail would grow outward from individual local efforts to eventually connect up with one another. To him, the trail's total length did not matter as much as how many communities were rallying to his vision. To Avery, though, local clubs were simply a means to an end. The end was the trail itself—complete, contiguous, marked, and measured.

In those early days, organizers planned to mark the trail with stamped metal insignia. The markers would help keep hikers on the path, but also with their distinctive design identify the AT as the special trail it was, not unlike the unique signs for United States highways. Avery became obsessed with getting these markers placed on every section of trail as soon as it was created.

Judge Perkins was paying out of his own pocket to have the markers made, then planning to be reimbursed by local clubs that would purchase them from him with whatever dues money they could raise. Sometimes Perkins would simply donate them. But this process could not keep up with the pace of new trail being cleared under Avery's insistent leadership, and to Avery it wasn't really the Appalachian Trail if it was not officially labeled as such. In August of 1930, while Perkins was recovering from his second stroke, Avery wrote him,

I am afraid that there is one detail of Club business which you will have to consider. I have written you for definite word as to whether you were going to start things off in Lynchburg with some markers. So that things wouldn't die out I advanced 120 from our stock. We are absolutely broke as a Club and I had to assure the Council that when more are made up that we will be reimbursed. Even if you decide not to donate any to Lynchburg, I suggest you have another batch made up and ready to sell. In fact you should have 500 on hand. As soon as other Clubs learn of the price requests for markers will come in and it will be annoying to wait two months to get them made up.

A couple of months later, more exasperated, Avery again hectored the ailing Perkins, "Now where are these markers coming from?"

Avery's manner was brusque and demanding, but his colleagues seem to have excused it as a by-product of a commitment to the project that none of them could match. To a small group of volunteers already dedicated enough to the Appalachian Trail to volunteer their time and hard work, Avery's intensity had to be both daunting and inspiring, if also frequently annoying. No other individual spent the hours that he did both in the woods and in the office; none had the knowledge he did of the overall trail effort, or often even of their own section.

In May 1932, Avery was notified by telegram that Judge Perkins had died. A few months earlier, Avery had been able to

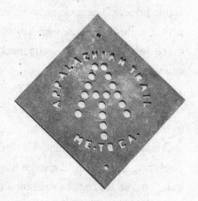

An early AT trail marker.

report to the ATC board that "with the exception of the link between the Smokies and Nantahala, which is being thoroughly scouted, the trail should be completed by August 1932 from Grafton Notch [just inside the Maine border] to the southern terminus." It had been less than five years since Avery's first trail-cutting trip near Harpers Ferry, when the AT was for practical purposes almost exclusively a New York–New England trail. And while the work of volunteers in local clubs was essential, it is impossible to imagine so much progress being made so quickly had Avery not been so persistently leading the work, in person and from afar.

One section of trail, though, seemed beyond even Avery's focus and stamina, and it was the one that provided his deepest connection to the mountains. "The 200 mile link from Grafton Notch to Katahdin seems hopeless," he wrote. Compared with the rest of the AT, the Maine section was impossibly distant from the kind of cities that could provide volunteers, deep in thick forest that required long and difficult journeys to reach. The very thing that made the AT a worthy project to all of its early backers—the proximity of its seemingly wild landscape to the population centers of the East—was also what made it a viable project. These cities provided people—and specifically people with middle-class lives, who had time and money to donate, and cars to transport volunteers—who marked and built the trail during weekend work trips.

But the ridgeline from Mt. Washington in New Hampshire to Katahdin in Maine ran nowhere near even small cities. Building the trail to that point had already been a monumental task, contingent on the enthusiasm for hiking that was welling up in the culture, and on the catalyzing qualities of both MacKaye's vision and Avery's drive. Without an urban backbone of volunteers to organize, the link to Katahdin seemed a bridge too far.

"Were it not for Katahdin's distinctiveness and the absence of a suitable northern terminus," Avery wrote in his 1932 report, "perhaps the abandonment of this Maine link would at this time be expedient."

His sense of discouragement did not last long. The next year, exercising the mix of willfulness and compulsion that defined his life, Avery led a small crew of PATC volunteers to the top of Katahdin, hauling a large wooden sign announcing the northern terminus of the Appalachian Trail. When Avery's party reached the summit, there were about 200 miles of remote wilderness separating them from the last section of existing AT. But this was a man who fully expected the world to yield to his own sense of what was right and necessary, under the unrelenting pressure of his own commitment. The crew of four men installed the sign, then hiked, scouted, and blazed south from Katahdin over a distance of 119 miles, coordinating their work with that of a Maine Guide (and Broadway actor), Walter Greene, who on his own had begun marking a substantial stretch of the new trail. A handful of others from Maine's forestry community contributed as well, so that by the end of 1934 a functional trail route had been marked.

As impressive as this accomplishment was, a marked route was not actually a trail, and clearing one through dense forest would require a great deal more work than Avery and his small band of volunteers could provide. Avery pieced together the funds to hire the labor to do the work, and arranged for the Civilian Conservation Corps, one of the Great Depression's signature work-relief programs, to clear some trail as well. In August of 1937, a CCC crew cleared a 2-mile stretch of trail in the high country between Spaulding and Sugarloaf Mountains, the last original section of Appalachian Trail to be opened.

By this time, Avery was the singular and unquestioned leader of the Appalachian Trail project, in part owing to his dedication and in part because he had alienated so many of his onetime collaborators. The turning point was the 1935 dispute within the Appalachian Trail

Myron Avery, center, with his trusty measuring wheel, atop Mt. Katahdin with fellow trail builders in 1933.

community over the federal government's building of scenic highways. Many of the key players in the building of the trail—including Avery's co-founder of the PATC, H. C. "Andy" Anderson, and Raymond Torrey, chair of the New York–New Jersey Trail Council—felt that these roads posed an existential threat to the AT. Unlike the philosopher MacKaye, Anderson and Torrey were trail builders and organizers with deep and long-standing ties to Avery. Like him, they had put in long, hard hours marking trail and felling trees, writing letters, and attending meetings, all on behalf of a vision of backwoods seclusion.

    Their faith in that vision was deeply shaken when the National Park Service built the Skyline Drive through Shenandoah National Park, bringing motorists and their vehicles to the same peaks, and along the same route, that the AT had only recently opened up to hikers. The trail was rerouted not far away, within earshot of the traffic. Appalled

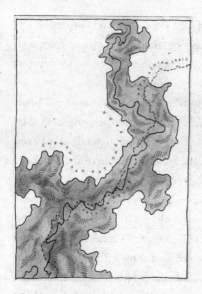

The AT and Skyline Drive in close proximity through Shenandoah National Park.

and offended, Avery's colleagues demanded that the Appalachian Trail Conference take a principled stand against any more construction of ridgeline highways by the Park Service.

Avery himself was no fan of scenic roads for their own sake, but he had long had a close working relationship with the leadership of the Park Service, and he resisted others' attempts to intrude. After all, the only reason the AT could proceed through a protected Shenandoah in the first place, and the Great Smoky Mountains farther south, was thanks to the creation of national parks. A negotiated, case-by-case solution was the best way forward, Avery argued. He had no interest in turning over his meticulously built organization to the forces of righteous indignation.

The activists, though, would not let the matter go. Why had they expended all of that time and effort on the AT if it could at any time be reduced to a sidewalk along a scenic drive? Moreover, what was the value in hiking the Appalachian ridgeline if it was just as overrun with cars as any other landscape?

Resolving this dispute inevitably raised the question of just who and what the Appalachian Trail Conference was: an organizer of trail work or an advocate for a wilderness experience? Avery argued for the former, his colleagues for the latter. In the past, whatever discomfort people may have felt with Avery's imperiousness was usually outweighed by the fact of his productivity, especially when everyone was essentially pulling in the same direction. But on a matter so central to the very meaning of the trail effort, his opponents resolved to confront Avery.

Under the old ways of doing Appalachian Trail business—a small band of committed volunteers, only as strong as the consensus they could agree to—the dispute might have resulted in paralysis, or even in Avery's resignation. But as the 1935 annual meeting of the ATC approached, Avery the attorney proposed a change to the organization's bylaws. Binding votes of the membership would be cast by representatives of each trail-maintaining local club, with the votes weighted by the mileage of trail that each club oversaw. Because so many of the clubs, especially from Maryland south, had come into existence under Avery's leadership, that format would cement his own control of the organization. And because the location of the 1935 conference was Skyland, the Shenandoah retreat not far from Washington, many of the attendees would be PATC members who would vote for the change in the bylaws. Avery's opponents had hoped to make the 1935 conference a showdown over skyline drives. Instead, the membership on hand voted 78 to 8 to change the bylaws, cementing Avery's position. Not only would his own policy on scenic highways carry the day, but on all matters the ATC was now unquestionably Avery's organization.

In a final, bitter exchange of letters, Benton MacKaye divorced himself from the ATC completely. Even Anderson, who had been with Avery on the very first trip to cut trail with dull axes near Harpers Ferry, left the PATC; Torrey bitterly denounced Avery and the ATC in his New York newspaper columns, though they later managed to work together again.

A few years later, the National Park Service announced an extension of the Skyline Drive. The Blue Ridge Parkway would reach more than 450 miles from Shenandoah National Park all the way to the Smokies, requiring a realignment of more than 100 miles of AT to a completely different route. Avery called it "the major catastrophe in Appalachian Trail history." It took until 1951 to finish the job of rerouting the trail.

While Avery managed to at some point alienate virtually every collaborator he ever worked with, there was one partnership that stood alone in its durability. Jean Stephenson, a fellow PATC volunteer, became Avery's indefatigable and loyal partner in the day-to-day management of the Appalachian Trail Conference for almost the entirety of his twenty-five-year involvement with the project.

In her professional life, Stephenson was an archivist and editor, roles that she took on for the ATC as well. She collected and edited trail data, oversaw the organization's publications, and managed publicity. These tasks were all critically important to Avery. Since he had first become interested in Katahdin as a law student at Harvard, he had been obsessed with documentation. His first publication was a bibliography of Katahdin literature, which he updated and expanded for years, fighting to keep it in publication. He also wanted his own knowledge published, always writing articles and harassing editors to get his and the ATC's worldview into print. His entrusting of that role to Stephenson, and the fact that the partnership endured over two decades, right up to Avery's death, was unique among the dozens of working relationships Avery built (and destroyed) over the years.

Avery's own family—he and his wife, Jeanette, had two sons—seems to have been largely left behind as he spent every waking moment not already spent on his professional career on the AT. One of his sons remembered that weeks would go by without his ever seeing his father. "He was gone in the morning before I got up and didn't come back until after I went to bed. We'd sometimes see each other on weekends, and it was kind of like we were having a reunion." When Avery was around, though, he was as demanding of his family as of everyone else in his life. He was, his son Hal remembered, a "very moral man, quite demanding of all of us, almost on a perfectionist level. And, he was equally demanding of himself. In the family, we treated him with a great deal of respect: It was, 'Yes, sir,' and, 'No, sir.' . . . It wasn't until later that I learned that other people never did that in their families, but we did."

Avery's demand for precision extended to the trail itself. He insisted that every section be well marked and precisely documented —trail mileages, shelter locations, points of interest. In most cases he insisted on doing the job himself, gathering data with his ubiquitous measuring wheel and notebook, hiking every section of trail as it was completed, on top of the earlier hikes he had made in the process of scouting and clearing the trail. Stephenson was then in charge of publishing the information in ATC guidebooks. To Avery, no section of trail was complete until it was fully documented in this fashion; its reality was in some sense constituted by its existence on paper, properly formatted. In his mind, to know the mountains was to catalog them, and the trail itself was something like an index, a way to organize and understand the landscape.

For this reason, Avery was obsessed with the published record. First with his Katahdin exploration and research, then with the Appalachians and their trail, it was exceedingly important to him to be the published authority on the topic. He was in constant contact and epistolary combat with editors seeking to have his articles published, both to set the record straight on some matter large or small, and to share his own hard-won knowledge. Perhaps it was self-aggrandizement that Avery was after, but it seems to have been equally important to him that the story be told the right way, up to his standards in form and content.

His crowning achievement in this regard, he expected, would be an article in one of the twentieth century's most esteemed publications, *National Geographic* magazine. He wrote an article in 1934 methodically describing the trail from north to south—the natural features along the way, some local history—in essence a lengthy encyclopedia entry. After submitting the article on Avery's behalf, Jean Stephenson received a courteous reply from the magazine, saying that the article as written was not appropriate for publication, but that other, more specialized, outlets might be interested. "I felt, upon reading the story, that it was too technical a paper, lacking in color, adventure, and human interest," the editor responded.

Avery and Stephenson might have either taken the editor's advice and looked for a different magazine to publish the article, or seen in the rejection the need to revise the article to make it more broadly appealing. Instead, Stephenson wrote back to point out that the editor had, in fact, come to the wrong conclusion. Stephenson made a lengthy case for the quality of Avery's article, its authoritativeness, and its appeal to a wide audience. Rather than pursue other magazines as an outlet, Stephenson wrote, she and Avery would seek to publish his work as a stand-alone book, "unless, of course, before that time the National Geographic can see its way closer to using it."

Book publishers were not interested, and two-and-a-half years later, Avery and Stephenson tried a second time with *National Geographic*. The response this time showed a hint of frustration. "To be frank with you, the article is not in shape for publication in the National Geographic and would probably have to be rewritten for our publication. If it is desired that any time in the future we would publish an article from you perhaps you would be given some suggestions as to our editorial policy and then proceed to do the job according to our specifications."

Another two years on, in the spring of 1939, Avery and Stephenson got word that the magazine was preparing its own article on the AT.

Others might have been thrilled, that their life's work was going to be profiled by a professional writer in such a prominent and well-regarded publication. But Avery and Stephenson were appalled. Stephenson wrote directly to the president of the National Geographic Society, insisting that Avery's article be published instead.

"Even if the article were not as well written as it is, there would be, I should think, a decided advantage in having any statement about such a unique and outstanding project made by a man who is not only at present Chairman of The Appalachian Trail Conference, but the one who is responsible for the carrying through and completion of the project, the one to whom the existence of it is due and who is entirely and thoroughly familiar with every phase of it."

Stephenson not so subtly pointed out that the information available from the ATC's guidebooks was copyrighted material, off-limits to a *National Geographic* writer. She said that while Avery was not interested in revising his article, he would be willing to make small edits.

An assistant editor replied, urging the ATC to cooperate in the preparation of an article, surely an odd plea to have to make when a magazine with a readership of five million is trying to write a positive profile. "If we once get in mind that the matter of the sale of this manuscript to The National Geographic Magazine is a closed incident, I think we then can proceed with a better understanding, and clear the decks to get an article which will be satisfactory to our Editor, to our readers, and to the Conference."

Avery and Stephenson, after five years, could not get that in mind; they insisted that Avery's article be published, or none. Not until August of 1949, a full fifteen years after the correspondence began, would *National Geographic* publish its article on the Appalachian Trail.

Perhaps the other great frustration of Avery's trail-building career was his attempt to have the region around Mt. Katahdin protected as a national park. Katahdin was doubly important to Avery as the northern culmination of the AT, and the defining inland feature of the state that he still proudly identified with. With justification, he considered himself the foremost authority on the area, based on his historical research and his demanding expeditions there over three summers in the late 1920s. But since that time, the mountain had become increasingly popular and accessible. Over the course of the 1930s, roads closer to Katahdin opened up, and the Appalachian Mountain Club developed a trail network on the rocky colossus. Already in 1932, an estimated 1,200 climbers had attempted Katahdin; five years on, that number was growing steadily.

The mountain was protected from development, but only to a limited extent. In 1930 a former governor of Maine, Percival Baxter, had purchased the land containing the peak and gifted it to the state. But the state government had no resources available to actually manage its new park. The same qualities that made Avery and Baxter enthusiasts of Katahdin — not just its status as Maine's highest peak, but its majestic profile — beckoned hundreds of visitors, most with a fraction of the mountaineering expertise Avery had needed for his earlier expeditions, bringing noise, litter, and disorder for several weeks every summer.

Avery determined that the solution to this problem was a new national park, protecting a territory much broader than the peak itself. The National Park Service had the means not only to protect the land, he reasoned, but to bring the kind of order that Avery so craved: managed uses, respectable facilities.

He enlisted the help of Maine congressman Owen Brewster, who in 1937 introduced a bill, drafted by Avery, to create a Katahdin National Park. Former governor Baxter, however, was staunchly opposed. A fervent anti–New Dealer, Baxter distrusted the federal government on principle, and was especially suspicious of the National Park Service's reputation for developing its parks so intensely that their wild character was lost. Baxter had begun working to make Katahdin a state park while Avery was still a schoolboy in Lubec. After failing first as a legislator and then as governor to accomplish the task in legislation, Baxter as a private citizen paid for the land out of his own pocket and created the park as a gift to the people of Maine. It required years of negotiations among landowners, himself, and the state. Baxter not surprisingly felt a deep personal stake in the park that bore his name.

Avery felt his own kind of ownership. He had through years of hard work become the most knowledgeable authority on the mountain and its history, explored its rarely visited surroundings multiple times, and directed the development of a 2,000-mile trail that would reach its figurative apogee at Katahdin's summit. He was accustomed to his twin advantages over others in knowledge and physical work making him the unquestioned leader on any given topic. When someone for whatever reason differed from Avery's preferred course of action, as in the Skyline Drive controversy or his tiff with *National Geographic*, he seemed to not understand, assuming that the more directly he explained himself, the more others would recognize the correctness of his preferred direction. The idea that someone else might have a different set of values, or even their own kind of expertise that Avery lacked, seemingly never crossed his mind. Others' failure to get on board with him, whether the president of the National Geographic Society or the namesake of Baxter State Park, quickly turned to bitter frustration and a seemingly bottomless capacity for further argument.

At the beginning of his campaign for a national park, Avery tried to enlist Baxter's support. An exchange of letters between the two men in the winter of 1936–37 began in a cordial tone — "Many of us who are interested in the Katahdin region have become quite concerned over its future," Avery wrote — but quickly turned more confrontational. Baxter replied that he was confident his own ongoing work to add lands to the state park would strengthen its protection, and he took offense at the idea of Avery and his allies at the federal level showing such disrespect toward the work Baxter had already done.

Avery argued that Baxter could not on his own act quickly enough to add more land, and regardless could do nothing about the state's failure to manage the park. He bristled at Baxter's resistance. "The need is so real and the project so tremendous that I am loathe to believe that you will irrevocably cast your influence across the path of this bill. . . . If you oppose this measure and your influence blocks an opportunity for the American people to acquire forever this area, this will rest on you a grievous responsibility."

Baxter was stalwart in his opposition, and he held much more influence in Maine than Avery. In this matter, Avery had the opposite position from the one he held in the Skyline Drive controversy with MacKaye. Now Avery was the one pleading his scheme from outside the process, and Baxter was the insider dealing in facts and practicalities.

"If you had worked twenty-six years on this project as I have done," Baxter wrote, "you too might have acquired some special knowledge of local men, conditions and motives—especially the latter—and might be in a position to profit by the experiences gained throughout the long period."

When Baxter rallied Maine's political leadership against the proposal, the National Park Service had no viable partner in pursuing the project. Brewster's legislation went nowhere, and though Avery continued to argue for a Katahdin National Park for years afterward, the matter was essentially closed. But in part to ward off any future interest from the federal government, Baxter continued to acquire land to expand the park, eventually reaching about 200,000 acres, compared with his initial gift of 6,000, and the State of Maine began to actively manage the park.

The battle between Avery and Baxter over Katahdin occurred in the same summer, 1937, that marked the "completion" of the AT in the wilds of western Maine. But as the Katahdin fight demonstrates, Avery's attention had by this point shifted from the opening of the trail to the maintenance and protection of it. At least three factors were at work fraying the link that Avery had so painstakingly stitched together from Maine to Georgia. The first was nature itself. Blowdowns blocked the trail; floods made sections impassible; undergrowth rapidly overtook previously cleared sections. While this was generally more of a challenge in the southern sections, the New England Hurricane of 1938 obliterated huge sections of trail in the north as well. It turned out that a path through nature required a lot of effort beating back nature just to keep it intact, and this was made more difficult by the second challenge — lack of use. In the Northeast, where there was a long-established and vibrant hiking scene, the AT tied together constituent trails that already had plenty of users and caretakers. But in the South, the AT was for the most part purpose-built. It made sense only as a part of a bigger idea, an idea strong enough to get it built (including long stretches with CCC labor) but not to attract a broad user base. At one point the head of the United States Forest Service warned that his southern forest managers were growing resistant to devoting scarce resources to a trail that was seeing so little use. The third challenge was the shifting use of the land through which the trail ran. Early outdoor hobbyists liked to think they were stepping off into a freestanding and more or less permanent nature, when in fact the backwoods had its own complicated history of human use, use that was ongoing and evolving. The same cars that had only recently made the hikers' weekend trips a possibility also enabled a different kind of outdoors constituent to take scenic drives. The backwoods through which the trail passed might seem timeless and remote, but in fact consisted of owned parcels that were subject to productive use, even in the national forests. A thick woodland one day might be a clear-cut the next, or the setting for a new mountain parkway.

From the beginning, then, the AT had to fight against its own contradictions. The nature to which it was meant to provide access proved at best indifferent, at worst hostile, to the trail's very existence. Only as a human thoroughfare—cleared, signed, maintained, rebuilt—could it continue to exist. But in that way it was no different than any other human use of the forests, one that had to contend in both land markets and policy circles for primacy over other, competing uses.

Avery embraced this challenge, envisioning an Appalachian Trailway that would provide a 2,000-mile corridor of protection, cobbled together from the federal, state, and private lands through which the trail ran. It would remain the foremost challenge of the Appalachian Trail community for decades.

Very quickly, however, far more pressing matters came to dominate the American consciousness. As Europe erupted into war, and American shipping to Great Britain took on strategic importance, Avery was required to move to New York to work out of the United States Attorney's office there. In 1942 he was called to active duty in the Navy, where he became the chief of admiralty law. His son remembered a special phone line being installed in the family home, where Avery could be reached at any time to deal with emergencies. Though he and the other trail volunteers did their best to keep work going on the Appalachian Trail, the war years by and large meant neglect for the trail only tenuously completed a few years earlier, and already facing considerable struggles.

In the years immediately following the war, Avery led the considerable efforts to rebuild and reopen the trail—clearing blowdowns, cutting back new growth, rerouting around changing land uses, and relocating the more than 100 miles displaced by the Blue Ridge Parkway. After years of work, Avery organized a ceremony atop a mountain called The Priest, in Virginia's Blue Ridge. "Here, on June 10, 1951, there was placed the last blaze which made the 2,025-mile Appalachian

Trail once again a completed unbroken footpath from Maine to Georgia." At that point Avery had twice, in the space of roughly fifteen years, led the efforts to clear a contiguous trail over the mountains from Maine to Georgia, with a singular mix of devotion, compulsion, and combativeness. In between, he had shouldered tremendous responsibility in the administration of the war effort.

His worldview did not, it seems, make any room for the inconvenience of ill health, but Avery in the postwar years learned that his pathological intensity was not sustainable. At various times, he and his ATC colleagues referred imprecisely to his "nerve fatigue," "hypertension," and "stomach trouble," ailments that required periodic breaks from his Navy duties and ATC leadership, even though he was only in his late forties. He was hospitalized multiple times, at one point checking himself out after three weeks, complaining that he was getting worse, not better.

Finally, in early 1952, Avery relinquished the chairmanship of the ATC and retired from the Navy. That summer, he took a driving trip with his son Hal to Nova Scotia, where he planned to do some genealogical research. "Letters indicated he had a restful, easy, trip and was enjoying his freedom to do as he pleased with no set schedule or deadlines to meet," Jean Stephenson wrote soon after. "But last Saturday morning, July 26, as he and Hal stood on the lawn of the hotel at Annapolis Royal, as he was calling Hal's attention to something, his face went blank and he dropped—and it was the end."

Avery "came to the end of his trail," as Stephenson put it in the ATC's obituary, at the age of fifty-two. "As Myron Avery, facing into the sunset, follows the trail over the hills into the land from which there is no return, we can see the long shadow of his erect and vigourous figure stretching back over mountain and woodland until it changes imperceptibly into a footpath from Maine to Georgia and Georgia to Maine."

The Thru-Hike:
Earl Shaffer and Emma Gatewood

///

Why not walk the Army out of my system, both mentally and physically, take pictures and notes along the way, make a regular expedition out of it?

—Earl Shaffer

I did it. I said I'd do it and I've done it.

—Emma Gatewood

For all their differences, Benton MacKaye and Myron Avery had one thing in common. Neither of them cared one whit about the spectacle of hiking the entirety of the Appalachian Trail in a single season-long excursion, and neither imagined that such an eccentric use of the pathway would come to dominate many people's understanding of the trail's purpose and meaning. But in increasing numbers over the second half of the twentieth century, hikers were drawn to the prospect of a transformative, immersive experience on a trail that was almost, but not quite, endless. Thru-hiking developed its own customs, language, and history—a subculture as rich and unique as any.

Earl Shaffer's story has for a long time been first and foremost in the lore of thru-hiking, drawing on the central elements of countless such tales: the young loner, seeking his own redemption, charts a course and sets a standard for others to follow. Shaffer's 1948 trek from Georgia to Maine is widely accepted as the first thru-hike. Just a few years later, though, Emma Gatewood took an excursion on the AT that ticked none of those conventional narrative boxes. She was an old woman, not a young man, and after a lifetime of dire hardship she seemed to care more about the freedom of a long walk than she did the mythology of woodsmanship or the purity of nature.

In the stories of these two people and their historic journeys on the AT—how they fit together and how they fail to—lies an interesting perspective on the thru-hike as a piece of American culture. Shaffer's has long been the more frequently told story, both feeding into, and being shaped by, the image of the Appalachian Trail as a site of natural renewal for the hale and hearty. But Gatewood's story, which has only recently come fully to light, shows that from the beginning the AT has been a more complicated place than that.

Emma Gatewood was, unusual for someone central to the history of the Appalachian Trail, actually from Appalachia, the southern highland region defined by both its steep terrain and distinct social economy. She grew up among the Allegheny foothills of far southeastern Ohio, and her everyday environment had much more in common with that of West Virginia just across the Ohio River than with the agricultural flatlands and industrial cities of the rest of her home state.

She was born Emma Caldwell in Gallia County in 1887, the twelfth of fifteen children, and grew up on a succession of farms as her fam-

ily moved repeatedly in search of better opportunities. For the Caldwells and the thousands of people who scratched out a living in the
hills, unlike their counterparts in towns and cities, the outdoors was a
workplace from which to wrest a livelihood, not a patch of scenery to
admire and explore. That work began at a young age, and in the case
of the Caldwells was too important to the household's well-being for
children to attend school in any but the most idle times. At eighteen,
with minimal education and limited prospects, Emma left home to do
domestic work.

She was earning 75 cents a week as live-in help for a rural elderly
woman when she met P. C. Gatewood, a college-educated teacher
whose family owned a small business. The two got married in the spring
of 1907, when Emma was nineteen, and within a year she was both preg-
nant and abused. Almost from day one of their marriage, according to
her descendant and biographer, Ben Montgomery, Emma Gatewood's
husband viewed her as a possession, and violence as his means of control. After he hit her for the first time, according to Montgomery,

> She thought of leaving him that day and that night and on into
> the next, but where would she go? She had no paying job, no
> savings, and her education had ended in the eighth grade. She
> couldn't return home and be a burden on her mother, who re-
> mained busy rearing children. So she bit her tongue and stayed
> with P.C.

Surviving her husband and providing for her steadily growing family would define Gatewood's married life for the next three decades.
She had eleven children and was responsible not only for their upbringing and running her family's household, but also extensive physical labor on the succession of farms the Gatewoods lived on. Through
it all, she was doing whatever she could to protect herself and her

children from her husband. She defended herself, she fought back, and she sometimes escaped to the woods, where the idea of refuge among the trees was no literary allusion, but an all-too-real matter of life and death. There were happy times as well. The children remembered their mother especially enjoying taking them for long walks outdoors.

P. C. Gatewood was convicted of manslaughter after he killed a man in 1924. He was given a suspended sentence because of the court's belief that he needed to be able to provide for his family, but the restitution he was ordered to pay required selling off half their farm, and began a steady cycle of worsening economic fortunes for the family.

Whatever else changed in the Gatewoods' life, P. C.'s violence toward Emma was a constant. In 1937, after nearly twenty years of marriage, she left her younger children in the care of their older siblings, who were now adults, and escaped to California, where her mother and two of her siblings lived. She corresponded with her children in letters that had no return address, and were carefully written to prevent P. C. from determining her precise whereabouts. Not only was he reading her letters, he was directing the children's replies. In the end, she returned home out of obligation to the children, knowing that it put her again in harm's way.

Not long after, P. C. moved the family, including Emma and the three youngest children, aged eleven to fifteen, to a small farm on the West Virginia side of the river. In 1939 he managed to have Emma arrested after a fight between the two of them that left her with a grotesquely battered face. But that turned out to be the beginning of the end for the Gatewoods' marriage, and P. C.'s presence in Emma's life. As local officials came to learn more about the Gatewoods' situation, they intervened on her behalf. P. C. left the family soon after, and in early 1941, after more than thirty years of marriage, Emma Gatewood secured a divorce. Now in her early fifties, she would set about building a new life on her own terms. Those terms would eventually include going for several very long walks.

In that same spring of 1941, about 325 miles away on the other side of the mountains in York, Pennsylvania, twenty-two-year-old Earl Shaffer was inducted into the United States Army. With the draft looming, he hoped to get a one-year hitch in the military over with so he could get on with his life. Instead, he would spend four-and-a-half increasingly embittered years in the Pacific Theater of World War II, and come out of it struggling to find a new path in life.

Shaffer was born in the small industrial city of York in November of 1918, the third of five children. His father did blue-collar work and served as a labor leader in York's factories, but beginning when Earl was five, the family lived in the countryside outside of town. Earl grew up roaming the fields and woods, hunting and trapping game as he got older, and working on neighbors' farms. His companion for much of that activity was a boy the same age, Walter Winemiller, who lived on a neighboring property. Earl, bookish and shy, deeply admired the more outgoing and physically capable Walter. "He seemed to know by instinct many things his pardner had to learn," Earl would recall.

> By night and by day we roamed the countryside, fishing, hunting, trapping, or just "bushwhacking" as we did every Sunday afternoon without fail for more than five years. We often walked as much as twelve or fifteen miles on these afternoon hikes, poking into every woodland or meadow so that we knew almost every woodchuck hole, squirrel tree, or similar attraction for miles around.

Adulthood came quickly for Earl. His mother died after a seemingly routine operation when he was fifteen, and he graduated from high school in York at the age of sixteen, having skipped eighth grade. In a later era, college would be the default option for someone with Earl's academic standing, but in a working-class family in the middle of the Great Depression, earning a wage was the top priority. He labored on farms and in construction for several years after high school, piecing together whatever jobs he could find to provide for himself and his family.

Earl Shaffer in the Pacific during World War II.

It became harder for Earl to find work after the United States began drafting soldiers in late 1940 for its likely entry into World War II; no one wanted to hire a young man who could be receiving an induction notice any day. So without any great enthusiasm he volunteered to be drafted into the Army, for what at that point was supposed be only one year. His more gung-ho pal Walter joined the Marines.

World War II was, to Earl, an exercise in almost ceaseless aggravation and discouragement. He was part of a crew that installed radar equipment on islands around the South Pacific, which was occasionally dangerous, and more often uncomfortable in a thousand different ways. From the time he showed up for induction in April 1941 until he returned home in September 1945, he was at the mercy of an Army bureaucracy that was constantly moving him around, frequently with no apparent rhyme or reason, and sometimes losing track of him altogether. His days consisted of some mixture of difficult outdoor work in the tropical heat, killing large swaths of time in between assignments, and traveling from one place to the next to endure more of the same. In one poem about his experience he wrote:

> We're just millions of young reluctants
> temporarily fighting men
> Who must shoulder the ugly burden
> for the right to go home again
> . . .
> The men who are faced with bullets
> are faced with a tangible foe
> But what of the ones who languish
> on an island a year or so?
> They look at the same grim faces
> and the same old barren view
> And must fight to retain their reason
> and something sane to do.

In early 1945, Earl received word that his friend Walter had been killed in the invasion of Iwo Jima. Several months later, the war over, Earl returned to his home in Pennsylvania a few months shy of his twenty-seventh birthday and tried to get his life restarted.

The end of the war also brought two of Emma Gatewood's sons home, one from a German prison camp, the other from the Philippines after taking a bullet in the leg. She had moved back to the Ohio side of the river by then, where her youngest child would finish high school. Free to fashion a life on her own terms, she spent the next several years moving around to different jobs and arrangements, living with a daughter for a while to help take care of a grandchild, tending to sick relatives, and working in healthcare.

At some point, probably while perusing magazines in a waiting room, she came across a 1949 article in *National Geographic* about the Appalachian Trail. It mentioned that a young man from Pennsylvania, Earl Shaffer, had the previous year become the first to hike the full length of the trail in a single trip. The article, which made no reference to Myron Avery and only briefly described the Appalachian Trail Conference, provided a gorgeously illustrated portrait of the trail as a continuous and well-maintained route through the mountains from Maine to Georgia. It was one version of what the trail aspired to be, but as both Avery and Earl Shaffer could have told readers, after years of neglect during the war years, the trail described in the article did not in fact exist.

Shaffer's 1948 thru-hike was the culmination of an abiding interest in the AT that had begun when he was a teenager in the '30s, the first few years of the trail's existence across Pennsylvania. Making his way in the outdoors, especially in the company of his friend Walter, had provided a sense of belonging for a young person whose family described him as something of a loner, diffident and argumentative. The AT, with its promise of ridgetop seclusion and extraordinary length, offered the possibility of a nearly boundless environment suited to Earl's needs; he and Walter had talked about hiking the whole thing one day.

By the time he was out of the Army, lacking direction and angry with the world, Shaffer searched for a way to make his mark and refocused his attention on the trail. He knew from a magazine article that no one had hiked the entire trail in one go, and hoped that if he could do it first, documenting his story in photos, he could get a book published and establish himself as a writer.

Setting off from Mt. Oglethorpe in Georgia on April 4, 1948, Shaffer almost immediately ran into the problem that would bedevil him for long stretches of his historic excursion: locating the trail itself. On the second day of the trip, he jotted in his diary, "Had tough time finding trail from Frosty Mt. north. Ranger showed me but still had difficulty."

Two days later, he "walked nearly ten miles before learning I was off trail. . . . Had to walk back hiked about 25 miles gained about 5."

Farther on in North Carolina, he later recalled, he was walking back to the trail after a stop for supplies in Horace Kephart's old stomping grounds of Bryson City when he missed his turnoff for the trail.

> The choice now was to backtrack or to bushwhack up the steep, high slope, which is what I chose and thereby jeopardized the entire expedition, instead of saving time. The greenbriers were incredibly nasty and the slope almost perpendicular. I must have been a pathetic figure, streaming with sweat, bleeding from scratches, every muscle aching, crawling endlessly in a back-slipping, bush-clutching struggle before coming out on top.

Part of Shaffer's problem, as Myron Avery was quick to point out after the hike was complete, was that he did not have the official ATC maps and guidebooks for reference. Shaffer had ordered them from the ATC before the hike, but they were lost in the mail before he left. But the larger issue was the state of the trail itself, which eleven years after its putative completion was riddled with blowdowns, overgrowth, detours onto roads, and being virtually paved over for long stretches by construction of the Blue Ridge Parkway. In fact, in Avery's mind there was no contiguous Appalachian Trail from 1938, when the New England hurricane wiped out large sections, until 1951, when the rerouting away from the parkway was complete.

In a sense, Shaffer was on a hopeless quest, seeking to hike in 1948 something that no longer existed: the completed Appalachian Trail of 1937. But it is hard to deny that even the patchy and discontinuous path of the late '40s was still in every important respect the AT. Physically it was badly frayed, but the idea that defined it, a ridgeline walking route from Maine to Georgia, was very much intact, and it was this combination of official pathway and imagined goal that Shaffer committed himself to that summer.

And it took a lot of commitment. He had to figure out how to stay fed, learn what gear was valuable and what wasn't, tend to his injuries (including a dog bite), and maintain steady daily progress on a trail that disappeared for long stretches. Heavy rain bedeviled him the most, more than once making him call into question the whole endeavor. Not far from home in Pennsylvania, a thunderstorm blew in and

> For an hour and a half it rained as fast as the air would let it fall, while I stumbled along over the rocky trail, my feet sloshing in my boots, rain dripping down my neck and all the while, mumbling to myself, Why oh why did I ever start out on this ridgerunner marathon anyway? And psyche answers in a mocking voice, to take pictures, amigo, to see if it can be done, for your health, to write a book, get along tough guy, get along.

It was not all hardship. Many individuals he encountered along the way, especially forest rangers and lone men staffing remote fire towers, expressed admiration for the challenge he had undertaken and opened up their homes to him. News of his journey traveled through the national forest network, and small-town newspapers, tipped off by a ranger of Shaffer's passing nearby, would write articles about him. In the White Mountains of New Hampshire, the Appalachian Mountain Club caretakers agreed to waive their usual fee for Shaffer to stay in their network of lodges.

As he approached the end in Maine, Shaffer's outlook continued to rise and fall. After a good night's rest in a shelter near Grafton Notch, he wrote in his diary, "In very good spirits. Thinking of Walter." A few days later on Mt. Spaulding, "Felt very lonesome, very grown up."

On August 4 he reached Katahdin Stream Campground. The ranger there notified a reporter in Millinocket who came out to interview him, along with a photographer, and the next morning he "climbed Katahdin in leisurely fashion, reached summit of Baxter peak about 1:30. Had pic taken by sign." And that was it.

Later generations of thru-hikers would look back on Shaffer's hike as the genesis of a tradition that they aspired to join, but at the time it seemed more a curiosity than anything. The ATC's newsletter included a report from Shaffer on an inside page of its January 1949 newsletter, with a preface presumably written by Jean Stephenson that acknowledged but did not celebrate the uniqueness of what Shaffer had done. It noted that Shaffer had struggled without the proper maps and guidebooks, and that the ATC discouraged solo travel on the trail. The greatest value of Shaffer's hike, from the ATC's perspective, seemed to be that he had provided an accounting of the trail conditions he encountered at different locations along the way. "This has been circulated to Conference officials and Trail maintaining officials to which it may be helpful."

While there was some newspaper coverage of the completed hike, because the article written by the reporter from Millinocket went out on the national AP wire, Shaffer's feat did not lead to widespread acclaim. *National Geographic* mentioned him at the start of its 1949 article, but only as a timely tie-in for a piece that had long been in the works. Shaffer wrote up his own book-length narrative of the thru-hike, but as with his World War II poetry, he could not find an interested publisher.

Still, Shaffer found a sense of purpose and belonging, perhaps for the first time since his weekend ramblings with a childhood friend, in the trail community. He took on a formal volunteer role with the

ATC as corresponding secretary, answering letter writers who needed guidance on long-distance hiking, and continued to report on conditions he encountered. In 1950 he returned to several stretches of trail to gather new material for his hoped-for book, and reported to Avery on what he had found. Avery appreciatively sent Shaffer's observations on to the various clubs in charge of maintenance.

> I wish to emphasize that Mr. Shaffer has written these letters, which involve considerable time and labor, at our request and for the sole purpose of assisting the Conference in affording the benefits of the observations of a very experienced Trail traveler. . . . I am sure that all who read the comments will appreciate his assistance and will not treat the matter as one which will require taking exception to any views expressed by Mr. Shaffer or imposing upon him the burden of further correspondence.

In the summer of 1953 Shaffer traveled to Shirley Center and visited at length with Benton MacKaye. MacKaye gave Shaffer a copy of his "An Appalachian Trail" article, signed "To Earl Shaffer of the A.T., one who did it from one who wrote it." The thru-hike had not altered the material circumstances of Shaffer's life, but it had enabled him to take on the AT as a central and treasured part of his place in the world.

Many others at that time were interested in taking an end-to-end hike on the trail. They were old and young, well educated and not, some on a break from a conventional career path, others not fully at home in the American mainstream. The term "thru-hike" did not exist yet, and for the most part these people did not know of one another. Each had decided, for their own set of reasons, that a months-long hike sounded like a good idea.

Three young men completed thru-hikes in 1951. The following year, a man and a woman together did what is now known as a "flip-flop," hiking part of the full trail in one direction, then traveling to the other end and hiking the remainder in the opposite direction. (The woman would later take on the name Peace Pilgrim, and make walking long distances in the name of peace her life's work.) That same year, 1952, a seventy-two-year-old retired professor thru-hiked the trail as well.

In 1954, sixty-six-year-old Emma Gatewood, apparently knowing nothing more about the trail than what had appeared in *National Geographic*, made her own decision to hike the full AT. She would never provide a singular answer as to why she was drawn to a thru-hike, beyond the fact that the trail sounded attractive to her, and she appreciated having the freedom to do as she pleased. The *National Geographic* article had organized its overview from north to south, and

A photo, captioned "All Hands Pitch In To Cut Short the Time till 'Soup's On!'" from National Geographic's *1949 article on the AT.*

in July Gatewood arrived at Baxter State Park in Maine to begin her trek. Though her first day on the trail was a success—she summited Katahdin in order to start at the very beginning—she quickly ran into trouble. On just her second full day of hiking after Katahdin, she inadvertently left the trail, one of the most dangerous situations one can find oneself in on that part of the AT. In the deep woods of Maine, being just a short distance off a trail can render it completely invisible, at which point the sea of surrounding trees becomes uniform and directionless, and disorientation quickly sets in. After two nights in the wilderness, and breaking her glasses, Gatewood somehow managed to rediscover the trail and return to where she'd started. With the strong encouragement of park rangers, including a ride to the nearest train station by the park's superintendent, Gatewood called off her hike and returned to Ohio.

The next spring she tried again, this time heading north from Georgia. As she had the previous year, Gatewood told no one, including her own family, what she was up to. She didn't want them to worry, and didn't want them to try to dissuade her from what she knew she wanted to do.

From the start, Gatewood made little distinction between the trail she was hiking on and the larger territory she was walking through. She sought food and shelter from the world around her, whether that was picking berries on the trail or asking to spend the night on nearby farms. Rather than outfit herself in special gear, she wore sneakers and slung her few belongings in a duffel over her shoulder. Gatewood had spent virtually her entire life in a working Appalachian landscape, getting around by foot, making do with what was at hand. Her hike on the AT would play out as an extension of that life, an indulgence in something that she enjoyed, rather than a self-conscious expedition into faraway nature.

Her first night, she lost the trail but came upon a house whose owners let her spend the night, and she hiked back in the morning. The second night, she used an abandoned shack near the trail for shelter. Later in Georgia she overnighted in a church, and another night was told by a man that she couldn't stay on his property, because she belonged with her family and not out hiking on her own.

Day in and day out, she proceeded up the trail, relying on her own grit and wits to get by, and relying on the generosity of those who lived nearby. Near Roanoke, Virginia, two members of the local Appalachian Trail club heard about her hiking through, spent half a day tracking her down, and shared her story with the local paper. As was the case with Shaffer, word of Gatewood's passage over the trail began to precede her, and local reporters caught up with her to write stories.

One reporter took an especially keen interest in Gatewood. Mary Snow covered women's sports for *Sports Illustrated* magazine, and could be an advocate for female athletes in her coverage. Tasked with covering the women's national track and field championships earlier that summer, Snow pointedly took note in her article of the resistance many young women had had to overcome just to participate in the competition. As Gatewood approached Bear Mountain in New York, Snow arranged to hike along with her for about 5 miles, then met her the next day on the mountain, bought her dinner, and paid for a cabin she could stay in.

Sports Illustrated ran a short back-page article under the caption "Pat on the Back." Unlike much of the coverage of Gatewood as an eccentric for thru-hiking the trail, Snow focused on the seriousness of the challenge she had undertaken.

> Mrs. Gatewood, alone and without a map, began following the white blaze marks of the trail early in May, and this week from Connecticut's Cathedral Pines, Grandmother Gatewood could look back on 1,500 miles of the best and worst of nature. She

had carefully avoided disturbing three copperheads and two rattlesnakes on the trail, flipped aside one attacking rattler with a walking stick. When caught without nearby shelter she had heated some stones and slept on them to keep from freezing. For snacks Grandma nibbled wild huckleberries, used sorrel for salad and sucked bouillon cubes to combat loss of body salt.

Gatewood proceeded into the mountains of New England in one of the worst possible years to be hiking there. Remnants of two different hurricanes dumped torrential rains, swelling creeks and rivers to record heights. Banding together with fellow hikers, she got through, made it across the fearsome Presidential Range of New Hampshire, and tackled the most desolate part of the trail, across western Maine, with a constantly sore knee.

When she got to Baxter State Park, she was met by both Mary Snow and the woman who had reported on the conclusion of Shaffer's hike seven years earlier, Mrs. Dean Chase. (Chase was known, as many women were at the time, by her husband's name. Snow's articles on Gatewood went without a byline.) The two women would accompany Gatewood off and on for the next several days, but she climbed Katahdin alone, for the second time in just over a year, to complete her hike on the morning of September 25, 1955.

Snow then rode the train with Gatewood to New York and showed her around the city. Reporting on the completed hike in *Sports Illustrated* a few weeks later, Snow celebrated Gatewood's "tremendous courage, ingenuity, and will power."

Asked why she undertook the trip, Grandma answered, "Because I wanted to,"—and because of the alluring things she had read about the Appalachian Trail. The reality was a disillusionment.... "I read about this trail three years ago in a magazine and the article told about the beautiful trail, how well marked it was, that it was cleared out and that there were shelters at the end of a good day's hike. I thought it would be a nice lark. It wasn't."

There was a great deal of news media attention to her feat, including an appearance on the *Today* show in New York, but Gatewood eventually settled back into her Ohio life. Then in the spring of 1957, she flew to Georgia again and thru-hiked the AT for the second time in three years, finishing a few weeks before her seventieth birthday. The following year she hiked a lengthy stretch of the AT in the Northeast, and in New York's Adirondack Mountains. In 1959 she walked along roads that followed the old Oregon Trail from Independence, Missouri, to Portland, Oregon, her progress tracked in newspapers, and the crush of onlookers near the end leaving her so frustrated that she hit one photographer with her umbrella. In 1964, at seventy-seven, she completed a section hike of the AT, traversing each part of the trail in a series of separate trips over the years, marking the third time she had walked the full length of the Appalachian Trail.

Emma Gatewood during her 1959 walk along the route of the Oregon Trail.

Earl Shaffer made his own repeat thru-hike, this time traveling from north to south, in the summer of 1965. Now forty-six, Shaffer was unmarried and continued to live at his childhood home with his sister and her husband. He never embarked on a formal career, working at various times in carpentry and stone work, dealing in antiques and clerking at auctions. For a long time, unpaid work for the AT was a central part of his life. In addition to corresponding with would-be hikers, he worked on trail relocations in Pennsylvania and built shelters. He always thought of himself as a writer but could never generate the interest in the stories of his life that he hoped to. The main outlet for his account of hiking the trail was a narrated slide show he would present to various groups.

It was only with the rise of thru-hiking, beginning in the late 1960s and accelerating in the '70s, that Shaffer's 1948 hike came to wider prominence. While there were numerous thru-hikers in the twenty years after his first trip, there were never more than a handful in any given year. But when a newer, more ecological version of the back-to-nature movement began to sweep the culture in the late '60s (Chapter 7), the popularity of hiking soared, to the point that hundreds of would-be thru-hikers were setting out from Springer Mountain each spring.

Shaffer's 1948 hike came to serve as the origin story for a thru-hiking culture that was playing a bigger and bigger role in the life of the AT itself. "Earl Shaffer's name is magic to hikers," Larry Luxenberg wrote in his book about thru-hiking. "No one better epitomizes the thru-hiker than this trail pioneer. . . . Earl Shaffer's life is a throwback to an earlier, simpler age, when people enjoyed the mountains unencumbered by bureaucracies and other modern trappings."

Emma Gatewood was not, in Shaffer's eyes, a bona fide part of that tradition. To Shaffer, the AT was a wilderness experience, a place where backpacking skill and know-how provided entree to a separate, higher realm of nature. Gatewood had not approached the trail in the same way, which disqualified her in Shaffer's eyes from the special status of a true thru-hiker.

"The image conveyed by various stories he heard portrayed an opportunistic woman who took advantage of what occasions came her way that might smooth her difficult journey," according to Shaffer's authorized biography. At the 1972 ATC meeting in New Hampshire, which included a gathering of the growing body of people who had hiked the entire trail, Shaffer and Gatewood did not speak to one another. "In Earl Shaffer's lexicon a 'thru-hike' unalterably referred to a journey on foot along the Appalachian Trail in a single trip, walking always in the same direction. In spite of her iconic status, Earl remained skeptical that any of Grandma Gatewood's three hikes met that minimum standard."

Perhaps what irked Shaffer was that, like so many who have been attracted to the idea of the Appalachian Trail, he had built it in his own mind to be a particular kind of place, and had hitched his life to the idea that he was uniquely defined by it. Gatewood's experience, and the attention showered on her, muddied the picture in which Shaffer had invested so much. Gatewood showed that the AT could be hiked in concert with the world of buildings and people that permeated it, not necessarily in opposition to them, and that it was a stage not just for the heroism of a young man, but for the mundane getting by of an old lady. Yes, it could be the object of a years-long quest to re-create oneself. But it could also be "a lark," taken up at the suggestion of nothing greater than a chance encounter with a magazine article.

Gatewood continued to hike and travel until the end of her life. She was a celebrity in the outdoor world, invited to various hiking gatherings around the country. Beginning in 1967, she led an annual winter hike along a trail, now named after her, in Ohio's Hocking Hills. The hike drew 2,500 participants in 1973, not long after which Gatewood embarked on a bus trip around the United States and parts of Canada. Within days of returning home, she fell seriously ill, and her condition quickly deteriorated. Emma Gatewood died in June 1973, at the age of eighty-five.

Whereas Gatewood's fame had come almost instantaneously after her first thru-hike, Earl Shaffer's grew much more steadily over his adulthood, as the AT and thru-hiking became more firmly implanted in the national imagination. In 1981 he literally self-published the book he had written on the 1948 hike, *Walking with Spring*, binding the books himself and giving them away. When the ATC got word of what he was doing, it agreed to publish the book and sell it, and Shaffer donated the proceeds back to the ATC.

Walking with Spring is very much in the tradition of Horace Kephart, whereby the outdoorsman's rugged interaction with the wild restores his soul, and imparts some of its majesty onto him. "The fog was burning off as the Lone Expedition crossed into North Carolina," Shaffer wrote, a lifetime of writing coming through in lyrical passages celebrating nature.

> The light of a clear dawn awoke me. The storm had settled into the surrounding valleys, leaving the highest peaks jutting like islands from a sea of fog. Then the sun rose, lighting a golden path across that misty sea. Seldom, even in the South Seas, have I seen anything to compare.

Shaffer sought an even closer connection with the AT in the 1980s, hoping to live near the trail and host a small hiker hostel on his property. The parcel in question was a top priority for the land acquisition effort that was then underway to provide permanent protection for the trail, a joint effort of the National Park Service and the ATC (Chapter 8). At one point it looked like the three parties had reached an agreement, but in the end Shaffer's preferred use of the property could not be reconciled with the needs of a natural corridor, and the plan fell through, leaving him disgusted with both the Park Service and the ATC.

By the mid-1990s, his legend steadily growing with the popularity of thru-hiking, Shaffer returned to more frequent involvement with the trail community, delivering his popular slide shows to appreciative audiences. With the fiftieth anniversary of his first thru-hike approaching, he resolved to do it again, and set out in 1998 at the age of seventy-nine. Though he surely would have hated the comparison, his fiftieth anniversary hike turned into a media sensation on the order of those Emma Gatewood had generated. Like her, he was flown to New York afterward to appear on the *Today* show, and the end of his trip at Mt. Katahdin was carefully orchestrated to be part of a feature on the *CBS Evening News.*

The story of Shaffer's first thru-hike, rekindled by the anniversary hike, proved as attractive to the mainstream media of the late '90s as it has to thousands of aspiring thru-hikers. But all foundation stories smooth away some rough edges to make for a better narrative, and Shaffer's is no exception.

A few years before the 1998 thru-hike, the ATC heard from an aging man who remembered hiking the full AT, which was missing only a short incomplete section in Maine, as part of a group of New York City Boy Scouts in the summer of 1936. To the extent they could verify the man's story, the ATC staff did, and published a newsletter article about this early group hike, celebrating another interesting piece of the trail's history. The ATC has never been in the business of certifying thru-hikes, though it does maintain a list of such reported hikes as an information source and a courtesy. But to those interested in what counts as a thru-hike and the records that go along with it, the news kicked off a bit of a tempest over whether Shaffer's 1948 hike was still The First.

There is also the question of just how much of the then-accessible Appalachian Trail Shaffer actually hiked in 1948. From the start, he made clear that while his goal was to walk the trail in its entirety, he had to make accommodation for the fact that it barely existed in many places. He wrote to the ATC shortly after the trip, "I am sorry that I cannot present to the Appalachian Trail Conference a record of a trip exactly planned and perfectly executed. I strayed at times and in getting back failed to cover every bit of the Trail route."

Jean Stephenson, after interviewing Shaffer to verify his travels before publishing his report on the 1948 thru-hike in *Appalachian Trailway News*, introduced his article this way:

> He emphasizes that he was not attempting a "stunt" of walking every foot of The Appalachian Trail, but was merely following the general trail route from Georgia to Maine.

Subsequent research, based on a detailed examination of Shaffer's trail diary and other sources, estimates that Shaffer may have missed 20 percent or more of the southern AT in his travels, including two car trips that skipped over almost 25 miles of trail.

Shaffer's own combativeness about what counted as a thru-hike may make it harder to reconcile the reality of his 1948 trip with a generous attitude toward such matters of verification. But even if Shaffer could be criticized for his prickly demeanor — which most everyone who came into contact with him took note of — the spirit behind his 1948 hike is unquestionably at the heart of the thru-hiking tradition.

Shaffer was never as well known as he was in the last few years of his life. After the publicity of the 1998 anniversary hike, friends and supporters, including the only member of his family with whom he got along reasonably well, organized a nonprofit to serve as the custodian of his legacy, and especially to get his writing out into the world. The only book by Shaffer that would ever be commercially published, titled (over his objections) *The Appalachian Trail: Calling Me Back to the Hills*, was released near the end of his life. Earl Shaffer died in a Veterans Administration hospice in May 2002, at the age of eighty-three.

The Government: Gaylord Nelson

We need a comprehensive, nationwide program to save the natural resources of America. We need this just as desperately as we
need a defense against atomic missiles.

—Gaylord Nelson

I
t is safe to say that Senator Gaylord Nelson, when he first introduced legislation in 1964 to provide federal protection for the
Appalachian Trail, had never heard of Earl Shaffer or Emma
Gatewood. Nelson had never set foot on the AT, was not close to anyone in the trail community, and represented a state, Wisconsin, that
was nowhere near the mountains. But when Nelson heard that the
trail's route was threatened by the incursion of postwar development,
he rallied to its defense. To him, the Appalachian Trail was a part of
something much larger, a new way of looking at the world that had the
potential to redefine American politics. In time, this new perspective
on the world would be termed "environmentalism."

The New Conservation, as it was called in the early 1960s, at first
seemed like simply a renewed commitment to the ideals of sensible
resource management that Benton MacKaye had learned about as a

young forester fifty years earlier. But there was a new dynamic at work in the sprawl of postwar America. Suburban development had allowed millions of people to live in a landscape of lawns and trees for the first time, but had also saddled them with a new set of problems: traffic, litter, pollution. For its residents, suburbia's promised perfect balance always appeared to be just over the horizon.

The political response that bubbled up from America's housing developments was twofold: a heightened demand for rustic landscapes to escape to, and a backlash against the noxious by-products of modern life, fouling what was supposed to have been the perfect city–country balance.

Gaylord Nelson was among the first politicians to pick up on this burgeoning sentiment in the body politic, and he found his calling by serving as one of its chief spokespeople. He recognized that a place like the Appalachian Trail was valuable not just for the recreational opportunity it provided its users. For the vast majority of people who would never hike on it, the simple existence of a virtually endless trail provided reassurance in an increasingly troubled age that some kind of natural order still prevailed.

Not long after the bill providing federal protection to the AT was passed in 1968, Nelson organized what would be the most full-throated expression of this new political sensibility. Embracing the new term that captured a much broader set of aspirations than mere "conservation," Nelson called it the Environmental Teach-In. The world would come to know it as Earth Day.

"Happy" Nelson, as he was known as a child, was born in the summer of 1916 in Clear Lake, Wisconsin, in the rural northwest of the state, about 50 miles from Minnesota's Twin Cities. He would later describe an idyllic childhood, consumed with carefree play in the fields and woods surrounding the small town. He and his friends hunted and fished, skied and skated, and went camping on their own. At the same time, the Nelson household was imbued with a serious ethic of service, and these two aspects of his upbringing, an easygoing demeanor combined with a sincerity of purpose, would very much define his adult life.

Nelson's mother had trained as a nurse and his father was a doctor. In addition to managing the household and assisting her husband when her advanced skills were required, Mary B. Nelson volunteered extensively, and opened her house to all manner of people needing a safe place and a warm meal. Anton Nelson worked as a physician seven days a week, making house calls by horse and buggy, or sleigh in the winter, before cars came along. He regularly turned down payment from those he determined could not afford his services.

Both parents were active and committed members of Wisconsin's Progressive movement, which would provide the unshakeable core of Gaylord Nelson's lifelong political beliefs. Progressivism valued the average citizen over the moneyed elite, open politics over backroom deals, and objective policy analysis over political power plays. It took especially strong hold in Wisconsin, and the Progressive Party was a viable third party in the state for a time.

Gaylord was a top athlete but an indifferent student in high school, and at first seemed ambivalent about taking the next step in life. Selected to speak at his high school graduation, he pretended to be sick in order to skip the ceremony. He made two attempts at starting college that fall, at first one and then another state teachers' college where football coaches had recruited him, but he did not feel comfortable at either place and returned to Clear Lake. After a winter on a road crew, Nelson made a second attempt at college, at San Jose State in California, where he lived with an aunt retired from teaching there. Once he became convinced he could handle it, he settled in and graduated four years later.

Nelson decided at that young age that he wanted to get into politics, and that a legal career could provide a professional home for his ambitions. He entered law school at the University of Wisconsin in Madison, and did the bare minimum to graduate on time. When he wasn't drinking beer with friends, he put most of his time and effort into politics, volunteering in campaigns and eventually heading up the campus Progressive Party.

Finishing law school less than six months after the Japanese raid on Pearl Harbor, Nelson was drafted into the Army upon graduation. He spent most of World War II stateside, eventually serving as one of four white officers overseeing an all-Black logistics unit. His troops' treatment in a segregated army gave Nelson a close personal view of American racism, and he would throughout his career be a forceful advocate for civil rights. His unit arrived on Okinawa less than a month before the war's end in the summer of 1945, and he spent just eight months overseeing a supply depot before his discharge from the Army, returning to Wisconsin in the spring of 1946, soon to turn thirty years old.

Eager to get his career in politics underway, Nelson immediately ran against the incumbent state assembly member from the Clear Lake area in the 1946 election. His family's good name got him only so far, though, and he lost. He headed to Madison regardless, knowing that the state capital and university town provided more fertile territory for his ambitions. He joined a small law firm with strong ties to organized labor, the perfect place from which to both earn decent pay and engage the political world. He was soon joined in Madison by Carrie Lee Dotson, a former Army nurse he had met during the war, and the two were married in the fall of 1947.

Nelson's political career got underway in earnest the following year, when at thirty-two he succeeded in his second attempt to get elected to the state legislature. He won a seat in the state senate representing the Madison area after lucking into the Democratic Party's nomination when the favored candidate had to drop out. At first glance, it wasn't much of a job. Democrats were a tiny minority in the Republican-dominated legislature, so actually passing legislation was never really possible. But Nelson found that it was the ideal spot from which to learn his trade. The routine of attending meetings, giving speeches, and conversing with politicians, frequently over an alcoholic beverage or two, perfectly suited his disposition. He patiently learned the workings of state government, while leading efforts to build the Democratic Party into a statewide electoral force and a home for Progressives.

By 1958, after ten years in the state legislature, Nelson decided the time was right for a run at the governor's office. The Democratic Party, thanks in part to his efforts, was beginning to have statewide success. There was nothing left for him to accomplish in the senate, and there was always the risk that today's rising star could be tomorrow's faded hope if he failed to advance his career.

Nelson's attempt to win the gubernatorial election combined tireless campaigning and savvy strategy on the one hand with a passionate commitment to good government and a keen understanding of the issues on the other. He could tell a folksy anecdote one minute, educate his audience on the finer points of some pressing issue the next, and conclude with a lacerating attack on the Republican Party. "For the first time in his life, Nelson was driven," his biographer Bill Christofferson has written, and the result was an upset win, by a comfortable margin, over the Republican incumbent.

The electorate that made Nelson governor in 1958, more than a decade removed from World War II and well into the postwar suburban boom, demanded a government that could keep up with modern life. Republicans, personified by President Dwight D. Eisenhower, were seen as caretakers of a system grounded in the past. Their small government, built around the self-reliance of business titans and farm owners, seemed deaf to the concerns of the rapidly growing class of people occupying the new suburban landscape. Without taxes and a capable bureaucracy, how would the roads be built? Where would new schools come from? Who would construct the water and sewer lines to serve the vast fields of single-family housing and shopping malls sprouting up across the countryside? A new landscape demanded a new kind of politics, and younger, dynamic politicians were elected across the country. The same year Nelson was elected governor, Democrats greatly increased their majorities in the United States House and Senate, and Massachusetts's young senator, John F. Kennedy, began mapping out a run for the White House in two years' time.

The forty-two-year-old Nelson had promised Wisconsin voters an ambitious agenda as governor—tax reform, improved public education, better roads—and he got to work on it immediately. Just one of the items on the new governor's to-do list, improving the state's opportunities for outdoor recreation, would prove to be the beginning of Nelson's career-long identity with the politics of the natural world. Up to that point, the political establishment had thought of the outdoors as the province of either the rural residents who hunted and fished in their own backyard, or wealthy individuals with the considerable means necessary to sojourn in the countryside. But now a burgeoning middle class with a vehicle or two in the driveway was heading to the woods and the lakes in previously unheard-of numbers. Parks and open space in postwar America, Nelson and others recognized, constituted a category of infrastructure like any other: a facility to be provided, requiring planning, funding, and management.

Nelson made limited progress on the issue in his first two-year term. Republican control of the state senate limited the legislation he could push through, and he had other, more important priorities. But the 1960 election was a wake-up call. With the presidential election dominating the headlines, state politics took a bit of a back seat. Though Kennedy won the presidency, he lost Wisconsin to Richard Nixon, and the Republican's success filtered down the ticket. Nelson was reelected, but by a smaller margin than two years earlier; both houses of the legislature came under Republican control.

For most of Nelson's legislative agenda, this new political environment meant a tougher road ahead. But he correctly intuited that the outdoors made for a different kind of issue. In what would turn out to be one of the most significant acts of his political life, Nelson staked his reputation on an ambitious new parks and recreation program, pitched directly to voters. The Outdoor Recreation Act Program (ORAP) would levy a 1-cent-per-pack tax on cigarettes (which were widely popular at the time) to generate $50 million over ten years to pay for the acquisition and protection of recreational land in every corner of the state. Nelson barnstormed the state to build support for his plans, and found widespread enthusiasm.

Part of ORAP's popularity stemmed from its largesse, delivering millions of dollars' worth of recreational facilities—forest campgrounds, preserved beaches, even urban parks—to Wisconsin's residents. But there was another factor at play. Turning open space into a park not only made it available for recreational use, it also protected it from private development. The automotive hordes heading out of town for the weekend required not just facilities to serve them, but a pastoral quality to their experiences. ORAP promised to be both an enabler of the trip and a protector of the destination.

In a speech to Wisconsin preservationists, Nelson argued that even the pressing needs of the rest of his agenda—highways, healthcare —took a back seat to land protection. "All these matters are urgent but they can still be solved later. In resource conservation, it's now or never. If we wait until later, the resources we are trying to save will be gone."

Hobbled in the state legislature by the 1960 election results, Nelson campaigned directly to the public on behalf of ORAP, and catalyzed a broad base of support. Editorial pages, civic groups, and voters with all manner of political leanings found outdoor recreation a worthy and sensible undertaking, and applauded Nelson for his policy invention. As conventional political battles over taxing and spending continued in their usual manner, the electorate rallied around ORAP.

There were only two groups opposed to Nelson's program: the tobacco industry, whose product was going to be taxed; and Republican politicians, who could not allow a Democrat to score such a resounding victory. But they were overwhelmed by the tide of popular support. The ORAP legislation passed both Republican-controlled chambers of the Wisconsin Legislature and was signed into law by Nelson in August of 1961.

With ORAP, Nelson put Wisconsin at the forefront of a preservation movement that was gathering steam across the country. Congress had undertaken a similar effort with the federal Outdoor Recreation Resources Review Commission. The Sierra Club succeeded in rallying nationwide opposition to the construction of Echo Park Dam on a major tributary of the Colorado River, the first time that preservationists had halted the juggernaut of dam building across the American West. And the Wilderness Society, co-founded by Benton MacKaye on a Tennessee roadside in 1935, was steadily winning support for a federal Wilderness Act to protect certain federal lands from development of any kind.

ORAP stood out because it had a broader base of popular support, and a broader range of implementation, than the typical conservation battles of the day. In this new political environment, outdoor recreation and landscape preservation were no longer the province of a relatively small group of enthusiasts; they were now at the heart of the relationship between citizen and government.

A second issue for Nelson had this same quality, a new challenge emerging from the demands of modern life: the phosphate pollution spilling into his state's waters, a by-product of the detergents powering suburban washing appliances. This was pollution not from a single source that might be controlled or at least isolated, but the cumulative effect of thousands of people going about their daily lives, distributed across the landscape in their single-family homes. Nelson convened Wisconsin's most knowledgeable officials to study the problem, and concluded that the solution lay outside any one state's lawmaking ability. The only effective approach would be a national ban on phosphates in detergents.

With the end of his second two-year gubernatorial term approaching in 1962, Nelson determined that the United States Senate was the appropriate venue for his ambitions. He was worn down from doing battle with Republicans in Madison, in particular over a fiscal reform package that imposed an unpopular sales tax, widely mocked as "three cents for Gaylord." JFK's New Frontier was attracting the best and brightest to Washington, and Nelson aimed to make his mark on the national stage. He ran against an aging longtime incumbent, in part on the wide popularity of ORAP, and won the race handily.

As Nelson campaigned in the summer and fall of 1962, a new book was attracting enormous attention.

"There once was a town in the heart of America," Rachel Carson's *Silent Spring* began,

> where all life seemed to live in harmony with its surroundings.
> The town lay in the midst of a checkerboard of prosperous
> farms, with fields of grain and hillsides of orchards where, in
> spring, white clouds of bloom drifted above the green fields.
> In autumn, oak and maple and birch set up a blaze of color

that flamed and flickered across a backdrop of pines. The foxes barked in the hills and deer silently crossed the fields, half hidden in the mists of the fall mornings.

... Then a strange blight crept over the area and everything began to change. Some evil spell had settled on the community: mysterious maladies swept the flocks of chickens; the cattle and sheep sickened and died. Everywhere was a shadow of death.

Carson went on to document, in alarming detail, the emerging scientific consensus that wanton spraying of the pesticide DDT was rapidly making her "Fable for Tomorrow" an eerie reality. Accumulating in the eggs of birds and killing their young before they could hatch, the chemical was dooming entire species, including the iconic bald eagle, to a rapid extinction.

"No witchcraft, no enemy action had silenced the rebirth of new life in this stricken world," Carson wrote. "The people had done it themselves."

The widespread popularity of *Silent Spring* demonstrated that it was about more than just DDT. It was Exhibit A in a much larger story: a fundamental breakdown in humanity's relationship with nature, a threat not just to wildlife but to that idealized little town and the civilization it represented. For a small but growing segment of the public, including the newly elected junior senator from Wisconsin, repairing that relationship was becoming the most important issue of the day.

Nelson made his first floor speech as a United States senator in favor of a bill to impose a national ban on phosphates in detergents, and delivered an impassioned plea.

The control of detergent pollution is just one part of what I consider the most urgent domestic crisis facing our Nation today—the preservation of our priceless natural resources and the defense of the environment in which we live against the most powerful assault in the history of our Nation. Unless this Nation girds for battle immediately, its people are not going to have clean water to drink, clean air to breathe, decent soil in which to grow their food, and a green outdoors in which to live a few decades from now.

Nelson's speech wove together two of the landmark initiatives of his time as governor—the fight against detergent pollution and ORAP's development of park space—into a single umbrella idea, "defense of the environment." At first glance, Nelson was on the fringe of

Senator Gaylord Nelson, right, with President John F. Kennedy and Wisconsin governor John Reynolds, during Kennedy's 1963 visit to Wisconsin's Apostle Islands.

the political mainstream; the detergent bill went absolutely nowhere. But in fact he was joining a movement that was steadily growing in influence. If 1962's *Silent Spring* signaled a popular awakening to the environmental idea, 1963's *The Quiet Crisis*, by Secretary of the Interior Stewart Udall, represented the political half of the equation. It, too, was a bestseller, written not from outside the establishment but from inside President John F. Kennedy's cabinet. JFK even contributed a short introduction, lamenting the fact that "new technical processes and devices litter the countryside with waste and refuse," while "our environmental standard of living—our access to nature and respect for it—deteriorates."

Kennedy's words perfectly captured the emerging sentiment: the more troublesome the downsides of modern life, the louder the calls for a refuge from it, and the more pure the escape needed to be. A natural area was no longer just a place to enjoy a certain kind of recreation; it was a talisman against the threat of a world gone awry.

The Appalachian Trail, winding seemingly endlessly over the mountaintops of the eastern mountains, was just such a place. And it was in serious trouble. Ever since Myron Avery had dedicated a rerouted and recleared Appalachian Trail in 1951, postwar development of every variety had been eating away at the pathway. Large tracts of wooded land were divided into individual lots for vacation homes; roads to reach the second homes crisscrossed the trail; ski resorts took over mountainsides, while radio and TV towers occupied summits; timber cutting to serve a voracious appetite for homebuilding removed the forest from around the trail. Constant relocations around these disruptions left the trail increasingly consigned to road shoulders.

Nelson knew next to nothing about the AT or its problems when it came up in a cocktail party conversation with a Washington-area physician and Wisconsin native, Cecil Cullander. "He knew I was interested in conservation, and we got to talking," Nelson recalled. "He expressed his concern about it, and I thought, well, hell, I might as well introduce a bill to preserve the Appalachian Trail."

The ATC leadership, which was just beginning to develop a strategy for securing federal protection of the trail, learned of Nelson's bill more or less out of the blue. While that was in part a quirk of happenstance, it also demonstrated the fact that the Appalachian Trail's identity was changing. The broader public, including those like Nelson from a relatively flat midwestern state who had never set foot on the trail, was beginning to feel a sense of ownership over the AT based on its reputation alone. This was just the sort of natural landscape, sharply contrasted with postwar sprawl, that adherents of the New Conservation venerated, regardless of whether they actually set foot on it.

Nelson's first AT bill was introduced in early 1964 and expired, as does most introduced legislation, with the conclusion of the two-year congressional session at the end of that year. But while the AT itself would have to wait, the New Conservation was gaining high-level support from a new occupant of the White House. When Lyndon Johnson succeeded to the presidency after Kennedy's assassination in November of 1963, he brought an agenda of domestic transformation, termed the Great Society, that placed New Conservation ideals front and center. At a major speech to the graduates of the University of Michigan in May of 1964, Johnson laid out his vision.

"We have always prided ourselves on being not only America the strong and America the free, but America the beautiful," Johnson bellowed to the football-stadium audience. But pollution and the loss of open space required the nation to fight for its future. "For once the battle is lost, once our natural splendor is destroyed, it can never be recaptured. And once man can no longer walk with beauty or wonder at nature his spirit will wither and his sustenance be wasted."

Later that year, Johnson signed into law two pieces of legislation, long in the making, that represented this new sense of urgency around nature as a depletable resource. The first, the Wilderness Act, was the culmination of Benton MacKaye's co-founding of the Wilderness Society thirty years earlier; it created a new category of federal land completely off-limits to roads and buildings. The second established the Land and Water Conservation Fund (LWCF), in essence a national version of Gaylord Nelson's ORAP, a pot of money dedicated to purchasing and protecting new parklands and recreational resources for the American public.

When the new two-year legislative session opened in 1965, Nelson reintroduced his bill to protect the AT, and in only a year the idea had grown from the stuff of cocktail party conversation to a national priority. Johnson convened a White House Conference on Natural Beauty in early 1965, and in his message to Congress on the topic argued that "we need to copy the great Appalachian Trail in all parts of America." In July, the Interior Department announced that its Bureau of Outdoor Recreation would conduct a study into a national network of trails.

For the Appalachian Trail Conference, this rush of activity was in many respects too much of a good thing. The fate of the AT, only recently the purview of a relatively small group of dedicated volunteers, had become caught up in a hypothetical national trails system that required study, planning, and negotiation among stakeholders across the country. While these potential other trails were planned, the actual Appalachian Trail continued to deteriorate. And the tricky questions of constructing new trails—siting them, building them, maintaining them—were ones the ATC had figured out for itself decades earlier. A one-size-fits-all national program ran the risk of upsetting the careful arrangements, especially with private landowners, that the Appalachian Trail community had stitched together over the years. The ATC's leaders wrote carefully worded letters expressing both appreciation for federal support and a desire for the AT to be protected on its own, rather than as part of a larger system. An eighty-seven-year-old Benton MacKaye even chimed in with a letter from Shirley Center, urging that the AT be treated separately in federal legislation.

But to both Nelson and Stewart Udall's Interior Department, what made the Appalachian Trail worth protecting also made it worth replicating. Nelson introduced a follow-up to his own bill, incorporating the AT into a proposed national trail system, and the Appalachian Trail, barely on the federal government's radar a few years earlier, was now the somewhat reluctant flagship of a nationwide trail-building initiative.

This larger effort required more time, especially for the completion of the Bureau of Outdoor Recreation study, and Nelson's second batch of legislation expired at the end of 1966. The "Trails for America" report was released in January of 1967, and it called for the immediate declaration of the Appalachian Trail as the first National Scenic Trail. Three others, including the Pacific Crest Trail (PCT), were identified as ready for development into full-fledged national trails, and several others were proposed for further study.

The bill to implement the report's recommendations and establish a National Trails System was introduced in March of 1967, but this time it did not have Nelson's name on it. Now that the legislation was a top priority of the Johnson administration and the Senate leadership, Senator Henry "Scoop" Jackson of Washington, chair of the Interior Committee, took on lead sponsorship of the bill. Nelson continued to be its chief advocate.

At the Senate committee hearing for the bill, just as the ATC had feared, concerns over a nationwide trail system, many of which did not apply to preserving the already-built AT, threatened to undermine the whole effort. The bill imagined a vast network not unlike what MacKaye had sketched out in his first 1916 article, of national trails, state systems, and urban pathways, all linking up together to provide a seamless experience at different levels of natural escape. "I see no reason why we cannot have a hiking trail within one hour of every American who needs one," Nelson said.

But the bigger the trail system's aspirations got, the greater the complications it had to wrestle with. If the AT and PCT served the two coasts, what trails would serve the middle of the country? How would historic routes like the Oregon Trail, through now-settled territory, be handled? In particular, would the federal government have the power of eminent domain to seize land from property owners? The bill's backers—Nelson, Udall, and others—struggled to craft a bill that would set out an ambitious program but not allow the uncertainties around it to stand in the way of immediate help to the AT and the only other trail with any actual development underway, the PCT.

Months of negotiations ensued. Against a backdrop of wrenching late-'60s turbulence—escalating war, political assassinations, cities on fire—the wheels of legislative maneuvering slowly spun. By the late summer of 1968, both houses of Congress had agreed to establish a National Trails System with at first two National Scenic Trails, the AT and PCT, as its anchors, and provisions for including new trails in the future. President Johnson signed the bill into law on October 2, 1968.

At the same ceremony, Johnson signed another bill for which Nelson fiercely advocated, the Wild and Scenic Rivers Act, which declared certain stretches of rivers, including the St. Croix near where Nelson had grown up in Wisconsin, off-limits to dams and other major developments. It was in many respects the perfect parallel to the trails bill, both of them protecting a human experience of nature by protecting the pathways weaving through it. In fact to some it seemed that these trails themselves almost created the wilderness. Frederick Eissler of the Sierra Club wrote that "The trail system, and the stream networks and dividing ridges that the trail systems follow, delineate the body of wilderness. In a real sense, 'trail country' is another term

Interior Secretary Stewart Udall, left, and President Lyndon Johnson at the signing of the National Trails System Act.

for wilderness." By this line of thinking, more trails seemingly created more wilderness. Notwithstanding the contradiction at the heart of that sentiment—the human use of an area is what establishes it as free of human use?—it proved to be a powerful idea.

A month after the signing of the national trails and wild rivers bills, Nelson was reelected to the Senate in a landslide. A mix of priorities that just six years earlier had only begun to find common ground as a political agenda—natural preservation, outdoor recreation, pollution prevention—had now risen to the forefront of America's cultural conversation. Moreover, they had coalesced into something greater than just a policy wish list. Nelson and the movement he was a part of began to speak not just of amenities to provide or problems to contain, but a singular, multifaceted, overarching ambition: the environment. If the New Conservation of the early 1960s was a policy program, the environment that emerged in the later years of that decade was a new reality altogether, a way of looking at the world that drew every aspect of human existence into conversation with the seemingly timeless truths of nature. It was a reality more Americans needed to become familiar with, in Nelson's estimation.

Since his first days in politics building a statewide Democratic Party from the remains of the Progressive movement, Nelson had been an organizer. Beginning his second term in the Senate in 1969, he looked for a way to catalyze Americans' nascent environmental aspirations into a new political force. By its very definition, the environment permeated every part of people's lives, which meant that it had the potential to define their politics. The question was: How to make that happen?

An early skeptic of the Vietnam War, and an advocate for civil rights since his time in the Army, Nelson appreciated the power of direct action to set the political agenda. The teach-in, an early tactic of the anti-war movement on college campuses, combined the protest of a mass gathering with the spirit of education, as experts empowered their audience with an understanding of what was happening and why. In the late summer of 1969, flying back to Washington after observing a California oil spill, Nelson resolved that what the country needed was a nationwide teach-in on the environment.

As with his Appalachian Trail bill, Nelson no sooner stumbled on the idea than he began acting on it. He tasked one of his Senate staffers with the work of organizing an event. Forty college campuses across the country would serve as the main centers of activity, and would in turn organize other schools nearby. In a model that coincidentally looked a lot like the effort to build the AT, leaders in Washington would coordinate and provide training, while the bulk of the work would happen in local organizations. In fact, the idea became so popular so quickly that looking back on it, Nelson would say that Earth Day organized itself.

In late September of 1969, Nelson mentioned his idea in a speech he gave in Seattle; an Associated Press report on the speech was the first anyone outside of Nelson's inner circle had heard of it. But just two months later, a front-page article in the Sunday *New York Times* about campus environmental activism noted that "already students are looking forward to the first 'D-Day' of the movement—when a nationwide environmental 'teach-in,' being coordinated from the office of Senator Gaylord Nelson, Wisconsin Democrat, is planned, to involve both college campuses and communities."

The effort quickly outgrew Nelson's Senate office, and he organized and found funding for a small stand-alone nonprofit, Environmental Teach-In, Inc., to serve as the national hub. Recognizing that young people might be in closer touch with the cultural moment than a fifty-something United States senator, he turned over management

The front page of the New York Times, *April 23, 1970.*

of the effort to a small group of budding activists in their twenties. One of their first actions was to change the name of the event to Earth Day.

On April 22, 1970, millions of people took part in more than ten thousand events, large and small, across the country. As many as 250,000 people streamed onto a stretch of Fifth Avenue closed to cars. Congress took a day's recess to allow members to speak in their districts. K–12 and college classrooms devoted the day or the week to environmental topics.

Earth Day unquestionably succeeded in the two central ambitions that Nelson had for it. First, in calling millions of people physically together in communities across the country, it provided an impossible-to-deny statement of the fact that the environment was a political force to be reckoned with—not just an issue of concern to a particular constituency, but an idea capable of organizing huge numbers of people. Second, the organization of thousands of Earth Day events across the country built a powerful network of environmental advocacy that would last well beyond the day itself.

Because it provides a convenient historical marker, it has been easy to overstate the impact of Earth Day, as if the modern environmental movement was immaculately conceived in the spring of 1970. Earth Day was in fact an expression of that movement, which had been steadily building in the fertile fields of postwar sprawl since the 1950s, as much as it was an organizer of it. But that was exactly what Nelson had hoped it would be: a statement of the public's growing concern that no politician could fail to notice.

Environmental enthusiasts did not just turn out for meetings and demonstrations; they headed for the hills as well. As masses of people sought to establish their own personal connection to nature, the popularity of backpacking skyrocketed, and the Appalachian Trail, so iconic in the national imagination that it warranted the protection of the federal government, became a magnet for a generation heading back to nature. Thru-hikers have always represented less than 1 percent of all trail users, but their numbers serve as a useful indicator of the trail's overall popularity. Between 1969 and 1974 there was a nearly fivefold increase in the number of thru-hikers; over roughly the same time frame the ATC's membership increased ten times over.

The AT was overrun with popularity, which meant not just more use but a different kind of use. By and large, the crowds heading to the woods had none of the sense of ownership or stewardship that the trail's earlier users had had. For previous generations, a backwoods expedition required an investment of time and money that relatively few people had; they joined together in clubs to make hiking a shared, collective endeavor. But with the technology of inexpensive, lightweight gear and an automotive landscape that made trailheads readily accessible, hiking became a relatively cheap counterculture consumable, not unlike the marijuana that went hand in hand with the outdoors experience. The historian Silas Chamberlin argues that over this period "the typical American hiker evolved from a net producer—of information, maps, well-maintained trails, advocacy, outings, and club culture—to a net consumer—of equipment, national magazines, and federally subsidized trails."

The National Trails System, then, was fighting an uphill battle from the day it went into effect. Land fragmentation threatened the AT from the outside, and overuse threatened it from the inside. As the trail became a haven for litter and loud noise, more private property owners kicked it off their land, and the nation's foremost "wilderness trail" increasingly took up residence on road shoulders.

It would take a robust and fast-acting policy to counteract those trends on the ground, but the National Trails System Act proved to be anything but. It would take a renewed commitment from Congress and the Carter administration to give the full federal protection to the AT that it enjoys to this day, a story told in the next chapter.

Gaylord Nelson, though, was not involved in that second round of legislation to protect the AT, beyond signing on as a cosponsor of the bill. The trail had grown enough in prominence and prestige at that point that it did not need a senator from far-off Wisconsin to stand up for it. But it was also the case that by the 1970s the environment had matured into an issue that required the kind of patient policymaking at which Nelson never really excelled. Other senators, especially Edmund Muskie of Maine, took on the role of negotiating complex environmental statutes, while Nelson found his niche in advocating more radical solutions than were politically practicable. He introduced a constitutional amendment declaring the public's right to "a decent environment," knowing full well it did not have a chance of being adopted.

Earth Day, in retrospect, proved to be something of a peak for Nelson's brand of environmentalism, which celebrated the very idea of environment as a rallying cry knitting together a wide array of frustrations with modernity. Turning that sentiment into action required laws, which had to be negotiated, and rules that had to be enforced, and disputes that had to be adjudicated. After Earth Day, the achievement of placing the environment at the heart of government meant that it increasingly operated like any other issue, with its own officials and lobbyists, friends and enemies.

As Nelson served his third Senate term from 1974 to 1980, and the environment became embedded in the inner workings of the liberal state, a backlash was slowly growing against that very state. Nostalgia for simpler times and resentment toward big government, especially in the American South and West, slowly grew into a potent ideology embodied in the sunny disposition and arch conservatism of former California governor Ronald Reagan. It was underestimated by many, including Nelson, as a worldview so simplistic and out of touch with reality that it would never be taken seriously by voters. The 1980 election proved otherwise. Reagan won forty-four states; twelve Democratic senators, including Nelson, were voted out of office.

As Reagan appointees did their best to unwind the federal involvement in environmental protection that Nelson and his colleagues had built up over the previous years, Nelson found what was for him the perfect post-Senate job. The Wilderness Society, once a threadbare association held together by the shared beliefs of Benton MacKaye and a handful of others, had grown into a permanent fixture on the Washington scene. The organization agreed to create the post of chairman for Nelson, a place from which he could offer counsel to the organization and have a platform to continue to argue the environmental issues of the day.

He continued to do so for the next twenty-five years. Gaylord Nelson died in 2005 at the age of eighty-nine.

8

The National Park: Dave Richie, Pam Underhill, and Dave Startzell

//

Those who worked with [Dave Richie] could not avoid being imbued by his nearly boundless optimism.

—Dave Startzell

I don't know that he ever raised his voice, whereas sometimes I could be found to go "What the fuck!" down the hallway.

—Pam Underhill

I t was a seemingly simple question. At a meeting of the Appalachian National Scenic Trail Advisory Council (ANSTAC) in June of 1972, representatives of the states through which the AT ran asked their federal counterparts whether any of the money authorized by Congress under the 1968 National Trails System Act would be granted directly to the states for land purchases. Or would all of that money be reserved for federal use?

It was not the first time the question had been asked, but nearly four years after Lyndon Johnson signed the NTSA into law, "neither the Bureau of Outdoor Recreation representative nor the Park Service personnel present could give a clear answer." The mood quickly soured.

"Half a dozen men jumped up and started shouting and waving papers in the air," an observer wrote. "Sensing that they were on sensitive ground, the Park Service personnel quickly offered a few pallid blandishments and changed the subject."

The Park Service promised to provide a definitive answer to the question in a forthcoming written report on the meeting. But when it arrived, the report stated only, apparently in all sincerity, that "a vigorous discussion with energetic input followed, in which the questions were well fielded." There was still no answer to the question.

That kind of bureaucratic dysfunction defined the entire effort to protect the Appalachian Trail in the first years of the NTSA. The federal government and the states were not on the same page. The Park Service and the Forest Service were at loggerheads. The Appalachian Trail Conference and its member clubs were barely in communication with one another. ANSTAC, which perhaps on the strength of its militaristic acronym alone was supposed to tie the whole thing together, almost never met. The Appalachian Trail's condition continued to deteriorate, and more miles were shifted onto road shoulders.

The AT's success, it turned out, depended not just on the enthusiasm of its caretakers or the power of the government, but on the delicate job of marrying those two forces together. The bureaucratic environment of the trail, as much as its natural environment, would determine its future.

More than any other individual, Dave Richie identified this as the central challenge for the Appalachian Trail in the modern era. A mid-level Park Service official when he came to the project in 1974, Richie was both a successful administrator and a reluctant one, savvy about what bureaucracy could accomplish and wary of what it could screw up. But he had faith, when almost no one else did, that a partnership could be fashioned between the Park Service and the Appalachian Trail Conference that would live up to the AT's loftiest ambitions.

Over a decade, Richie worked to build the foundation of that partnership, and after his retirement his protégés took up the task of acquiring and managing a permanently protected corridor for the Appalachian Trail. His eventual successor as the Park Service's head of the AT, Pam Underhill, was both administrator and advocate, fiercely arguing for the trail's needs within her own agency and with the general public. Her counterpart at the Appalachian Trail Conference, Dave Startzell, steadily built an organization that could responsibly manage such a significant national asset, and worked the halls of Congress to ensure the flow of funds to buy up the necessary land.

It was at times a messy process. A swath of land owned in perpetuity by the federal government was far less welcome in many communities than a simple trail through the woods had been. Voices were raised; protests were held; lawsuits were filed. But in the end, Underhill, Startzell, and the organizations they led would prove Dave Richie's faith justified, and the Appalachian Trail came to represent not only a wilderness footpath, but a protected and managed corridor, a very narrow national park, from Maine to Georgia.

When Dave Richie first took charge of the National Park Service's Appalachian Trail project in 1974, there was no reason to believe he would shepherd its turnaround. In a sign of how far down the agency's priority list the AT had fallen, the project was meant to occupy only 10 percent of Richie's time as the deputy director of the Park Service's regional office in Boston.

The Park Service's confusion and indifference regarding the trail effort came down to one basic stumbling block: the Appalachian Trail was not, in any obvious way, a park. Conventional national parks—old ones like Yosemite out west, newer ones like Great Smoky Mountains down south—were chunks of land clearly marked on a map, controlled by the agency and managed by it according to a well-worn set of rules and procedures. The AT, though, had no fixed location; it was controlled by a mishmash of public agencies, private landowners, and trail volunteers; and what little guidance had been provided for its development in the National Trails System Act had proven mostly unworkable. In short, the trail did not fit the bureaucracy, and when its supporters in Stewart Udall's Interior Department left town with the Johnson administration after 1968, so did the mandate to take the effort seriously.

To Richie, however, the problem contained its own solution. If the trail did not fit the bureaucracy, then the task at hand was to make a bureaucracy that fit the trail.

Born in 1932 outside Philadelphia, Richie grew up in a family with deep and prominent roots in American Quakerism, a tradition that valued quiet humility and service to others. He seems to have been both fully at home in the expectations of his upbringing and wanting some distance as well. A top athlete and class president at his private Quaker school, he bolted for the gold fields of Alaska with a couple of friends the summer after high school graduation. He enrolled at the Quakers' prestigious Haverford College, only to drop out in order to become a Marine Corps jet pilot, then returned to complete his degree.

A lifelong lover of nature, Richie embarked on a career in federal land management at the Interior Department in Washington, and headed out west for postings at Mt. Rainier National Park and Coulee (now Lake Roosevelt) National Recreation Area in Washington State.

After a brief detour to teach at his old high school, Richie returned to the Park Service as superintendent of George Washington Memorial Parkway outside Washington, DC, in 1971.

The linear park along both sides of the Potomac River not only preserved the shoreline landscape but also housed two increasingly busy roadways. It was a complicated environment, with commuters, neighbors, two state governments, and the federal District of Columbia all voicing their own needs and requirements. Amid those political crosscurrents, Richie consistently put faith in the ability of volunteers to shape the park with their own work. When a vacant former amusement park came under the parkway's jurisdiction, Richie invited 125 "local artists, architects, and ecology freaks" (in the *Washington Post*'s description) to spend a weekend brainstorming ideas. In championing a new bike path along the Virginia riverfront, "Richie said 'we're responding to considerable public demand' for the new trail, and said he hoped the public would respond by helping to spread the gravel."

Promoted to Boston in 1974, Richie began his work on the AT just listening to the various parties—the Appalachian Trail Conference, individual trail clubs, state officials—whose experiences during the first five years of the NTSA had been so frustrating. The partners, after countless unproductive meetings, had become disillusioned with the Park Service's inability or unwillingness to move the project forward. Both the NTSA and Richie's personal disposition imagined the AT as a public–private partnership, but the public half of that equation, Richie's own National Park Service, was not living up to its end of the bargain.

Richie argued for more and more of his time to be devoted to the trail project, and he had the credibility within the Park Service to win the argument. By 1976 it was a full-time assignment, and a couple of years later he opened a stand-alone Appalachian Trail Project Office in Harpers Ferry, West Virginia, alongside the Appalachian Trail Conference. In fact, the two shared space for a while.

At first Richie's doggedness was enough to make the federal government a more reliable partner in the trail protection effort, but it soon became clear that it wasn't just the Park Service's disinterest that had allowed the project to stagnate. The National Trails System Act itself was not up to the job.

There were two significant shortcomings. First, the NTSA was structured around the assumption that the Park Service would coordinate and promote trail protection efforts but individual states would take the lead in acquiring the land. In practice, though, the states for the most part waited for Washington to act; it was the Appalachian *National* Scenic Trail, after all. The second problem grew out of the first: the NTSA had authorized only $5 million to pay for trail land, a paltry sum compared with the task at hand.

In 1978, thanks to the lobbying of the AT community, the enthusiastic support of the Carter administration, and renewed confidence in the project's viability thanks to Richie's leadership, Congress passed a new and improved NTSA. It authorized $90 million to pay for trail land; tasked the National Park Service with directly acquiring the necessary property; and allowed for a corridor of 500 feet on either side of the trail, five times wider than in the original legislation, to insulate the pathway from incompatible nearby uses. It had taken ten years and two tries to pass the necessary legislation, but beginning in 1978 the federal government was a fully invested partner in the Appalachian Trail.

Shortly after the legislation passed, a new member of the clerical staff came to work in Richie's Harpers Ferry office. Pam Underhill was a young single mother who lived nearby, and after a year of commuting back and forth to the Interior Department's Washington office, was thrilled to be able to work closer to home. Underhill took the job "not because I knew a damn thing about the AT, or I was a hiker, or anything like that. It sort of suited my life needs at the moment." Over the ensuing years, Underhill's allegiance to the Appalachian Trail would grow steadily alongside her increasing responsibilities for it, until by the mid-1990s she was the Park Service's superintendent of the AT, and one of its fiercest defenders.

She had grown up in New Jersey until her father took a job in Stewart Udall's Interior Department and the family moved to the Washington area. A. Heaton Underhill was assistant director of the Bureau of Outdoor Recreation, the office that wrote the "Trails for America" report setting the stage for the National Trails System Act. Though Pam would eventually find herself working in the same field as her father, her path there was anything but direct. She attended the prestigious Wellesley College, where she was two years behind Hillary Clinton, before transferring to Cal-Berkeley for her senior year and graduating in 1971. She kicked around for a few years after that, eventually settling in Harpers Ferry with her leathersmith husband and having her first child. When the marriage broke up, she was determined to find the kind of employment that would reliably provide for her and her daughter. She rode the commuter train to Washington, took the civil service exam, went next door to the Interior Department, and knocked on doors until she had a job.

When the 1978 legislation passed, the Park Service needed a bigger staff working on the AT, and Underhill took the job in Richie's office. She was a secretary at first, but every time some new job needed doing, or someone left for a new position elsewhere, Underhill would take on new responsibilities, steadily rising up the civil service ranks, her own career intertwined with the growth of the AT as a unit of the National Park Service. By the end of her career almost twenty-five years later, she referred to the trail as her middle child.

While Underhill was riding the train to Washington, Dave Startzell was on the other side of the country, biking to work as a city planner in Oxnard, California, outside Los Angeles. He had only recently arrived there from Tennessee, where as a graduate student he had done some work for the Appalachian Trail Conference. The ATC, like the Park Service, needed to increase its staff to meet its responsibilities under the new legislation, and they invited him to return. Less than a year into the California job, Startzell quit and moved back across the country, driving through a snowstorm that followed him much of the way. He would work for the ATC for the remainder of his professional life, most of that time as its executive director.

Startzell had also grown up in the Washington area, where his father steadily moved up the ranks in J. Edgar Hoover's FBI. As the elder Startzell's career required postings around the country, Dave followed along, so the Cleveland FBI office for his father turned into college at Ohio's Miami University. When Dave was looking at graduate programs in urban and regional planning, there was in-state tuition at the University of Tennessee—his father was heading up the FBI's Memphis office—and Dave wound up in Knoxville on the western flank of the Appalachians. A recent graduate of the same program was working as the ATC's executive director, and Startzell helped out on trail projects from time to time. After the yearlong detour to California, he took on the job of ATC education director, organizing the trail community into a reliable partner of the federal government.

"ATC had made assurances to the government that if you spend all this money on land acquisition, we'll really beef up our volunteer capabilities and care for these lands, so it won't be an ongoing burden," Startzell recalled in a 2019 interview. "The problem is," he chuckled, "we had no capacity." The ATC, if it was going to be the bridge between the Park Service and its member clubs doing frontline trail work, needed to be a far more professional organization, with the money, people, and expertise to coordinate trail maintenance from Maine to Georgia.

Previous Park Service personnel had thrown up their hands at the situation, but Dave Richie piloted a new approach. He took some of the budget allocated to his office and passed it on to the ATC in the form of grants. The federal government became an investor in the Appalachian Trail Conference. The grants paid for specific work that the Park Service needed done, and provided a critical mass of funding to allow the organization to grow into its new responsibilities.

Underhill, soon after starting work on the AT, took a position in the Park Service's land acquisition office for the trail, a stand-alone unit whose job was to use the funding and authority of the 1978 law to buy up a corridor for the trail. It would seem to have been a relatively straightforward undertaking. Map the trail's location. Identify the owners of the underlying property. Negotiate with the owners to buy their land, or at least a portion of it, to protect the trail and a buffer surrounding it. If all else failed, use the government's power of eminent domain to force landowners to sell, in return for the fair market value of the property.

There was a problem, though, of the chicken-and-egg variety. It wasn't only the case that the trail's route determined where the protective corridor needed to be. The reverse was equally true: the acquisition of a new corridor would determine where the trail would go. For example, the trail had long relied on roadside segments (increasingly so in the 1960s and '70s) to connect its more remote stretches. But a wilderness footpath, which is what the federal law called for, needed to replace road segments with newly acquired woods and countryside. Moreover, the trail's routing from day one had been built around whatever ad hoc agreements could be pulled together by Myron Avery and his minions, not always reaching the ridgeline heights or the most

McAfee Knob.

scenic vantage points. The new acquisition effort meant that those earlier shortcomings could be addressed; it was both an opportunity and a mandate to create the best possible version of the trail.

But there was an inherent contradiction between protecting a trail that already existed and building a new trail to meet some vaguely specified ideal. Owners of property that had never before hosted the AT, had perhaps never even heard of it, might find out one day that in the interest of protecting a supposedly already existing trail, they were going to have to give up their land to accommodate the building of a brand new route.

For example, McAfee Knob, a ship's prow of exposed rock jutting out from southwestern Virginia's Catawba Mountain, is a gorgeous spot with an expansive view of the valley below and a parallel ridge, North Mountain, on the other side. It is just the sort of place one would imagine being part of the Appalachian Trail, but at the beginning of the acquisition effort, it was not. The trail was actually located across the valley on North Mountain, which was inside Jefferson National Forest, while the land on Catawba was split among several private owners.

If the AT that the federal government had committed to protecting was just any ridgeline path from Maine to Georgia, the North Mountain route already had that covered. But if it was the most scenic version of that path, then the trail needed to include McAfee Knob, and the Park Service was going to have to acquire a corridor across Catawba. That is exactly what happened, and as with everything else in this period, it was a joint decision. The trail community, represented by both local volunteers and the ATC, worked hand in hand with the Park Service not only to determine the route, but to meet with landowners and build credibility for the effort.

The process almost stopped as quickly as it had started, however. After Ronald Reagan won the presidency in 1980 on a tide of resentment toward the federal government, his interior secretary, James Watt, imposed a moratorium on all new land acquisition. Watt would not last long in the job, and the moratorium would soon be lifted, but for a brief period the AT effort ground to a halt.

"All of the sudden, all of us in the land acquisition process didn't really have a whole lot to do," Pam Underhill recalled, and she moved back into the trail's management office, part of the team coordinating the day-to-day oversight of the trail with the Park Service's various partners, especially the Appalachian Trail Conference, which was struggling under the weight of its new responsibilities.

Startzell was just coming to terms with the bare-bones nature of the ATC operation. In addition to the executive director and himself, "we had a bookkeeper, and an editor for the magazine, and a shipper, and that was about it. And our relationships with the clubs were almost non-existent. They just viewed us as some foreign entity." He remembers the bookkeeper struggling to decide which overdue bills to pay and which to hold onto for another week.

Marrying these two vastly different organizations into a coherent partnership on behalf of the Appalachian Trail was no easy task. The Park Service was a multimillion-dollar professional agency, while the ATC was a small nonprofit representing a hardy band of self-directed volunteers. The idea that the two groups could work productively together, bringing the power of the federal government to the trail's defense without losing the grassroots spirit that defined its success, was a massive leap of faith, as big as the assumptions that had unwittingly sunk the first protection effort.

Dave Richie had that faith, and the personal disposition to see it through. He shepherded the creation of two documents that would define the Park Service–ATC partnership: a master plan to guide the trail's physical development, and an agreement delegating to the ATC responsibility for the lands the Park Service was acquiring.

The comprehensive plan that Richie sent to his Park Service superiors in 1981 announced from the get-go that it was no ordinary plan. On the first page, a quotation from the ATC declared that "The body of the Trail is provided by the lands it traverses, and its soul is in the living stewardship of the volunteers and workers of the Appalachian Trail community." Body and soul are not the typical starting points for a land-use plan, but Richie was keen to establish the fact that the Park Service's role in this project, distinct from its usual way of doing business, was to support and facilitate the trail community's leadership, not supplant it.

Rather than prescribe what should happen where, as a traditional park plan would, the AT plan described a process for making decisions, grounded in consensus among the stakeholders particular to any

Dave Richie.

given section of trail. The trail ran through federal, state, local, and private lands; over mountains, across fields, and through towns; under the responsibility of dozens of different trail clubs, large and small. A single comprehensive plan for the whole trail could not hope to detail the right solutions for the myriad different circumstances that would arise, and it didn't attempt to. Instead, it outlined a process for individual trail clubs to develop a series of local management plans, supported and overseen by the ATC, and guided by the principles of the comprehensive plan.

"Richie liked principles—broad, almost poetic doctrines of conduct and perspective," Startzell recalled. "When they speak about volunteer leadership, he meant it. He really believed that volunteers were capable of pretty much anything if you didn't overly constrain them or patronize them."

Richie made it clear within the Park Service that their job was to foster the AT's volunteer stewardship as much as it was to protect the trail itself. "Those of us who worked for Dave had it very much instilled in us," Underhill said. "I learned that mantra from him and it never left me, that what was important was to keep that tradition alive for the trail."

The second foundational document for the new AT was the delegation agreement spelling out responsibility for the trail land the Park

Service was acquiring. The government was in effect making a new national park out of disconnected lengths of newly acquired trail corridor, stopping and starting wherever other agencies—national forests, state parks—had already provided protection. As a solution to the AT's problems it made a lot of sense, but as a single park unit to be managed it was unusual to say the least.

The delegation agreement basically off-loaded that responsibility from the Park Service to the ATC, which would in turn pass it on to the individual clubs responsible for each section of trail. It was a sensitive agreement to negotiate. The Park Service could not just turn over government property to a private organization to do with it whatever it pleased. But at the same time the ATC did not want trail land, which for decades had been tended by volunteers, to suddenly be subject to layers of federal oversight. And for that matter the local trail clubs were not thrilled about having to answer to the faraway ATC.

The final document, typical for something Richie was at the center of, was brief and more suggestive than prescriptive. The formal memorandum of understanding described only the legal basics of the relationship, while an appendix, which could be modified more easily as the project evolved, contained the guiding principles of the partnership. Trail clubs would take the lead on managing their sections of trail, but "ATC will serve as guarantor to the National Park Service that the Trail and corridor are being adequately managed. If there is a problem with a trail club's performance, ATC will be accountable to NPS in rectifying the problem." Richie had the ATC draft the side document "to have ATC tell NPS what it proposes to do rather than to have NPS tell ATC what it cannot do."

It was and remains a landmark agreement, a unique partnership between the federal government and a private nonprofit to jointly steward a significant park asset in the national interest. The signing ceremony in January of 1984 was held at the Washington headquarters of the American Institute of Architects, the original publisher of Benton MacKaye's AT proposal.

Ten years after Dave Richie inherited an Appalachian Trail initiative in almost total disarray, while much work remained to be done, the bureaucratic structure that would protect and shape the trail for the indefinite future was firmly in place. The Appalachian Trail Project Office he headed reported directly to Park Service headquarters in Washington, outside the usual chain of command, and a stand-alone land acquisition office worked exclusively on the unique challenges of building a trail corridor through fourteen states. Despite some initial fears, the project had survived the arrival of the Reagan administration, thanks in part to its firm foundation outside the government in the volunteer sector.

In 1986, Richie finished hiking the full length of the AT, a personal ambition that meshed nicely with his professional responsibilities. He retired from the Park Service the following year, at fifty-five ready for new adventures outside of government.

A few months before Richie's retirement from the Park Service, Dave Startzell was elevated to the ATC executive director's job. He had expected to get the job five years earlier, and planned to quit when it went to someone else. But Richie, who had a reputation for recognizing and cultivating talent, had personally intervened and convinced Startzell to stay on. Startzell would direct the ATC for the next twenty-five years.

A key part of his job over that period was convincing Congress to keep the money flowing, year after year, to pay for land acquisition. The NPS–ATC partnership conjured by Richie was an increasingly smooth-running machine, but it could only do its job of acquiring and managing a new trail corridor if it was fueled by annual appropriations from Congress.

The ATC became in some respects a lobby like any other, building relationships with elected officials and their staff people, both in Washington and in district offices up and down the trail. Each year Startzell and different representatives of the trail community would put on a presentation for the House Interior Appropriations Subcommittee ("it was literally a smoke-filled room"), outlining a collection of acquisition targets carefully cultivated to curry a wide range of support. The Park Service would receive and spend the money, but Startzell's lobbying made it clear that this was not an agency seeking funds for its own sake, but instead for a preservation project that would have a broad public impact. The trail ran through fourteen states; if Startzell could get all the senators from those states to sign on, that was more than a quarter of the United States Senate.

Startzell proved to be a consummate player of the appropriations game, building long-term relationships among both Republicans and Democrats that ensured a steady stream of acquisition dollars. Pam Underhill, meanwhile, steadily rose through the ranks in the Park Service's Appalachian Trail office until she was named its director in 1996. Starzell and Underhill would lead their respective organizations side by side for the next sixteen years. Startzell, though he headed the outside advocacy organization, had a reputation for a calm demeanor and smooth relations. And while Underhill was the lifelong civil servant, she played the role of fiery advocate for the AT, more than once getting in trouble for remarks in the heat of battle that did not reflect well on the agency.

"I was like a momma bear when it came to the Appalachian Trail," she recalled. "Anything that was a threat to it, . . . I said any of these things that involve social discussions about different points of view, about what's gonna be in the best overall interest of society, I said my voice in that conversation is on behalf of the Appalachian Trail. My interest is very long and narrow and very simple. And somebody else can advocate for all the other interests in this conversation because this is what I'm advocating for. And that's the way I felt about it."

The day-to-day work of acquiring the trail corridor required the sort of things that bureaucracies, for all their limitations, are good at: persistence over time, procedures that ensured some semblance of fairness, and when the circumstances called for it, the power to get things done. In hundreds of transactions, all unique in their own way, the Park Service slowly pieced together a permanent trail route.

There were hiccups, large and small, along the way. In the Cumberland Valley of Pennsylvania, a long stretch of trail across rural lowlands required years of frequently confrontational public process before a corridor was finally agreed to. In the Hudson Valley north of New York City, a Franciscan monastery encroached on a stretch of trail corridor it had previously signed over to the Park Service. When Underhill promised to use the power of eminent domain to secure a fully protected route across the friars' land, headlines pitting the federal government against a serene band of monks ensued; a negotiated solution, basically along the lines of what the Park Service had sought from the start, quickly came to pass. In Vermont, a federal judge ruled the Park Service could not seize more land from a property owner than it had initially offered to purchase; an appeals court, though, decided that an offer made to entice a voluntary deal should not artificially tie the government's hands in securing the corridor that best served the interests of the AT.

The trail underwent its greatest transformation in Maine, where a vast realm of forest allowed for a wholesale rerouting away from the opportunistic passages of Myron Avery's first rush to completion, and onto the highest, most compelling, terrain. Such a route by definition included Saddleback Mountain, home to both a unique summit ecosystem with stunning views and a ski operation with expansion-minded owners intent on fighting the government at every turn. It would take fifteen years of bitter acrimony, political posturing, and eventually a special act of Congress to finally resolve the situation.

To the builders and protectors of the Appalachian Trail, Saddleback represented an almost perfect embodiment of the project's aspirations. Towering above sparsely settled forest and a scattering of crystalline lakes, its rocky ridgeline home to a distinct alpine community of inches-high vegetation, Saddleback is as naturally unique as it is visually impressive.

But since 1960 the mountain had been home to a small, slowly growing ski operation, which was purchased by Massachusetts businessman Donald Breen in 1978, the same year Congress kicked off the new AT acquisition program. Skiing in the Northeast was at the beginning of an explosion in popularity, and Breen saw in Saddleback's slopes the ski runs and condominiums of a booming real estate investment. At first Breen only leased the land for the ski operation from the timber company that owned the mountain. But in 1984, even though the Park Service had initiated talks with the timber company for an AT corridor, Breen bought the property outright.

It is obvious in retrospect that the Breen family did not fully appreciate the commitment the Park Service was making to the mountain they had just purchased. In the positions they staked out over the years, the Breens made clear that to them the trail was no more than a right-of-way, a conduit for hikers to pass through their land, which they could and would develop to its maximum profitability. Chairlifts, pipes for snowmaking, lodges, and parking lots should be of no concern to the trail community, they argued, so long as the owners accommodated a route across their property. The National Trails System Act, however, required the Park Service to acquire and protect the

Appalachian National *Scenic* Trail, and provided the legal authority to make that happen. The whole point of the reinvigorated acquisition program was to place the trail in as natural a setting as possible, and to protect that setting in perpetuity. David Field, a giant in the AT community but also a local landowner who could see the issue from the Breens' perspective, said of them in 1987, "They happened to come along at the wrong time. This is a resource of national significance."

The two sides negotiated intermittently, and unsuccessfully, for several years after the Breens purchased the land. The AT issue was not the only thing complicating the investors' plans, however. The State of Maine approved only a portion of their proposed expansion of the ski area in 1989, and after a downturn in the real estate market, the Breens declined to pursue even that limited development. In the meantime, two other Maine ski resorts had developed ahead of Saddleback and soaked up much of the available demand. In 1991, perhaps seeking to make the best out of an investment that turned out to be more complicated than anticipated, the family tentatively agreed to scale back their expansion and sell 2,000 acres to the Park Service for the trail and surrounding scenery. But a professional appraisal of the land's value, which was all that the Park Service was legally allowed to pay, came up well short of what the Breens were hoping for. They rejected the offer.

At this point the Saddleback dispute was not unlike countless others the Park Service and ATC had worked through in the process of cobbling together a 2,100-mile corridor. The public's interest in a national scenic trail was bound to bump up against private property owners' interests in their own land. A respectful give-and-take could usually yield an agreement, and when it couldn't, there was an established way of resolving the situation, in court. When the government seizes land—whether for a highway or a civic center or a park—it brings a lawsuit to do so, and a judge determines what the appropriate price to be paid is. The public's interest is not unfairly hamstrung by one individual's recalcitrance, but owners' interests in the value of their property are protected as well. In fact, because judges could order sale prices higher than the appraised value that the Park Service was limited to, even successful negotiations sometimes ended with an agreement to go to court to establish the fairest price.

The longer the negotiations with the Breens dragged on, and the longer Saddleback stuck out as the most significant AT section not yet protected, the more the Park Service came to believe that the only way forward was to use the power of eminent domain to take the necessary land from the Breens and let the courts figure out the appropriate level of compensation. But the Breens were determined to avoid that outcome, and in 1995 launched a well-funded influence campaign aimed at delegitimizing the acquisition effort and demonizing the Park Service.

With the help of political strategists and PR consultants, favorable articles began appearing in local and national newspapers. The Breens announced to the media, but not to the Park Service, a seemingly generous donation of land that would more than meet the AT's needs, they said. They conveniently forgot to mention that a condition of the donation would be continued access for ski infrastructure through the trail corridor, the same as if they had made no donation, and ignoring the AT's scenic requirements. They conjured visions of a massive resort development that would rival the finest in the Rockies, if only the National Park Service would get out of the way, without producing any firm business plans. Most significant, they succeeded in convincing many of the residents of nearby Rangeley, for whom their hypothetical resort would provide a significant employment base, that the federal government's unreasonable demands were blocking the community's economic future.

In 1997 the publisher of the local Rangeley newspaper told a national reporter that Donald Breen's failure to develop Saddleback was not a big deal in the community. "He would have been a good steward to Saddleback," she said. "But over the years the town simply went on to other things like promoting snowmobiling." But just two years later the controversy had been stoked to such a fevered pitch that local residents, with the help of an outside activist who proudly described himself as "Mr. Rent-A-Riot," angrily took over a Park Service public hearing in Rangeley; a journalist reported seeing a participant lean in and push Underhill.

The more the Park Service fell back on the kind of studies that bureaucracies are good at — a formal evaluation of the scenic quality at different spots on the mountain, an independent consultant's report on economically viable options for expansion of the resort — the more the Breens raised the political heat. Maine's senior senator at the time, Republican Olympia Snowe, at first entered the fray squarely on the Breens' side. Over time, though, she backed away from embracing the entirety of their position and devoted considerable time to trying to broker a solution.

In the end, the Breens succeeded in moving the dispute outside the usual channels for handling these disputes. The Park Service did not have the political support to use its power of eminent domain, which would have ordinarily been its last resort, and the relationship between the two parties had become so toxic that direct negotiations were fruitless. The Breens' hiring of former Maine senator George Mitchell — a Democratic heavyweight, broker of Northern Ireland's Good Friday Agreement in 1998, and a one-time Senate colleague of Interior Secretary Bruce Babbitt — helped break the logjam. In 2000 a political appointee at the Interior Department was tasked with working out a deal, which was concluded in the late stages of the Clinton administration, and the $4-million price tag was inserted into a special appropriations bill.

Underhill was livid that her political superiors would cut such a

Dave Startzell and Pam Underhill at the AT's southern terminus on Springer Mountain, Georgia.

deal, feeling until the end that the Breens were not entitled to such a large payout outside of the normal channels. But others were content that the matter had finally been resolved. "I was just sort of relieved," Dave Startzell recalled, "even though it was a little galling that they probably got twice what the property was worth." For that money, the government did not get all that the trail's advocates desired, but it did secure protection of the most significant scenic and natural assets on Saddleback, preserving a unique hiking experience. The Breens sold the resort shortly thereafter to a local family, which led a more limited expansion of the facilities.

There were several unique factors that made the Saddleback battle so lengthy and bitter, but in the end it came down to the fact that there is a lot more tied up in the idea of the Appalachian Trail than the pathway itself. What makes the AT valuable is the experience of hiking it, a huge component of which is the scenery that, while it is visible from the trail, may lie a considerable distance away. Is it the AT's job to provide only a relatively rustic walking path from Maine to Georgia, or does it have the additional mandate to stamp out development that might occur in its surroundings?

That question played out in another Maine controversy that served as something of a coda to the Saddleback drama. In 2005 a wind-energy company proposed building turbines on Mt. Redington, not far from Saddleback and the AT, which would have been visible to hikers for miles around. Underhill staked out a clear and uncompromising position for the Park Service against approval of the plan by Maine's land-use regulators. When some environmental advocates argued that, in an era of climate change, scenic preferences might have to give way to more pressing needs, Underhill was having none of it. Renewable energy was all well and good, she argued, but not in the AT's backyard. "I do not know why the Natural Resource Council of Maine decided to toss the Appalachian Trail under the bus on this one," she said in a formal hearing, "but it is not something we will forget any time soon." She was reprimanded by her superiors for her threatening tone; the State of Maine ultimately ruled against the proposal.

At the time Congress committed to protecting the AT in 1978, 55 percent of the trail's current 2,100-mile length was in public ownership; nearly all of the remaining 45 percent has been acquired since. Together with the United States Forest Service and state governments, the Park Service acquired the land to protect more than 900 miles of trail, and while the critical acquisition effort is essentially complete, building and protecting the trail are ongoing ventures. Minor reroutings are commonplace, as are trail improvements of various kinds, but the more significant challenges concern the larger environment through which the trail passes. The Park Service and ATC work with a variety of partners—state and local governments, land conservancies —to protect new parcels near the trail that can add to its experience. And the demands of modernity to cross the trail environment, with things such as roads, power lines, and pipelines, require a constant examination of the trail's balance between naturalistic seclusion and the needs of the wider world.

But thanks to the work that Dave Richie did in building a public–private partnership on the trail's behalf, and the day-in, day-out work of acquiring and managing the trail corridor that Pam Underhill, Dave Startzell, and many others carried forward, the Appalachian Trail became a permanent feature of the American landscape in a way that it never was before. Such permanence certainly comes with costs—to those both inside and outside the trail community who may chafe at how the Park Service and the ATC conduct their business—but it is clear that there would be nothing like today's AT in existence had that robust partnership not come into being.

Dave Richie and his wife enjoyed several years of retirement before he died of cancer at the age of seventy in 2002. Pam Underhill and Dave Startzell retired from their respective positions with the Park Service and the ATC in 2012.

9

The Bestseller: Bill Bryson

//

I was still going to hike the Appalachian Trail; I just wasn't going
to hike all of it. Katz and I had already walked half a million steps,
if you can believe it. It didn't seem altogether essential to do the
other 4.5 million to get the idea of the thing.

—Bill Bryson

Bill Bryson was a hugely successful writer, in Britain. In three
books chronicling his travels, he had proved to be a terrifically
entertaining tour guide not only of the places he saw, but of
the baby boomer psyche as it slouched into middle age. That success
had not, however, translated across the Atlantic from Bryson's adopted
home in England. The United States market was the logical next step
in his quest for publishing success, and he sought an American venue
for his unique brand of storytelling.

The Appalachian Trail would prove to be the perfect setting. Once
the relatively obscure domain of dreamers and enthusiasts, by the
mid-1990s the AT was a fixture of the American landscape, both literally and figuratively. Public ownership and professional management
gave the trail a physical permanence it had previously lacked, and in-

creasing popularity brought the trail's attractions steadily closer to the mainstream. In the hands of a skilled and ambitious writer at the top of his game, the AT was poised, seemingly out of nowhere, for a blockbuster role on the American cultural stage.

Bryson published *A Walk in the Woods* in the United States in 1998, and it was a massive bestseller. Irreverent and sarcastic, but with an enduring core of sincerity, Bryson crafted an Appalachian Trail that was a backdrop for human foolishness—not least his own—as much as it was a gateway to natural wonder. That the book's popularity owed more to the author's comic timing than the physical realities of the trail did not sit particularly well with the AT community. But like Horace Kephart at the beginning of the twentieth century, Bill Bryson at its end delivered what his audience desired, and the Appalachian Mountains became the setting for a decidedly ironic outlook on the world.

Bryson grew up in a household where writing for others' entertainment was the family business. He was born in Des Moines, Iowa, in 1951, to parents who both had prominent roles with the local newspapers. His mother, Mary, wrote for and then edited the *Des Moines Register*'s so-called women's pages, covering topics of interest to homemakers, while his father, Bill, was the national baseball writer for the *Tribune*.

Baseball dominated fans' attention at that time like no other sport, the game so prominent that even a newspaper in Des Moines, with no Major League team of its own, would assign a top writer to cover it. Bill Bryson Sr. traveled the country covering the game, celebrated among his sportswriting peers from big cities even though he wrote for a regional paper. The younger Bryson would later lament that by staying in Iowa, his father had missed out on a chance to shine on the national stage.

Bill's was a charmed childhood in many respects. The Bryson family lived comfortably on two good incomes, and he occasionally got to tag along with his father, flying on airplanes when that was a rare luxury, entering Major League locker rooms, meeting the sporting giants of the day. As a teenager he worked for the *Register*'s sports section, drank too much and got in trouble with his friends, and did just enough schoolwork to get into college. "I was a shit, really," he says now of his high school self, unimpressed with Des Moines and impatient to get out and see the world.

He embarked on a backpacking trip around Europe one summer during college, and was intrigued enough to return the following year, this time with a childhood friend in tow. Matt Angerer, who would later be immortalized and assigned a starring role in *A Walk in the Woods* under the pseudonym Stephen Katz, was in many ways Bryson's opposite. Angerer was outgoing where Bryson was introverted, but also reckless and destructive where Bryson was merely cavalier and detached. When, in their high school years, a band of teens had participated in a beer heist from the local railyard, Bryson and most others kept enough distance to enjoy the beer but avoid any serious consequences; Angerer was sentenced to juvenile detention.

The two young men caroused across the Continent in the summer of 1973, Bryson making it back to their hostel every night, Angerer sometimes only turning up the following day, or the day after that. Bryson grew increasingly frustrated with his friend, but appreciated that Angerer helped give him entree to the wider world. "I would spend my whole life not talking to another human being if I could get away with it, whereas he was exactly the opposite, so all of the friendships we made along the way, it was because of his being outgoing."

At the end of that summer (after Angerer's drunkenly pushing Bryson through a shop window in Istanbul, which netted Angerer a night in handcuffs), Bryson was in London, waiting for his flight home. He met up with a couple of acquaintances from Iowa, two women working as student nurses at a mental hospital far outside the city. He learned that the hospital was always hiring entry-level staff to help look after the patients, and that the job came with housing. Two weeks before he was slated to return to Des Moines for his senior year of college, Bryson opted to stay in England instead; he showed up hung over and a bit late for his first day of work.

He met a nurse there named Cynthia Billen, and the two were married sixteen months later. They moved to Des Moines so that Bill could complete his college degree, then immediately returned to England, where he embarked on something of a two-headed career. Having grown up around the newspaper business, he found salary-paying work as a copy editor, first for a regional newspaper in Bournemouth, then at bigger papers in London. But from the start, Bryson also began carving out a freelance writing career of his own.

Freelancing is a mercenary business, a constant hustle to identify topics that are within reasonable reach of the writer's knowledge, while simultaneously of interest to editors who will pay for the work. Bryson (using a "Jr." in his byline to distinguish himself from his father) soon established a niche for himself as a chronicler of curiosities, with an eye for the absurdities of life. On St. Patrick's Day in 1978, the *Detroit Free Press* ran a piece by a twenty-six-year-old Bryson on the fuzzy history surrounding Ireland's patron saint. "On March 17 (probably) in the year 461 AD (or thereabouts), M. Sucatus Patricius (better known as St. Patrick) breathed his last, which is why the world is honoring him (or them) today." The next year the *Los Angeles Times* featured Bryson's short essay on the many oddball statistics that scientists seemed to be churning out every day, like toilet paper production measured in terms of an imaginary unrolling around the equator. "It pains me to think that the world might be so short of undiscovered facts or so long on scientists that some of our best minds have nothing better to do with their time than circle the earth with hypothetical toilet paper." The writing was meant to be entertaining, and it sold.

"I didn't particularly want to be a writer," Bryson says. "I wanted to make a living as a writer. And it was the one skill I had that I knew I could get income out of. And it seemed like that would give me a pretty good life if I could make it work."

As his editing career inside newspapers steadily progressed, so did his freelance work, yielding bigger assignments for more substantial publications. He began writing travel pieces for the *Washington Post* and published a handful of small novelty books (*The Book of Blunders*, a *Dictionary of Troublesome Words*), but his goal was to write something more substantial—fewer articles and bigger books—and eventually leave behind the daily grind of the newsroom.

He sent out book proposals to publishers in both the United States and United Kingdom, and developed a handsome collection of rejection postcards. "They always looked like invitations, and in a sense they were invitations, cause they were inviting you to fuck off." But one British publisher saw potential in a book Bryson pitched that would be something of a travel memoir, a portrait of America from the perspective of an expat returning home and road-tripping between out-of-the-way places. He left the newspaper world behind and devoted himself full-time to making a living from his writing.

In the spring of 1988, the widely read and respected British literary magazine *Granta* published an excerpt from Bryson's forthcoming book about America, which would be called *The Lost Continent*. (Among the literary luminaries in the same issue was the Czech dissident playwright Vaclav Havel, soon to become his country's first president after the fall of the Berlin Wall.)

"I come from Des Moines," Bryson wrote to open the piece.

> Somebody had to. When you come from Des Moines you either accept the fact without question and settle down with a local girl named Bobbi and get a job at the Firestone factory

and live there forever and ever, or you spend your adolescence
moaning at length about what a dump it is and how you can't
wait to get out, and then you settle down with a local girl
named Bobbi and get a job at the Firestone factory and live
there forever and ever.

In a style that was by turns acerbic and poignant, Bryson conveyed
a world-weariness that, while it could come across as contempt toward Bobbi and her ilk, at its best captured a heartfelt reckoning with
a perplexing world. The publishing industry took note. The book at
that point was only slated to be published in the United Kingdom, and
American publishers began a bidding war to get the North American
rights. Bryson was on a reporting trip in Belgium, in a small hotel bar
with a handful of patrons, when his wife called with the news that the
auction was over. The winning bid was $300,000.

"I was so, just, transfixed by what had happened that I did something, you know, 'Drinks on the house!', which they didn't understand
at all." There would be no more living from freelance check to check,
though Bryson would continue to write magazine articles for a few
more years. After a decade of striving, Bill Bryson was an overnight
success.

In the end, *The Lost Continent* would succeed in the British market
but was not well received in the United States. For many readers, what
came across as bracing sarcasm in a single chapter degenerated into
mean-spiritedness when repeated for every new town Bryson drove
into. Rhetorical antics that elicited a chuckle on the first encounter,
such as humorously made-up names for people and places ("Draino,
Indiana"), came to seem repetitive and tiresome. Multiple reviewers
argued that Bryson seemed far more interested in inventing a gag than
in learning or sharing anything of real value to the reader.

The *Washington Post*'s Pulitzer-winning book critic Jonathan Yardley came to the conclusion that, outside of the jokey turns of phrase and stale criticisms, there just was not enough substance in Bryson's work. "Coming to the end of *The Lost Continent*, it's hard to imagine what he had in mind when he started out except the prospect of making some money. Which makes him just as American as all those benighted people at whom he so merrily sneers."

Though Bryson later expressed regret over his dismissive tone and learned to temper it, the basic outlines of a Bill Bryson book had been established, and publishers eagerly signed up for more. In 1991's *Neither Here Nor There*, he retraced much of the route of his 1973 European travels, with occasional humorous reference to "Katz" and their long-ago shenanigans. He published a pair of popular books on the English language and its American offshoot, and in 1995 turned his traveler's gaze on Britain itself. *Notes from a Small Island* was Bryson's third book in this vein, and he was fully in command of his craft. The book was a massive bestseller in the United Kingdom, celebrated as both a delightful read and a window into the country's soul. It was still a top-five bestseller in Britain two years after its publication. Selling books "by the truckload," the *Guardian* said, "Bryson is not just a hugely successful author but a brand name."

Success did not come quite so readily in the United States market, however. The tone and style Bryson had been honing for a British audience did not capture Americans' affections to nearly the same extent. In one respect, that didn't matter. If his only aim had been to make a decent living as a writer, Bryson had already succeeded beyond his wildest dreams. But that was not the case.

"I got more and more ambitious as I started to have success," he said. "It was a little bit like, you know, pushing on the door and realizing it's not locked, and you go through it. . . . Really, all I ever expected in the beginning was just, will I be able to pay my bills and make a living. But little by little, I was able to do more than that and actually, might actually get famous at this, I might be really successful, so I'll just keep pushing to see where it takes me."

Because his family wanted to live in the United States for a time, they decided to move to the New England college town of Hanover, New Hampshire. His next book would be targeted to an American audience, but his stock in trade was the humorous travel narrative, and he had already published, to a very mixed reception, his take on the classic American road trip. Bryson needed a journey to undertake, one with a distinctly American character.

He says the idea came to him while out for a walk in Hanover, when he noticed the Appalachian Trail heading up into the woods on the outskirts of town. Thru-hiking the AT, he wrote in the opening pages of the ensuing book,

> would get me fit after years of waddlesome sloth. It would be
> an interesting and reflective way to reacquaint myself with the
> scale and beauty of my native land after nearly twenty years
> of living abroad. It would be useful (I wasn't quite sure in what
> way, but I was sure nonetheless) to learn to fend for myself in
> the wilderness.

And it would, in the vein of Kephart's retreat to the Appalachians some ninety years earlier, provide a venue for Bryson's publishing ambition.

He recruited his old friend Angerer to be his hiking companion, and the two set out from Georgia's Springer Mountain in March of 1996. Like so many long-distance AT hikers, they spent the first several days getting accustomed to the trail, figuring out what worked for them and what didn't, establishing the routine of their hiking days. And then it dawned on Bryson: virtually all there is on the AT is the routine of the hiking day. Walking, eating, sleeping. Trail, trees, and more trail. There was none of the rapid-fire change of scenery and cast of characters that his earlier travel narratives had relied on.

"Every night when I'd crawl into my tent, I'd just think, 'I don't know what the hell we're doing out here, cause I'm not going to get a book out of this. There's *nothing* going on." The deeper satisfactions of the trip were not entirely lost on him, but he was first and foremost a writer on assignment, not a long-distance hiker for its own sake. Unable to envision how life on the trail would plausibly lead to any book at all, let alone one on a par with his considerable success to that point, he began to doubt the whole enterprise.

His hiking partner, meanwhile, was not in a good place. Angerer had spent his adult life wrestling with addiction, occasionally in trouble with the law, and had agreed to join Bryson on the hike in part so that a change in scenery would help him stay sober. His outlook on the world at that point was not especially bright. Instead of the carefree raconteur Bryson had been expecting, Angerer was, for the bulk of their time together on the trail, depressed and withdrawn.

Morale did not improve when the two novice trekkers hiked into a spring snowstorm in North Carolina, a genuinely dangerous situation that eventually necessitated a few bored and idle days off the trail in a motel. Ultimately, though, the hardest part for Bryson was the loneliness of being separated from his family. That had always been the least attractive aspect of his writing career, but the isolation of life on the trail proved to be a step beyond what he could live with.

"I have never been so wretchedly homesick," he recalled. Talking to Cynthia in faraway New Hampshire required a reluctant detour away from getting trail miles underfoot, in the hopes of finding a pay phone. "And you call home and nobody answers, cause they don't know when I'm going to call, so she's gone to the grocery store or something, and you just think, 'Do I go back on the trail and try again in a few days, or do I sit here for a half an hour, hour, what do I do? I just want to hear my wife's voice.' It was terrible. It was awful."

Discouraged and demoralized, after reaching the center of Great Smoky Mountains National Park, 200 miles along the 2,100-mile trail, Bryson pulled the plug.

"It was like somebody hit me in the forehead with a sledgehammer. It was just like, 'I'm never going to do it.'"

He was not going to hike the entire AT, but Bryson still had a book to deliver. In fact, freeing himself from the requirement of trudging every last inch of trail made it possible for him to engage the trail—as both a hiking challenge and a writing subject—on his own terms. He and Angerer would skip ahead to hike the trail through Shenandoah National Park in Virginia, then part ways while Bryson tackled smaller trips on his own, and meet up to hike a concluding segment in Maine. As a long-distance hiker, Bryson had been considerably out of his element. But as a peripatetic gatherer and teller of stories, he was back on the authorial home turf that had won him such success in Britain. Hiking on the AT would be central to the book's structure, but not always its content; the trail was the scaffolding on which Bryson could array his signature pieces of research, observation, and humor.

An annoying fellow hiker with whom the two men had shared the trail early on yielded several pages of comic ridicule. The Park Service and the Forest Service came in for rants against clueless bureaucracy. The possibility of a bear attack called for copious research and the darkly humorous recounting of Bryson's anxiety. Perhaps most significant for the success of the book, the dejected, sullen Angerer transformed into the hilariously grumpy Stephen Katz. *A Walk in the Woods* became something of a buddy comedy.

Bryson had initially drafted a more realistic picture of Angerer/Katz but came to the conclusion that such a downer of a character would sink the book.

He was quite depressed at this time, he was struggling with chronic alcoholism, he'd had a long-term relationship fall apart, he was feeling sorry for himself, he hadn't had a decent job for years, he just felt like life had kicked him in the balls and he wasn't doing very well. And I portrayed all of that. And it was just depressing. And I just thought, this is just terrible, this isn't going to work at all. And then my revelation with that was, instead of making him just depressed, I just made him angry, which he also was. I made it much more that he was angry with the trail rather than angry with life. Cause he was. He was angry at the trail, cause it was so hard, and I just sort of dropped off the other reasons that were making him an angry person in life. And so it really became the two of us against the trail. And then it started to work much better, I think, as a narrative.

His massaging of the source material notwithstanding, Bryson retained a piercingly intelligent commitment to rendering the world — Angerer, the AT, himself — in a sincere way. The conclusion of the book, featuring the two men's second abandonment of the trail after nearly losing Angerer to Maine's 100-Mile Wilderness, touchingly comes to terms with some uncomfortable truths, not least nature's complete indifference to whatever convenient tales of redemption one might want to imagine for it.

A Walk in the Woods was released in the United States in the spring of 1998, two years after Bryson and Angerer had set off from Springer Mountain, and it was a triumph. One reviewer called Bryson "a satirist of the first rank, one who writes (and walks) with Chaucerian brio." Another wrote that for all Bryson's humorous hijinks, "it is a serious book. . . . By playing on our fears, he captures the ambivalence of our feelings about the wild. We revere it but we're also intimidated." Several appreciated that the book gleefully dispensed with the need to describe every inch of the trail.

The buying public couldn't get enough of the book. It hit the *New York Times* bestseller list almost immediately and stayed there for thirty-five weeks, eleven of them in the top five; the paperback version was a bestseller for over two years. Bryson's is, by orders of magnitude, the most-read book about the Appalachian Trail. For many people it is almost synonymous with the trail itself, the instant association they make when the AT is mentioned.

For those within the AT community, however—resolute long-distance hikers, trail maintainers, and club volunteers—the book was a massive shock to the system, the uninvited guest who turns the music up to eleven and invites all his friends over. *Appalachian Trailway News*, the ATC's newsletter, diplomatically took note of the book's excesses, while appreciatively stating that it contains "the best history of the Trail ever held to three pages."

But letter writers from the ATC membership were appalled. They called out Bryson for his lazy and demeaning caricatures of southerners, his ill-informed complaints, and his apparent disinterest in the trail's larger ideals. Perhaps his greatest sin was that he was an interloper turning their beloved trail into slickly produced fodder for the pop culture. "There are those who hike the A.T.," one correspondent wrote. "There are those who hike the A.T. and write meaningful, accurate books about it. And, there are those who don't bother hiking the A.T., but, what the heck, they write about it anyway."

Another said that "the last straw was the typical quitter rationalization, 'I didn't quit; my goals changed.'"

As a practical matter, what the book meant for the AT community was a surge in popularity, and the attendant problems of wear and tear that had to be managed. In the first hiking season after the book's release, the ATC estimated a 45 percent increase in starting thru-hikers, which is roughly representative of the overall increase in trail use. Estimated trail use peaked in 2001, three years after the book's release, before the *Walk in the Woods* bump receded.

By that time, Bryson had already published his next bestseller, adapting his by now well-worn formula to travels around Australia. At one point the Australia book was on the hardcover bestseller list while *A Walk in the Woods* was on the paperback list. *A Walk in the Woods* stayed on the paperback list so long that the Australia book soon joined it there. And Bryson's earlier books that had not succeeded in the United States began to sell as well. It didn't hurt that he had name-dropped their titles into the body of *A Walk in the Woods.*

He was somewhat ambivalent about repeatedly mining the same vein of publishing gold in these witty travel narratives. But his publishers were always interested in the equivalent of the next hit single, and the travel books were a bankable commodity.

"In the beginning, I guess I was fairly passive, maybe even happy about being pigeonholed, because it was going well, and each book did a little bit better," he recalled. But by this point in his career, it was his name on the cover that was selling books, whatever the topic, and that gave him the freedom to embark on a different kind of work altogether.

In 2003 he took a tour not through some mildly exotic land, but through the world of science. *A Short History of Nearly Everything* aimed to explain to readers the fundamentals of how the world worked, and succeeded wildly. It was like a lecture series on the breadth of scientific knowledge neatly distilled into 600 pages of humorous writing, with Bryson again as the moderately clueless protagonist. *A Short History* was translated into several languages and received multiple awards for science communication; it became and remains Bryson's all-time global bestseller, even as *A Walk in the Woods* is tops in the United States.

A Short History also elevated him to a new role in public life, not just as a successful writer but as an ambassador for education and scientific literacy, including several years in the ceremonial post of chancellor of England's Durham University.

The books kept coming over the ensuing years, indulging his wide-ranging interests, but for the most part did not involve the travel genre anymore. (He likes to joke that he cannot interest anyone in a book about Canada.) An essay about his father in *The New Yorker* in the early 2000s might have signaled a turn to more sober literary fare, but his work stayed firmly rooted in the mass market of sometimes glib, always sharply observant reporting.

A Walk in the Woods seemed ideally suited to a film adaptation, but it took Hollywood seventeen years to make and release a movie. The legendary actor Robert Redford acquired the rights in 2005, hoping he had finally found the vehicle to reunite himself on screen, starring as Bryson, with his equally legendary friend Paul Newman as Katz. The two actors' bickering repartee in 1969's *Butch Cassidy and the Sundance Kid* was a classic of the buddy-comedy form, a storytelling device that Bryson had so effectively used to structure his own book. The plot would be reworked around aging pals, and Redford and Newman's first film together in more than twenty-five years would be a major event.

But before they could get the picture made, Newman grew too ill to take part, and died in 2008. Redford persisted in developing the film, as several writers took a crack at adapting a screenplay, and different top directors were attached to the project at various times. Bryson, having signed over the rights to his book, said he was comforted by the fact that Redford was in charge, but he had no direct involvement in the filmmaking.

In 2015 Redford premiered the movie at his Sundance Film Festival, with Nick Nolte in the Katz role. The real-life Bryson gamely participated in publicity for the film, giving interviews about the hike

and Katz. Reviews were mid-
dling, as the various elements
that had been knit together so
elegantly in the book seemed
rather incoherently jumbled
together in the movie. "There
are a few chuckles along the
way, but only the scenery has
any real depth," one critic
wrote. With help from a low
production budget that seems
painfully obvious in the mov-

Robert Redford and Bill Bryson at the
Sundance Film Festival premiere of A
Walk in the Woods *in 2015.*

ie's look and feel, it earned a decent profit at the box office.

The film's release also provided an excuse for the *Des Moines Register* to visit Matt Angerer and see how life had turned out for him. He
reported that he was happily married and ten years sober, bemused at
the success of Bryson, with whom he was still in occasional contact,
and mostly focused on the stability and contentment of his household
life.

Bryson fondly recalls Angerer's autograph being more in demand
at a Des Moines book-signing than the author's own. He says that
Angerer has never been upset with him about the oafish caricature in *A
Walk in the Woods.* "I would argue that all that stuff that I said about him
in the book is fundamentally true, but it's just looking through a kind
of slit at him. And he's a much broader character, any human being is
much broader."

He says he assigned his friend the role of comic relief, "and he did
me a great favor by playing that role. So in a sense I did use him, and
he was very generous in letting me do that. And once I'd written the
book, I thought, oh Jesus, I hope he's not going to hate me now. And
him not hating me was one of the nicest things anybody's ever done

Matt Angerer in 2015.

for me. Cause I wouldn't have been so generous if it had gone in reverse."

Looking back on his writing career, Bryson plays down the fame he achieved, either because he has adopted the British requirement to express an abundance of modesty, or because the kind of drive that leads to the success he has had is never satisfied. "Being a writer is a really strange thing," he says, "because, no matter how successful I get, more than 99 percent of people have no idea who I am. Being a famous writer is, you're only famous inside Barnes and Noble, or in a small circle. Go out into the wider world, and there's almost no name recognition anywhere. And certainly no physical recognition. So I don't feel successful. I mean I know my books sell enough to give me a comfortable living and all of that and that people are buying them, and when I do a public event, people come, I realize, so there are people out there. But they're a very small proportion of the wider community."

More than twenty years after he was effectively done with it and moved on to other projects, Bryson continues to be identified with the Appalachian Trail. He is to some extent tired of talking about it, but at the same time gracious in his appreciation. When the ATC published a coffee-table book on the trail and its history in 2012, Bryson wrote a thoughtful foreword, expressing gratitude for what the trail had taught him, and celebrating its unique environment. "We have a sacred duty —that is not putting it too strongly—to see that it remains healthy and vibrant for all time," he wrote.

10

On the Trail

////////////////////////////

> For it seems to me that neither the frontiers between the wild
> and the cultivated, nor those that lie between the past and the
> present, are so easily fixed.
>
> —Simon Schama, *Landscape and Memory*

O n a humid July day, three young women kicking off a multiday backpacking trip on the Appalachian Trail arrive at
the top of Georgia's Springer Mountain, the trail's southern
endpoint. Like so many mountaintops, Springer's summit does not an-
nounce itself with a craggy peak and a 360-degree view. The ground
is gently, almost imperceptibly rounded across a partial clearing, and
aside from a couple of small plaques, the site is unremarkable.

"Is this it?" one asks.

It is.

"So random!" another replies.

Not quite how I would have put it, but the young hiker's phrase
does capture the feel of this place. So freighted with significance in
the context of the AT, the landscape of Springer's summit is, in per-

son, very ordinary. Based on the visual surroundings alone, it seems you could have placed the trail's endpoint on just about any southern mountain and the experience would be the same.

Yet those hikers are here, as am I, taking notes, and soon a group of middle-school-aged summer campers, and back in the spring dozens of aspiring thru-hikers per day, all of us here for the plaques, and what they signify. As with so much of the AT, it is the status of the trail, its identity *as* the Appalachian Trail, that attracts visitors to this point, more than anything extraordinary in the surroundings.

It was to get at this identity, the collage of aspirations and associations that have drawn successive generations to the AT, that I began looking into its history. And in the summer of 2019, I consulted a final historical source, the trail itself, in a series of day hikes from Georgia to Maine. Each day I hiked a short section of trail for five or six hours, drove up the road a ways, and hiked a different stretch the next day. My goal was not to attempt any sort of definitive understanding of the AT. Even a summer-long thru-hike could not accomplish that, and my trip compared to a thru-hike like a stroll around the block compares to a marathon.

Instead, I treated the trail like one of the many archives I had investigated in researching this story. As when leafing through old letters or newspaper articles, I tried to observe the trail and its environment for the insights it had to offer. What seemed noteworthy? What patterns emerged? How does history shed light on today's trail, and how does the contemporary trail help us understand its history?

I got lost on the first day.

Parking for the AT at Springer Mountain sits well inside the Chattahoochee National Forest in north Georgia, requiring a drive along dirt and gravel Forest Service roads that, in the thick of the woods, all look the same. My carefully prepared directions, written out ahead of time knowing navigation by phone would be unlikely in the forest, had proven less than adequate. About a half-hour after leaving the nearest state highway, I drove with a waning belief that the trailhead might be just around the next bend. Then a fence appeared along the road, displaying clear no-trespassing warnings; behind it, a United States Army Ranger sign hung in the trees.

It turned out to be Camp Merrill, home of the Army's elite Ranger mountain training school, and obviously not a part of the AT. But a little ways on, an armed civilian guard reassured me that they see would-be hikers like me all the time. I had missed my turn some ways back and was about 12 miles away from the trailhead. He pointed me in the right direction, but in the end it was the fortuitous discovery of cellphone service that provided a glimpse of a map and a clear sense of where the heck I was.

An hour later than I'd planned, I parked in the small lot adjacent to the AT, less than a mile from the top of Springer. A steady stream of hikers left from or passed by the parking area, in small and large groups, one middle-aged guy arriving on his motorcycle for a short hike. It was Georgia in the summertime, so the air was hot and sticky, but quite bearable up here in the forested uplands. (Having learned my lesson on Mt. Greylock a few years earlier, I carried ample amounts of water.) I hiked to and observed the Springer summit for a while, then returned to the parking lot on a side loop, the Benton MacKaye Trail, which fittingly charts its own course through the southern mountains. I enjoyed the forest's wildflowers and the occasional view, became acquainted with the unnerving company of large hoverflies, and appreciated a return to the singular pleasure of experiencing the outdoors at the scale and pace of walking.

MacKaye would have been pleased, I suspect, at a forest big enough to jostle a twenty-first-century driver out of his comfort zone, and providing a simple footpath on which to become re-grounded in the world.

Just over 100 miles of trail distance to the north, the AT up Wayah Bald in North Carolina crosses back and forth over a gravel road. The road doesn't connect to any others; like the trail, its purpose is just to get recreational visitors to the top of the mountain, where a historic stone fire tower offers impressive views of the surrounding Nantahala National Forest. (On this day, the view was of a vast sea of mist.) Walking across one of these trail–road intersections, I noticed how the roadcut had exposed the roots of a large hillside tree. Erosion had washed away the soil on that side almost completely, leaving tree roots hanging forlornly in the air.

A bit farther up the trail, an uncomfortable reality set in. The footpath was itself extracting a toll on the natural surroundings, and it looked surprisingly similar to the road's. Thousands of footfalls had kicked the soil away to expose roots and rocks; rainwater seeking the fastest route down the mountain had scoured away even more dirt. In places the trail sat several inches below the ground on either side, a human-made gully through the forest. In my travels it was a daily occurrence to see a chunk of a trailside tree's root structure exposed to the air. The culprits here are trail blazers rather than road builders, boot treads instead of tire treads. Notwithstanding the considerable effort that goes into minimizing trail impacts by the AT's legion of caretakers, the pattern persists nearly everywhere the trail goes.

We often talk about how different a trail is from a road: it requires walking instead of driving, moving our bodies instead of sitting, human power instead of machine power. Those distinctions are important and undeniable; there can be no doubt that my experience of Wayah Bald was different, and for my purposes far more rewarding, having hiked to the top rather than driven.

But what isn't different is the fact that my trip required a cleared right-of-way, as a car trip would, and that the trailway is an intrusion on the landscape that does ongoing damage. The trail may not be as distinguishable from the road as we hikers like to think.

Ever since MacKaye and his colleagues helped define wilderness in opposition to cars and roads, we have tended to think of trails as taking us into nature, and roads as a

Appalachian Trail erosion on Wayah Bald.

destruction of nature. The trail is a portal that somehow disappears from our consciousness while we observe nature's bounty around us. A road does the opposite, seemingly blotting out its surroundings so that all we notice is the Industrial Age incursion. But is the woodpecker perched along the forest road any less natural than it is along the AT? Is the tree any more natural when its roots are exposed by the trail than when they're exposed by the road?

Of course a road is wider than a footpath, so it does more damage, and roads as a whole have transformed the landscape to an almost incomprehensible degree. But assigning trails to the Nature category in our brain, by definition the opposite of and antithetical to roads in the Destruction category, is a distinction that may not be as cut-and-dried as we'd like to think.

Damascus, Virginia, is a small town in the far southwestern corner of the state that has embraced the AT's passage down its main street.

Billing itself as "Trail Town USA," Damascus plays host to the annual Trail Days festival of AT enthusiasts, and is chock full of businesses catering to both hikers and bicyclists on a popular nearby rail trail. The section of AT just east of town is itself not especially noteworthy, taking the hiker through the trees up to, along the shoulder of, and down from a ridgeline that parallels a creek below.

As countless long-distance hikers on the AT have learned, the vast majority of the trail is like this: wooded but not fantastically scenic. With little to occupy my brain along this stretch, no peak or landmark to look forward to as a destination, I found myself tuning in to the everyday qualities of the surrounding landscape. Periodically, as the trail meandered along the south side of the elongated ridge, it would reveal a V shape in the mountain's side, the wedge slowly deepening and widening as it descended to the creek valley below. These notches, formed by and channeling the runoff of rainwater, are an utterly routine feature of the mountain environment, but passing around and through them felt like walking among the architectural innovations of some old cathedral. They provided a deeper sense of the mountain, as a system of land and water together, the geography of each inseparable from the other.

I have taught students the basics of stormwater runoff, but there is a difference between knowing something and experiencing it. Your piano teacher can point to how these three notes together make a pleasant harmony. But it is another thing to hear it, and another still to play it with your own hand.

As the trail descended back to Laurel Creek, it crossed one of these tributary streams near the bottom of its run. The most noticeable change in the surroundings was the sound. On the trail you are always watching where your feet go, so picking out rocks on which to step across the water felt pretty routine. But the sound of running water unmistakably announced an all-new environment, the layers of burble and gurgle drowning out the usual ambient sounds of insects and footfalls. As I paused and looked upstream, my mental horizon shifted, away from the two-dimensional forest floor and the three-dimensional mountain to the one-dimensional stream, receding toward its origin near the ridgetop, a part of, yet distinct from, its surroundings.

MacKaye's most famous adage, written well into his old age, seemed made for this day: that the purpose of hiking the Appalachian Trail was "(1) to walk; (2) to see; (3) to see what you see."

About 100 miles northeast of Damascus as the crow flies, nearly 250 miles as the AT hiker walks, lies perhaps the most photographed location on the trail. McAfee Knob features both a tremendous view of a picture-postcard valley below, and a dramatic profile of the Knob itself, jutting majestically out into the sky. The silhouette of McAfee Knob, usually with a hiker or two proudly surveying their domain, is an icon of the Appalachian Trail like a moody Brooklyn Bridge is of New York City.

And like with the Brooklyn Bridge, access to McAfee Knob is relatively democratic. A large parking lot off a state highway, 15 miles from downtown Roanoke and 6 miles off the interstate, welcomes visitors to a nearby trailhead. It takes only a couple of hours to get to the lookout from there, and while it is a strenuous walk, it does not require any special knowledge or a particularly high level of fitness. On the hot and clear summer day I was there, three not-obviously fit young men spilled out of a well-worn pickup truck in the parking lot, apparently fueling their hike with nothing more than a bottle of Mountain Dew and a pack of cigarettes among them. They provided a sharp and, to my eyes, welcome contrast to the typical REI-adorned denizens of the trail (myself included).

Whom the trail is for, usually couched in terms of what it is for, has been a topic of debate among its users and stewards since its inception. Long-distance hiking or short-distance? Using obvious blazes for navigation, or requiring orienteering skills? Featuring steep ascents or more gradual switchbacks? Depending on how we answer these questions, and countless more, we stake out larger and smaller subsets of the population that are welcomed on the trail. It is not an easy calculus. Err on the side of accessibility and you take away the physical challenge that is the whole point of the trail for many of its users. Make it too forbidding and you've excluded a broad swath of the population from the benefits the trail is meant to provide.

To me, there are two things arguing for a widely accessible trail, not necessarily across its entire extent but for much of it. First, a more remote and demanding AT is unavoidably a more socially exclusive one. Have you got the right gear? Do you know what you're doing? Do you understand the customs? These are the kinds of questions that define country club membership, or middle-school social strata for that matter. To whatever extent they provide a feeling of accomplishment and belonging to those who master a difficult environment, they to an equal extent wall off and exclude others. We live in an era seemingly bereft of places where folks from different walks of life can experience their shared humanity; our home address, our online affiliations, even our eating habits signal our distance from one another. If the AT provided a way for an academic chomping granola and a laborer swilling an oversized soda to meet as equals before a nature that recognizes none of those social markers, I would argue that is a good thing.

The second argument for trail accessibility is particularly well illustrated by McAfee Knob. This iconic location is a part of the trail only because the federal government, using the threat of eminent domain and the power of tax dollars, purchased it on the public's behalf. As with any natural attraction, the challenge is to balance the public's use and enjoyment against protection of the remote qualities that make the trail worth visiting in the first place. But we can be more confident that the public spirit of the National Trails System Act is being lived up to when we see many different types of people embarking on many different kinds of hikes.

A day later, in Shenandoah National Park, the trail environment did not feel so inclusive.

Like the cast of characters who have populated this book, and its author, it was a strikingly white place.

Oriented north–south around the summits of Virginia's Blue Ridge about 75 miles from Washington, DC, Shenandoah is home to more than 100 miles of Appalachian Trail, nearly 5 percent of the trail's total length. The AT runs down the middle of the park, separated from but roughly parallel to the Skyline Drive parkway, with its RV campgrounds, lodges, and restaurants.

During an afternoon in the park, an overnight stay at one of the lodges, meals in the restaurant, and a short hike the following morning, I encountered roughly 250 people, including other guests, employees, hikers, and picnickers. Only one of them, a restaurant busser, looked African American to me, in a country where the African American population is 13 percent. No one appeared to be Latin American or Arab American or any version of American with a darker shade of skin color than my own.

In an era when the global diaspora is present not just in big cities but suburbs and small towns, such uniform whiteness seemed wildly off kilter. It suggested that the history of the American outdoors is very much alive in the present. Like so many aspects of the twentieth-century built environment, outdoor recreation and the parks to accommodate it were, to a great degree, created by and for the white middle class. Their biases and blind spots were designed into the landscape, in parks distant from cities, oriented around car travel, motivated by a sense of refuge not only from noise and smokestacks, but from the less refined and the lower class.

Over the course of my travels on the trail, I did see a more diverse group of people than that one day in Shenandoah, and both the Park Service and the AT community have gone to significant lengths to foster a more inclusive outdoors. But this one day served as a reminder that race, class, and nature have a complicated history with one another, and that past is by no means entirely in the rearview mirror.

The single unbroken mountain chain at the heart of the Appalachian Trail story occasionally has to make room for a more complicated reality, and Pennsylvania's Cumberland Valley, about 25 miles from where Earl Shaffer grew up, is a prime example. Surrounded by human habitation rather than expanses of forest, the AT winds through here like a shy person crossing a crowded bar.

Just south of the small town of Boiling Springs, the northbound trail descends into the valley from a state forest, exiting into a large tilled field, and jogging at right angles along the edges of farm plots for about a mile. Signs warn hikers that these are working agricultural areas, complete with pesticide use. On the day I walked through, a farmer on his tractor was working the fields just a stone's throw from the trail.

In Boiling Springs the trail passes through a town park, then meanders for several miles across the exurbia of greater Harrisburg, Pennsylvania, a region of more than half a million people. Skirting the farm fields and large-lot residential developments that typify the edges of metropolitan America, the trail is oddly incognito. You would never know, observing the otherwise nondescript line of woods at the back of these properties, that the world-famous Appalachian Trail was passing by.

Soon, though, the journey gets more complicated. The same break in the mountains that brings the trail down from its heights provides an ideal opening for the arteries of commerce. Two interstate highways run roughly east–west through the valley, making a flattened X on the map as they intersect. A third highway connects to both interstates, and is the ideal spot for various truckstops, distribution centers, and other outposts of the United States shipping industry. Weaving through this landscape of logistics is a thin ribbon of federally protected woods, shielding the AT's passage between parking lots of 18-wheelers and warehouses the size of multiple football fields. North of the highways, which the trail crosses on two road bridges and a purpose-built pedestrian bridge, it returns to the borderlands of sprawl, then ascends again to the protected forests of higher ground.

The AT's 12-mile journey across the Cumberland Valley brings into sharp relief an important aspect of the trail's whole existence. Conjuring a "wilderness footpath" from Georgia to Maine is in part an exercise in wishful thinking and selective perception. Even in the trail's earliest days, imagining a pristine alpine realm required not seeing the native history of the Appalachians, or the so-called mountain people eking out an existence deep in the woods, or the logging roads that provided crucial early trail connections. As postwar development pushed deeper into the countryside, threatening to break up the AT forever, the protection effort became more urgent and, by definition, more contrived. Isolating the trail from the change all around it meant carving out a narrow strip of exclusion from the actual landscape, an exercise not just in preservation but illusion.

That should not, in my view, undermine the trail's value or diminish the accomplishment of protecting it. But it does put the trail in a somewhat different light, in places as much about the inward-facing scenery as the outward-facing experience of the world.

• • •

As one gazes east from Kittatinny Ridge across the wooded landscape below, rolling hills gently recede in the distance, the green of the trees gently fading into the blue of the sky at the horizon, a classic mountain vista. One would never guess that this scenic vantage point is in New Jersey, or that over the horizon lies New York City, or that just 10 miles south of here, the AT is a sidewalk on an interstate toll bridge, with a waist-high concrete barrier separating hikers from I-80 traffic hurtling toward Gotham about 60 miles away.

It is surprising how quickly that world fades from consciousness up here, and takes its place in a much bigger story. Ascending the rocky trail, feeling the rise of the land in one's muscles and breathing, emerging from the forest to see the shape of the land as the tectonic

Looking east toward New York from New Jersey's Kittatinny Ridge.

plates and the glaciers made it, the fact of nature registers in a visceral way.

That this realization hits home in New Jersey, of all places, is a testament to its power. Even here, watching airplanes descend into Newark, one can sense a larger natural world, operating at its own scales of time and space, shaping and constraining our collective life even as we try to bend it to our will.

The AT alongside Interstate 80 at Delaware Gap.

Not for the first time on this trip, I discovered the trail prodding me in much the way Benton MacKaye intended. The power of nature suggested by the Appalachians' impressive heights was meant not just to provide an escape from the cities down below, but a better perspective on them, and an opportunity to reflect on the relationship between these two poles of our existence.

"There would be a chance to catch a breath, to study the dynamic forces of nature," he wrote in his 1921 article. And industry "would come to be seen in its true perspective, as a means in life and not an end in itself."

On the other side of the vast New York metropolitan area skirted by the AT, outside the quintessentially quaint New England town of Salisbury, Connecticut, the trail climbs to that state's highest peak, Bear Mountain. As it meanders up through the woods, the trail navigates around a handful of low rock walls that may or may not register in a hiker's pursuit of the higher ground ahead.

The walls are remnants of the farmlands that not too long ago were the defining feature of this land. Much of today's New England forest, including the section the AT winds through here, is of very recent vintage, grown on top of land shorn of its trees by early immigrants building a farm economy. Rocks pried from the land to make room for crops were piled at field edges, markers of property lines and progress. But by the mid-1800s, the agricultural clearing of New England had reached its peak. Farming largely moved elsewhere, abandoned fields reverted to woods, and the only reminders of yesterday's landscape are these trailside fragments.

The straight lines and stacked order of the walls, surrounded and overgrown by the forest's fecundity, are a little disorienting. Am I walking through nature here, or history? Whose history? The colonial settlers? The native populations that shaped their own environment for centuries but whose stories are ignored in our zeal to identify a seemingly pristine nature?

If the history represented in the walls in some sense doesn't count —if previous generations' devotion to their own visions of the best life are essentially meaningless—what does that say for this trail? The wall and the trail are both products of people's attempts to craft a home in the world, different outcomes for different times, but grounded in the same underlying aspiration to make the best of one's surroundings. Seeing yesterday's human endeavor subsumed under nature's inexorable advance is a sobering reminder that today's works, including this trail, are destined for the same fate.

A mile or so farther on, climbing toward a rocky outcrop called Lion's Head, I hear Willie Nelson singing. A local hiker, smartphone in hand, is streaming music out of his phone's speaker as he descends the trail. We talk briefly; he says he gets good data coverage up here, enough to keep the tunes flowing as he walks. From prehistoric landforms to Willie Nelson in the digital ether, the outdoors here seems not timeless, but the opposite: a jumble of multiple times all occupying a single place.

Two-hundred-and-fifty miles north in Franconia Notch, New Hampshire, it is the craggy, severe version of New England that is on display. The AT's route up Mt. Liberty from the valley below is a more or less straight line of steady, relentless ascent. No switchbacks, no leveling off, just a steep, mile-long staircase of jumbled rocks. The trail's job here is to get up to the White Mountains ridgeline, where the AT reaches its greatest northeastern heights. It does so with an admirable if challenging directness.

Near the peak, the Appalachian Mountain Club maintains one of several tenting sites aimed at concentrating and containing the crush of hikers that seek out the Whites' beauty each summer. Hundreds of hikers pitching their tents alongside the AT would turn a narrow pathway into a long, linear campground, so the White Mountains National Forest and the AMC work together to provide a small number of tent sites with platforms and privies, and require that hikers use them. It is a different way of doing business than on most of the rest of the AT, where pitching a tent gives you the freedom to do your own thing, one of several ways in which the AT takes something of a back seat to the AMC network of trails that preceded and helped inspire it. Another is the fact that the trails through here maintain their original AMC names, even the white-blazed ones serving as the AT. Directional signs point the way to three or four different AMC trails at a time, with just an "(A.T.)" appended after one of them. It sends a pretty clear message. The AT is not the only or even the most important hiking venue here. It is welcomed but also managed by the AMC.

At the Liberty Springs tent site this rainy day, the management job falls to Natalie, a recent college graduate and former student of

Liberty Springs Trail (A.T.).

mine, working as an AMC summer caretaker. She physically maintains the site and the nearby trail, organizes campers' use of the platforms, and serves as a resource to those passing through, educating hikers about the rules and best practices aimed at protecting this unique environment.

As we chat, a solo male hiker comes through. Natalie offers him granola bars from the stash left behind by last night's group, and lets him know this is the last good opportunity for water for a while. He seems a touch offended at the suggestion that he could be anything less than fully informed and self-sufficient, and marches on.

The caretaker resides in a roughly 8-foot-square tent on a wood platform perched on the side of the mountain, a short ways off the trail. There is just enough platform left over for a sort of front porch, and over a welcome cup of hot tea, she and I renew a conversation that began a few years earlier when she was planning her own successful thru-hike. I've been curious since I began work on this book about the Internet-ization of the AT, how the digital world shapes the trail experience, and she has acted as a sort of interpreter of that scene for me.

I learned about thru-hikers stocking up in trail towns not just on food and supplies, but on battery-pack charge and downloaded shows; trail shelters lit from the inside by the glow of smartphone screens; influencers building online followings to secure sponsorship from gear companies; and full-time streaming of a hiker's step-by-step location to the web. Between satellite connections, cellphone networks, and in-town WiFi, the blanket of data over much of the AT is considerable.

Based on Natalie's reports and my own online explorations, it seems there are three big changes the Internet has brought to the trail. The first is just how quickly and easily trail knowledge moves around. Getting a reliable map, informing loved ones of one's progress, and doing pre-trip research all happen in a digital instant, with practically no limits. Today's hiker is far less alone than in earlier times, with the expertise and support of the outside world vastly more readily available.

The second change is the inverse of the first: not only can hikers draw more easily on the wider world, they can broadcast back into it. The public performance of hiking, shared through and shaped by social media, to varying degrees determines hikers' experience of the trail, as people craft content to bolster their personal brand. (One can imagine Myron Avery for once being rendered completely speechless trying to make sense of such a thing.) The combination of these two factors—the massive support that became available and the unique social media fodder that it provided—likely helps explain the soaring popularity of thru-hiking in the 2000s and 2010s.

The third change wrought by the ubiquity of digital communication is the steady blurring of the dividing line between civilization and nature that has always defined the AT. City life—doing business, meeting people, and so on—used to depend on the physical proximity of face-to-face interaction, so all it took to excuse yourself from that world was to head out to the woods. But now that so many of these interactions happen virtually, through the devices in our pockets, separation becomes a lot harder. Civilization (and a nature defined as its absence) was once dependent on its physical setting; now it is wherever there is data, and that is just about everywhere. Of course you can always turn your phone off in the woods, or leave it behind altogether. But that is an option available at home as well. The distinction between the two places, once a fact of the physical circumstances, increasingly is just yet another personal choice.

As I descended from Mt. Liberty, my phone buzzed. It was my eighty-three-year-old mother, who lives alone, no doubt calling to be reminded about the details of my upcoming visit. I put off talking to her for a couple of hours, a child's responsibility sheepishly cast aside in favor of a belief that one doesn't take calls on the Appalachian Trail. (Justice was served when I lost track of the trail a short while later.) It was a reminder that the entanglements of everyday life do not disappear at the forest's edge.

Another 150 miles of trail distance to the northeast, and still more than 200 from Katahdin, the last stop on the day-hiking tour was Saddleback Mountain in Maine. Saddleback's peak was the site that in all of my travels, including hikes in previous years, most evoked the Appalachian Trail we carry around in our heads. The mountains in western Maine are not as high as their New Hampshire peers, nor as densely packed. They felt, on this day at least, less intimidating. But still from Saddleback's summit above the tree line, the patchy eye-level clouds would clear to reveal a stunning 360-degree view made up almost entirely of remote forest and alpine lakes. The AT stretched away in either direction, tracing the ridgeline into the distance, white blazes painted onto the occasional rock on the ground.

Eleven days' worth of zigzagging along the AT, ducking into and out of its peculiar environment, had left me with one overall impression: a century after they were first articulated, the trail's original ideals remain intact. Understanding the history of the trail can't help but puncture some of the mythology that has built up around it, but the opposite is also true, and to a greater degree. For all that the AT is a human construction, its opening up to nature still has the power to inspire. We do not need a simplistic fantasy of unsullied Creation to appreciate the parts of the universe that aren't us. It is enough to hold the contemporary world somewhat at bay, to make the intentional effort to see a bigger picture. Over 2,100 miles, in landscapes majestic and ordinary, that is the opportunity the trail affords us.

The AT on Saddleback Mountain.

ACKNOWLEDGMENTS

Thanks to Regina Ryan for agreeing to represent me and this book, to Lisa White at Houghton Mifflin Harcourt for acquiring it, and to everyone at HMH who shepherded it to publication.

A number of people in the AT community were gracious in sharing materials and stories with me. In particular, Brian King was very accommodating of my inquiries even as I presumed to delve into his area of expertise from out of the blue.

Thanks to George Ellison for showing me around Bryson City as I researched Horace Kephart.

Andrew Fedurek and Michelle Helner participated in the early research for Chapters 2 and 3, respectively. Natalie Burr patiently and capably answered my questions about the thru-hiking experience in the twenty-first century.

Many colleagues at the University of Michigan listened to me bounce ideas off them or let me quiz them on their knowledge of various topics relevant to the book. I won't attempt to list them here because I would surely leave someone out, but I am genuinely thankful. U-M's Institute for the Humanities Summer Fellowship, and the writing group that emerged from it, was an especially valuable collaboration. Thanks to Jason Tallant for his help with Jenny Kalejs's map illustrations.

Alan Hogg was the first reader for virtually every word here, acting as both perceptive critic and skilled editor.

Geoffrey Bankowski and I began a conversation about ambition, doubt, and the meaning of life way back in 1986; it continues to this day, and provided an invaluable anchor throughout the conception and writing of the book.

Avery and James Farmer endured their father blathering on about his book project with grace and wit, well beyond what I could have mustered at the same age, for which I am deeply appreciative.

Alicia Farmer put up with all the blathering and more, providing both savvy counsel and seemingly bottomless support, including pitching in near the end to wrangle the artwork. It is a simple fact that the book would not have happened without her and the partnership that we've built up over the years. I am grateful beyond words.

ILLUSTRATION CREDITS

NOTES

The two Europeans: Kohlstedt, *The Formation of the American Scientific Community.*

18   *Entering the wilderness:* Nash, *Wilderness and the American Mind.*

19   *"Geography ought to be":* Guyot, *The Earth and Man,* 21.

"Science thus comprehends": Guyot, *The Earth and Man,* 29.

It was translated: Jones, "Arnold Henry Guyot," 40.

21   *Sometimes the whole range:* Walls, "On the Naming of Appalachia."

"One of my first labors": Guyot, "On the Appalachian Mountain System," 159.

"the lamentations": Jones, "Arnold Henry Guyot," 32.

22   *On a typical:* Grant, "With Professor Guyot."

24   *In just one expedition:* Guyot letter to Henrietta Stillman Dana, Oct. 1859. Dana Family Papers, Box 2, Folder 61.

"which form a second forest growth": Avery and Boardman, "Arnold Guyot's Notes," 290.

There can be no doubt: E. Watson, "Mitchell, Elisha."

"My trip in the Smoky": Guyot letter to James D. Dana, Oct. 3, 1859. Dana Family Papers, Box 2, Folder 61.

25   *"When studying a group of mountains":* Guyot, Letter to the Editor of the *Asheville News,* 139.

His 1861 article: Guyot, "On the Appalachian Mountain System."

26   *"with a winning manner":* Jones, "Arnold Henry Guyot," 42.

He secretly prepared: Avery and Boardman, "Arnold Guyot's Notes"; Schulten, "Mapping Appalachia."

Charles Darwin had: Darwin, *On the Origin of Species.*

28   *"Let us not":* Guyot *Creation,* 6.

"The invisible is father": Guyot letter to James D. Dana, Feb. 16, 1880. Dana Family Papers, Box 2, Folder 61.

"even last year": Dana, *Memoir of Arnold Guyot,* 35.

"The marvelous unity": Guyot, *Creation,* 117.

2. BACK TO NATURE: HORACE KEPHART

29   *"I love the wilderness":* Quoted in Ellison and McCue, Introduction to *Camping and Woodcraft,* xxiv.

30   *Kephart was born:* General biographical background is drawn from Ellison, Introduction to *Our Southern Highlanders;* Ellison and McCue, Introduc-

tion to *Camping and Woodcraft*; and Stephens, "Librarian as Barbarian." The now-definitive source is Ellison and McCue, *Back of Beyond*.

"*I had no playmates*": Kephart, "Horace Kephart," 49.

"*not without misgivings*": Kephart, "Horace Kephart," 50.

31 "*enjoying the blessed privilege*": Kephart, "Horace Kephart," 50.

Fiske's tenure at Cornell: Cornell University Libraries, "The Passionate Collector."

32 "*A bell rings*": Kephart, "Continuity."

"*gives me what my*": Quoted in Stephens, "Librarian as Barbarian," 29.

33 "*Each month he was buying*": Miller, "Horace Kephart," 307.

"*My father was not*": Quoted in Ellison and McCue, Introduction to *Camping and Woodcraft*, xxv.

34 "*meeting point between savagery*": Turner, "The Significance of the Frontier in American History," 200.

Turner's lament: Marx, *The Machine in the Garden*, 19–24.

"*Frontier nostalgia*": Cronon, "The Trouble with Wilderness," 78.

"*Surrogate adventurers*": Schmitt, *Back to Nature*, xi.

35 "*The fire was all right*": Kephart, "Notes from Camp Nessmuk H.-Housing," 408.

"*Kephart's aura*": Miller, "Horace Kephart," 307.

37 "*In default of any other name*": Frost, "Our Contemporary Ancestors," 311. See also Batteau, *The Invention of Appalachia*.

"*He was much interested*": Miller, "Horace Kephart," 306.

38 a "*recent illness*": *Library Journal*, "Librarians," 270.

39 "*DRAWERS must fit*": Kephart, *Camping and Woodcraft*, 130.

"*A mountain settlement*": Kephart, *Our Southern Highlanders*, 30–31.

40 "*Any danger of this roost*": Kephart, *Our Southern Highlanders*, 71.

41 "*A camper should know*": Kephart, *Camping and Woodcraft*, 18.

42 "*at the first sign*": Quoted in Ellison and McCue, Introduction to *Camping and Woodcraft*, xxx.

43 *By this time*: Schmitt, *Back to Nature*.

"*Yesterday, after dipping into*": Letter to Kephart, July 12, 1919, illegible signature. Kephart Papers, MSS 80-24.1, Folder 5.

44 "*As a delighted reader*": Martin Baker to Kephart, Nov. 16, 1921. Kephart Papers, MSS 80-24.1, Folder 7.

"In the summer of 1904": Kephart, "Horace Kephart," 51.

45 *"Kep was his own":* Margaret Gooch to George Ellison, Feb. 6, 1977. Casada Collection, Box 2, Folder 30.

 The founding of: M. L. Brown, *The Wild East;* Pierce, *The Great Smokies.*

46 *At the heart of the campaign:* Kephart, *A National Park in the Great Smokies.*

47 *"It was a big undertaking":* Kephart letter, Sept. 12, 1928. Kephart Papers, MSS 80-24.1, Folder 11.

 "The Board seldom": Will C. Barnes, U.S. Geographic Board, to Kephart, Feb. 14, 1929. Kephart Papers, MSS 82-2.1, Folder 4.

 It had been lobbied: I. K. Stearns to Frank Bond, U.S. Geographic Board, Dec. 2, 1930. Kephart Papers, MSS 82-2.1, Folder 5.

48 *11-page historical monograph:* "Origin of Place Names in the Smoky Mountains." Kephart Papers, MSS 82-2.1, Folder 5.

49 *Masa, like his mentor: The Mystery of George Masa.*

 Kephart brought his expertise: Mittlefehldt, *Tangled Roots,* 46–48.

50 *"His writing in the camping field":* Kephart, "Then and Now," 57.

 "When I was a boy": Kephart, "Then and Now," 52.

51 *"The urban population":* Kephart, "Then and Now," 52.

 "Well, why should not": Kephart, "Then and Now," 57.

3. THE LONG TRAIL: JAMES P. TAYLOR

52 *"If patriotism is love of country":* Taylor, "Green Mountain Glimpses."

54 *Taylor arrived in Vermont:* Taylor Collection, "Biographical Sketch."

 As a child: Letter from Taylor's nephew, July 4, 1973. Green Mountain Club Records, Doc 225, Folder 20.

 Outside the classroom: Taylor to Walter H. Crockett, Aug. 12, 1930. Taylor Collection, Doc T7, Folder 13.

 Taylor attempted a new life: Taylor Collection, "Biographical Sketch."

 a "most valuable man": "Report of the Principal of Colgate Academy for the Academic Year ending June, 1907." Colgate University Board of Trustees Records, Box 15, Folder 72.

 back to graduate school: Colgate University Board of Trustees Records, Box 15, Folder 72.

 a letter of introduction: James C. Colgate to Harper Brothers Publishing, Nov. 1, 1907. Taylor Biographical File.

55 *a system of "degrees"*: "Mountain Club Degrees." Taylor Collection, Doc T2, Folder 25.

"A nonathletic boy": Untitled notes, Taylor Collection, Doc T2, Folder 24.

56 *"a Fifth Avenue of a trail"*: Taylor, "The Blazing," 6.

to the top of Killington Peak: Taylor, "The Blazing," 7.

the sense of Heimat: Wilson, *The German Forest*; Confino, *The Nation as a Local Metaphor*.

58 *now known as the* Westweg: Paris, "The Green Mountain Club"; Deutscher Wanderverband, *125 Jahre*.

further along the path: Schama, *Landscape and Memory*.

The Vermont that Taylor encountered: Harrison, *The View from Vermont*; D. Brown, *Inventing New England*.

59 *The Appalachian Mountain Club*: Waterman and Waterman, *Forest and Crag*; Isserman, *Continental Divide*; Chamberlin, *On the Trail*.

he conceived the idea: Taylor, "The Blazing"; Paris, "The Green Mountain Club"; Nuquist, "The Founding of the Green Mountain Club, 1910"; Waterman and Waterman, *Forest and Crag*; Curtis et al., *Green Mountain Adventure*.

"the Vermont mountains": Taylor, "The Blazing," 11.

"The Green Mountains": Taylor, Speech to University of Vermont Dinner 1911, Taylor Collection, Doc T2, Folder 24.

60 *a decidedly cool reception*: Taylor, "The Blazing."

aristocratic Alpine Club: Isserman, *Continental Divide*.

61 *"A little sensitive"*: Taylor, "The Blazing," 15.

The clinching event: Waterman and Waterman, *Forest and Crag*.

62 *Another outsider to the state*: Waterman and Waterman, *Forest and Crag*.

"He painstakingly combed": Waterman and Waterman, *Forest and Crag*, 365.

63 *"It is your job"*: R. Watson, "A Woman's 'Hike' in Vermont."

his next big idea: Waterman and Waterman, *Forest and Crag*.

64 As she approached: Davis, "Women of the Long Trail," 17–19.

"It is very kind": Green Mountain Club Records, Doc 229, Folder 49.

65 *Benton MacKaye took note*: MacKaye, "The Recreational Possibilities of Public Forests."

"pestered the life out of": Rutland Herald, "Jim Taylor."

hints at furtive intimacy: H. F. Miller to Taylor, Dec. 15, 1932. Taylor Collection, Doc T7, Folder 13.

66 *a frequent guest:* Cowles, "Green Mountain Chronicles."

    one friend urged him: Lucius Wilson to Taylor, Apr. 29, 1920. Taylor Collection, Doc T7, Folder 13.

    "Summer evenings": Taylor, "Green Mountain Glimpses."

    "supersalesman trailsman": Waterman and Waterman, *Forest and Crag,* 344.

67 *Green Mountain Parkway:* Goldman, "James Taylor's Progressive Vision"; Post, "The National Park That Got Away."

    Virginia's Shenandoah National Park: Simmons, "The Creation of Shenandoah National Park."

68 *"mysterious psychology":* Quoted in Goldman, "James Taylor's Progressive Vision."

70 *a testimonial dinner:* Taylor Collection, Doc T7, Folder 15.

    his last fight: Goldman, "James Taylor's Progressive Vision," 176.

    Again a round of fundraising: Taylor Collection, Doc T7, Folder 19.

    One morning in September: Associated Press, "Jim Taylor, State C. of C. Secretary, Believed Drowned"; *New York Times,* "Body of J.P. Taylor of Vermont is Found."

4. THE BIG IDEA: BENTON MACKAYE

71 *"Our job in the new exploration":* MacKaye, *The New Exploration,* 214.

72 *MacKaye was born:* The definitive and superb account of MacKaye's life is Anderson, *Benton MacKaye.* See also Bryant, "The Quality of the Day."

74 *He died soon thereafter:* Malloy, "Buffalo's Steele MacKaye."

    "a meeting house": MacKaye, *From Geography to Geotechnics,* 46.

    "from whom I received": Quoted in Bryant, "The Quality of the Day," 28.

75 *"I shall always recall":* MacKaye, *From Geography to Geotechnics,* 21.

    Forestry at that time: Hays, *Conservation and the Gospel of Efficiency.*

76 *"Forestry may be defined":* MacKaye, *From Geography to Geotechnics,* 26.

    Benton's brother James: MacKaye, *The Economy of Happiness.*

77 *the Weeks Act:* Bramwell and Lewis, "The Law that Nationalized the U.S. Forest Service."

    "The geologists, however": MacKaye, *From Geography to Geotechnics,* 31.

78 *"He had used his technical skills":* Anderson, *Benton MacKaye,* 74.

    the social economy of the forest: MacKaye, "Employment and Natural Resources."

80   *"The mountain land":* MacKaye, "The Recreational Possibilities of Public Forests," 10.

81   *"The series of roads and trails":* MacKaye, "The Recreational Possibilities of Public Forests," 29.

    "Here, then, with the mountain lands": MacKaye, "The Recreational Possibilities of Public Forests," 30.

82   *Jessie Hardy Stubbs:* In addition to Anderson, *Benton MacKaye,* see Schultz, "The Physical is Political."

83   *Betty had a nervous breakdown:* MacKaye to Ethelberta Hill, Apr. 23, 1921. MacKaye Family Papers, Box 165, Folder 6.

    a dispute erupted: Anderson, *Benton MacKaye,* 129–136.

84   *In the spring of 1921:* MacKaye to Ethelberta Hill, Apr. 23, 1921. MacKaye Family Papers, Box 165, Folder 6.

85   *"When we were married":* MacKaye to Ethelberta Hill, Apr. 23, 1921. MacKaye Family Papers, Box 165, Folder 6.

    "its threatened approach": Karl Karstens to MacKaye, Apr. 19, 1921. MacKaye Family Papers, Box 165, Folder 6.

    "You would adore the spot": Charles Whitaker to MacKaye, May 19, 1921. MacKaye Family Papers, Box 165, Folder 9.

    "Memorandum on Regional Planning": MacKaye Family Papers, Box 177, Folder 2.

86   *"Working out Appal. trail":* MacKaye Family Papers, Box 177, Folder 13.

    "Resting now on the top": MacKaye, "An Appalachian Trail," 326.

87   *"And this is the job":* MacKaye, "An Appalachian Trail," 327.

89   *His collaborator, Stein:* Larsen, *Community Architect.*

    "As a result": MacKaye to Stein, Feb. 26, 1922. MacKaye Family Papers, Box 165, Folder 11.

    "I am immensely interested": Stein to MacKaye, Mar. 2, 1922. MacKaye Family Papers, Box 165, Folder 11.

90   *"Upon my return":* MacKaye to Stein, Mar. 5, 1922. MacKaye Family Papers, Box 165, Folder 11.

    Torrey and Welch: Scherer, *Vistas and Vision.*

91   *a Washington meeting in 1925:* B. King, *The Appalachian Trail,* 33–34.

92   *a loose confederation:* Spann, *Designing Modern America.*

    "the fundamental world": MacKaye, *The New Exploration,* 71.

    "First it occupies": MacKaye, *The New Exploration,* 73.

93   *Arthur Perkins:* B. King, *The Appalachian Trail,* 34–35.

94   *The AT community was divided:* B. King, *The Appalachian Trail,* 60–65; Anderson, *Benton MacKaye,* 230–237; Ryan, *Blazing Ahead,* 157–170.

95   *"This clash of Trail":* Quoted in Bryant, "The Quality of the Day," 210.

96   *The Wilderness Society:* Sutter, *Driven Wild.*
     a multivolume work: Anderson, *Benton MacKaye,* 337.

97   *When a writer:* Stallings, "The Last Interview with Benton MacKaye."

5. THE ORGANIZATION: MYRON AVERY

98   *"A trail and its markings":* Avery, "Report of the Chairman to the Twelfth Appalachian Trail Conference," May 30, 1952. Appalachian Trail Conservancy Archives, Myron Haliburton Avery Memorial Volume.

99   *Avery was born:* The main events of Avery's life are drawn from Rubin, "The Short, Brilliant Life of Myron Avery."
     "Let us go forth": Quoddy Light high school yearbook, 1916. Avery Collection, Folder C221.
     worked every summer: Avery to New England Trail Conference, July 5, 1932. Avery Collection, Folder 19.

100 *"plugging away to win":* Quoted in PATC Bulletin 25th Anniversary issue, 1952. Appalachian Trail Conservancy Archives, Myron Halliburton Avery Memorial Volume.
     Katahdin was to many: Hakola, *Legacy of a Lifetime.*

101 *"Presenting a new country":* Avery memorandum on "Shenandoah National Park Trip." Appalachian Trail Conservancy Archives, Box 4-3-1.

102 *Perkins had come to hiking:* Rubin, "The Short, Brilliant Life of Myron Avery."
     "I sat with the Judge": Quoted in Niedzaliek, *A Footpath in the Wilderness,* 64.
     "I know there are lots": Perkins to Avery, Oct. 15, 1926. Avery Collection, Folder 11D.
     Potomac Appalachian Trail Club: Niedzaliek, *A Footpath in the Wilderness.*
     "Our first real work trip": Niedzaliek, *A Footpath in the Wilderness,* 12–13.

103 *an opening address:* "Appalachian Trail Conference Record of Annual Meeting." Kephart Papers, MSS 82-2.1, Folder 4.

104 *The new constitution:* "Constitution of the Appalachian Trail Conference." Kephart Papers, MSS 82-2.1, Folder 4.
     "The purpose of this organization": Kephart Papers, MSS 82-2.1, Folder 4.
     "had denigrated into": Avery, "The Appalachian Trail."

Judge Perkins suffered: Rubin, "The Short, Brilliant Life of Myron Avery."

105 *Avery hiked 70 miles:* Avery to Perkins, June 27, 1930. Appalachian Trail Conservancy Archives, Avery Correspondence General 1930–32.

"*which we shall polish*": Torrey to Perkins, Nov. 1, 1930. Appalachian Trail Conservancy Archives, Avery Correspondence General 1930–32.

106 *hiked 200 miles:* B. King, *The Appalachian Trail*, 55.

107 "*I am afraid*": Avery to Perkins, Aug. 30, 1930. Appalachian Trail Conservancy Archives, Avery Correspondence General 1930–32.

"*Now where are these markers*": Avery to Perkins, Oct. 27, 1930. Appalachian Trail Conservancy Archives, Avery Correspondence General 1930–32.

108 "*with the exception of*": Avery letter to ATC Board of Managers, Feb. 15, 1932. Appalachian Trail Conservancy Archives, Avery Correspondence General 1930–32.

"*The 200 mile link*": Avery letter to ATC Board of Managers, Feb. 15, 1932. Appalachian Trail Conservancy Archives, Avery Correspondence General 1930–32.

"*Were it not*": Avery letter to ATC Board of Managers, Feb. 15, 1932. Appalachian Trail Conservancy Archives, Avery Correspondence General 1930–32.

109 *crew of PATC volunteers:* Field, *Along Maine's Appalachian Trail*, 18.

Walter Greene: Ryan, *Blazing Ahead*.

the 1935 dispute: B. King, *The Appalachian Trail*, 60–65; Anderson, *Benton MacKaye*, 230–237; Ryan, *Blazing Ahead*, 157–170.

112 *the organization's bylaws:* Ellis, "The Path Not Taken."

113 "*major catastrophe*": Quoted in B. King, *The Appalachian Trail*, 76.

an archivist and editor: Washington Post, "Jean Stephenson, Retired Editor, Dies."

"*He was gone*": Quoted in Rubin, "The Short, Brilliant Life of Myron Avery."

115 "*I felt, upon reading*": William Showalter to Stephenson, Nov. 2, 1934. Appalachian Trail Conservancy Archives, Jean Stephenson Correspondence 1934–47.

"*unless, of course, before that time*": Stephenson to Showalter, Nov. 9, 1934. Appalachian Trail Conservancy Archives, Jean Stephenson Correspondence 1934–47.

"*To be frank with you*": Leonard C. Roy to Avery, May 7, 1937. Appalachian Trail Conservancy Archives, Jean Stephenson Correspondence 1934–47.

116 "*Even if the article*": Stephenson to Gilbert Grosvenor, May 5, 1939. Appa-

lachian Trail Conservancy Archives, Jean Stephenson Correspondence 1934–47.

"If we once get in mind": J. R. Hildebrand to Stephenson, June 22, 1939. Appalachian Trail Conservancy Archives, Jean Stephenson Correspondence 1934–47.

Katahdin protected as a national park: Hakola, *Legacy of a Lifetime.*

117   *an estimated 1,200 climbers:* Hakola, *Legacy of a Lifetime,* 126.

118   *"Many of us":* Avery to Baxter, Jan. 12, 1937. Avery Collection, Avery Papers, vol. 7, Jan.–Apr. 1937.

119   *"The need is so real":* Avery to Baxter, May 3, 1937. Avery Collection, Avery Papers, vol. 7, May–June 1937.

      "If you had worked": Baxter to Avery, May 12, 1937. Avery Collection, Avery Papers, vol. 7, May–June 1937.

120   *Forest Service warned:* B. King, *The Appalachian Trail,* 80.

121   *special phone line:* Rubin, "The Short, Brilliant Life of Myron Avery."

122   *He was hospitalized:* Rubin, "The Short, Brilliant Life of Myron Avery."

      "Letters indicated": Stephenson to Mrs. Stubbs, Maine State Librarian, July 30, 1952. Avery Collection, vol. 30, Avery miscellaneous correspondence.

      "came to the end of his trail": *Appalachian Trailway News,* "Myron H. Avery."

6. THE THRU-HIKE: EARL SHAFFER AND EMMA GATEWOOD

123   *"Why not walk":* Shaffer, *Walking with Spring,* 8.

      "I did it": Snow, "Pioneer Grandmother."

124   *actually from Appalachia:* Williams, *Appalachia: A History;* Raitz and Ulack, *Appalachia: A Regional Geography.*

      She was born: The details of Gatewood's life come primarily from Montgomery, *Grandma Gatewood's Walk,* and the chapter on Gatewood in Luxenberg, *Walking the Appalachian Trail.*

125   *"She thought of leaving him":* Montgomery, *Grandma Gatewood's Walk,* 34.

127   *Shaffer was born:* Shaffer's authorized biography is Donaldson and Forrester, *A Grip on the Mane of Life.*

      "He seemed to know": Undated manuscript. Shaffer Papers, Box 3, Folder 1.

129   *"millions of young reluctants":* "Plea for Valuation." Shaffer Papers, Box 10, Folder 11.

130   *a 1949 article:* A. Brown, "Skyline Trail from Maine to Georgia."

      "Had tough time": Shaffer, 1948 Hike Diary, 9.

"walked nearly ten miles": Shaffer, 1948 Hike Diary, 9.

"The choice now": Shaffer, *Walking with Spring,* 25.

Avery was quick to point out: Avery to ATC officers, Nov. 23, 1948. Shaffer Papers, Box 6, Folder 2.

in Avery's mind: Report to ATC Board, "Controversy over account of 1936 Boy Scout thru-hike," Nov. 2000. Shaffer Papers, Box 13, Folder 11.

132 *"For an hour and a half":* Shaffer, 1948 Hike Diary, 57.

Appalachian Mountain Club caretakers: Shaffer, *Walking with Spring,* 126.

133 *"In very good spirits":* Shaffer, 1948 Hike Diary, 89.

"Felt very lonesome": Shaffer, 1948 Hike Diary, 90.

"climbed Katahdin": Shaffer, 1948 Hike Diary, 95.

"This has been circulated": *Appalachian Trailway News,* "Georgia to Maine in One Trip."

134 *"I wish to emphasize":* Avery to ATC officers, Sept. 1, 1950. Shaffer Papers, Box 6, Folder 2.

Shaffer traveled to Shirley Center: Anderson, *Benton MacKaye,* 363.

MacKaye gave Shaffer: Shaffer, *Walking with Spring,* 3.

Many others at that time: Appalachian Trail Histories, "Early Thru Hikers."

136 *Gatewood arrived at:* The accounts of Gatewood's hikes are drawn from Montgomery, *Grandma Gatewood's Hike,* and Luxenberg, *Walking the Appalachian Trail.*

137 *Mary Snow covered women's sports: Sports Illustrated,* "Memo from the Publisher."

pointedly took note: Snow, "The Girls at Ponca City."

"Mrs. Gatewood, alone": Snow, "Pat on the Back."

138 *"tremendous courage":* Snow, "Pioneer Grandmother."

140 *hundreds of would-be thru-hikers:* Mittlefehldt, *Tangled Roots,* 103.

"Earl Shaffer's name is magic": Luxenberg, *Walking the Appalachian Trail,* 100.

"The image conveyed": Donaldson and Forrester, *A Grip on the Mane of Life,* 210.

141 *"In Earl Shaffer's lexicon":* Donaldson and Forrester, *A Grip on the Mane of Life,* 210.

142 *"The fog was burning off":* Shaffer, *Walking with Spring,* 19.

"The light of a clear dawn": Shaffer, *Walking with Spring,* 24.

a top priority: Don King to Shaffer, Apr. 17, 1985. Shaffer Papers, Box 2, Folder 12.

reached an agreement: Don King to Shaffer, Jan. 7, 1985. Shaffer Papers, Box 2, Folder 12.

143   *Shaffer returned:* B. King, *The Appalachian Trail*, 83.

the end of his trip: Donaldson and Forrester, *A Grip on the Mane of Life*, 280.

the ATC heard from: Report to ATC Board, "Controversy over account of 1936 Boy Scout thru-hike," Nov. 2000. Shaffer Papers, Box 13, Folder 11.

144   *"I am sorry":* "Report of Hiking Trip Via Appalachian Trail," Nov. 1948. Shaffer Papers, Box 6, Folder 2.

"He emphasizes": Appalachian Trailway News, "Georgia to Maine in One Trip."

may have missed 20 percent: McNeely, "Report on a Study of the Record," 19-2.

7. THE GOVERNMENT: GAYLORD NELSON

145   *"We need a comprehensive":* Nelson, "An End to Detergent Pollution," 4,835.

146   *"Happy" Nelson, as he was known:* The authoritative life of Nelson is Christofferson, *The Man from Clear Lake*.

149   *"For the first time":* Christofferson, *The Man from Clear Lake*, 82.

The electorate that made Nelson governor: For more on the emergence of environmental politics in this period, see Rome, *The Bulldozer in the Countryside*; Hays, *Beauty, Health and Permanence*; and Sellers, *Crabgrass Crucible*.

151   *Outdoor Recreation Act Program:* Christofferson, *The Man from Clear Lake*, 141–147.

"All these matters": Streyckmans, "Wisconsin Governor Outlines."

152   *Outdoor Recreation Resources Review Commission:* Olson, "Paper Trails."

federal Wilderness Act: Turner, *The Promise of Wilderness*.

153   *"three cents for Gaylord":* Christofferson, *The Man from Clear Lake*, 160.

"There once was a town": Carson, *Silent Spring*, 1.

154   *"No witchcraft":* Carson, *Silent Spring*, 3.

"The control of detergent pollution": Nelson, "An End to Detergent Pollution," 4,834.

156   *"new technical processes":* Udall, *The Quiet Crisis*, xii.

eating away at the pathway: Mittlefehldt, *Tangled Roots*, Chapter 3.

"He knew I was interested": Nelson, transcript of interview, Dec. 12, 1983. Nelson Papers.

157   *out of the blue:* Nelson, transcript of interview, Dec. 12, 1983. Nelson Papers.

Lyndon Johnson succeeded: Melosi, "Lyndon Johnson and Environmental Policy."

"We have always prided": Johnson, Remarks at the University of Michigan.

158 *"we need to copy":* Johnson, Special Message to the Congress on Conservation.

carefully worded letters: In Nelson Papers: Stanley Murray to Nelson, Jan. 30, 1965, Box 144, Folder 13; Walter Boardman to Senator Alan Bible, May 23, 1966, Box 144, Folder 12.

159 *a letter from Shirley Center:* MacKaye to Ed Garvey, Apr. 26, 1966. Nelson Papers, Box 144, Folder 18.

report was released: Bureau of Outdoor Recreation, "Trails for America."

160 *"I see no reason":* Nelson press release, May 24, 1968. Nelson Papers, Box 144, Folder 19.

"The trail system": Eissler, "The National Trail System Proposal."

162 *a nationwide teach-in:* Rome, *The Genius of Earth Day.*

163 *a front-page article:* Hill, "Environment May Eclipse Vietnam as College Issue."

165 *fivefold increase:* B. King, *The Appalachian Trail,* 110.

membership increased ten times: Mittlefehldt, *Tangled Roots,* 112.

"the typical American hiker": Chamberlin, *On the Trail,* 157.

8. THE NATIONAL PARK: DAVE RICHIE, PAM UNDERHILL, AND DAVE STARTZELL

168 *"Those who worked with":* Startzell, "The Long Journey of Dave Richie," 37.

"I don't know that he": Underhill, interview.

169 *"neither the Bureau of Outdoor Recreation":* Fairfax, "Federal-State Cooperation in Outdoor Recreation Policy Formation," 128.

"Half a dozen men": Fairfax, "Federal-State Cooperation in Outdoor Recreation Policy Formation," 145.

"a vigorous discussion": Fairfax, "Federal-State Cooperation in Outdoor Recreation Policy Formation," 128.

170 *10 percent of Richie's time:* Foster, *The Appalachian National Scenic Trail,* 32.

171 *Born in 1932:* The basics of Richie's life and career are drawn from Startzell, "The Long Journey of Dave Richie."

the gold fields of Alaska: Marina Richie, interview.

172 *"local artists":* Shales, "Glen Echo Coming to Life."

"*Richie said*": Hodge, "Bike Path to Extend South of Alexandria."

Richie began his work: Foster, *The Appalachian National Scenic Trail*.

173   *two significant shortcomings*: Fairfax, "Federal-State Cooperation in Outdoor Recreation Policy Formation."

new and improved NTSA: B. King, "The A.T. Bill of 1978."

a young single mother (and other life details): Underhill, interview.

174   "*not because I knew a damn thing*": Underhill, interview.

175   *Dave Startzell was on the other side* (and other life details): Startzell, interview.

"*ATC had made assurances*": Startzell, interview.

176   *passed it on to the ATC*: Foster, *The Appalachian National Scenic Trail*, 105; Startzell, interview.

178   *split among several private owners*: Mittlefehldt, *Tangled Roots*, 122; D. King, interview.

"*All of the sudden*": Underhill, interview.

"*we had a bookkeeper*": Startzell, interview.

179   *The comprehensive plan*: National Park Service, "Comprehensive Plan."

"*The body of the Trail*": National Park Service, "Comprehensive Plan," epigraph.

180   "*Richie liked principles*": Startzell, "The Long Journey of Dave Richie," 12.

"*When they speak*": Startzell, interview.

"*Those of us*": Underhill, interview.

181   *local trail clubs were not thrilled*: Startzell, interview.

"*ATC will serve*": "Memorandum of Agreement Between the National Park Service and the Appalachian Trail Conference Concerning the Appalachian Trail." Appendix F in Foster, *The Appalachian National Scenic Trail*, 162.

"*to have ATC tell NPS*": Quoted in Foster, *The Appalachian National Scenic Trail*, 96.

182   *convinced Startzell to stay on*: Startzell, interview.

183   "*it was literally*": Startzell, interview.

"*I was like a momma bear*": Underhill, interview.

184   *Cumberland Valley of Pennsylvania*: Mittlefehldt, *Tangled Roots*, 139–152.

a Franciscan monastery: Kilgannon, "Friars Locked in Dispute Over Land"; Risinit, "Friars, Feds Find Path to Common Ground"; Underhill, interview.

a federal judge ruled: U.S. Department of Interior vs. 16.03 Acres of Land.

its greatest transformation: Field, *Along Maine's Appalachian Trail*.

185   *It would take fifteen years*: This summary is based on a review of 55 news ar-

ticles in local and national publications about the Saddleback controversy, identified through a search of online newspaper databases.

186 *"They happened to come along"*: Quoted in Ellement, "Appalachian Trail: 50 years, 2,099 Miles."

188 *"He would have been a good steward"*: Quoted in Holmstrom, "Path With a View Is Center Of Maine Ski Resort Dispute."

"Mr. Rent-A-Riot": This is the late Chuck Cushman, founder of the American Land Rights Association. landrights.org/Staff.htm, accessed June 16, 2020.

push Underhill: Chappell, "Hearing on Trail Protection Disrupted."

Underhill was livid: Underhill, interview.

189 *"I was just sort of relieved"*: Startzell, interview.

190 *"I do not know why"*: Maine Land Use Regulation Commission, "Public Hearing," 453.

She was reprimanded: Underhill, interview.

has been acquired since: National Park Service, "Appalachian National Scenic Trail Protection Progress Report."

9. THE BESTSELLER: BILL BRYSON

192 *"I was still going"*: Bryson, *A Walk in the Woods*, 114.

193 *Bryson grew up*: Longden, "Famous Iowans."

his father had missed out: Bryson, *The Life and Times of the Thunderbolt Kid*, 265.

a charmed childhood: Bryson, *The Life and Times of the Thunderbolt Kid*.

194 *"a shit, really"*: Bryson, interview.

sentenced to juvenile detention: Bryson, *The Life and Times of the Thunderbolt Kid*, 257.

The two young men caroused: Bryson, *Neither Here Nor There*; Bryson, interview.

"I would spend": Bryson, interview.

a night in handcuffs: Churcher, "How a Drunken Drug Addict."

195 *hung over and a bit late*: Bryson, *Notes from a Small Island*, 53–54.

"On March 17": Bryson, "St. Patrick."

"It pains me": Bryson, "These Are Heady Times."

196 *"I didn't particularly want"*: Bryson, interview.

leave behind the daily grind: Bryson, interview.

"They always looked": Bryson, interview.

published an excerpt: Bryson, "Fat Girls in Des Moines."

"I come from Des Moines": Bryson, *The Lost Continent*, 3.

197   *his wife called:* Bryson, interview.

198   *"Coming to the end":* Yardley, "The Trashing of America."

"by the truckload": Donegan, "Bill Bryson: Lost in the Woods."

"I got more and more ambitious": Bryson, interview.

199   *"would get me fit":* Bryson, *A Walk in the Woods,* 4.

200   *"Every night":* Bryson, interview.

depressed and withdrawn: Bryson, interview.

"I have never been": Bryson, interview.

201   *"It was like somebody hit me":* Bryson, interview.

202   *"He was quite depressed":* Bryson, interview.

"a satirist": Garner, "Thinking on His Feet."

"it is a serious book": Lehmann-Haupt, "On the Trail, with Wit and Insights."

203   *"the best history":* B. King, "Book Reviews."

"There are those": *Appalachian Trailway News,* "Letters from our readers," 7.

"the last straw": *Appalachian Trailway News,* "Letters from our readers," 7.

204   *45 percent increase:* *Appalachian Trailway News,* "1999 Annual Report."

peaked in 2001: DeGagne, "Hiking Benton MacKaye's Hike."

his next bestseller: Bryson, *In a Sunburned Country.*

"In the beginning": Bryson, interview.

205   *a major event:* Gajewski, "'A Walk in the Woods' Director."

at various times: Gettell, "Ken Kwapis is Directing 'A Walk in the Woods.'"

206   *"There are a few chuckles":* Kermode, "'A Walk in the Woods' Review."

contentment of his household life: Kilen, "The Real Life of Bill Bryson's 'Stephen Katz.'"

Bryson fondly recalls: Bryson, interview.

"and he did me": Bryson, interview.

207   *"Being a writer":* Bryson, interview.

"We have a sacred duty": B. King, *The Appalachian Trail,* 12.

10. ON THE TRAIL

208   *"For it seems to me":* Schama, *Landscape and Memory,* 574.

212   *in opposition to cars:* Sutter, *Driven Wild.*

214   *"(1) to walk":* B. King, *The Appalachian Trail,* 112.

220   *"There would be a chance":* MacKaye, "An Appalachian Trail," 327.

221   *the forest's fecundity:* See Annie Dillard, "Fecundity," in *Pilgrim at Tinker Creek.*

BIBLIOGRAPHY

Anderson, Larry. *Benton MacKaye: Conservationist, Planner, and Creator of the Appalachian Trail.* Baltimore, MD: Johns Hopkins University Press, 2002.

Appalachian Trail Conservancy Archives. Appalachian Trail Conservancy, Harpers Ferry, WV.

Appalachian Trail Histories. "Early Thru Hikers." Online exhibit, available at https://appalachiantrailhistory.org/exhibits/show/hikers/hikerintro; accessed June 15, 2020.

Appalachian Trailway News. "Georgia to Maine in One Trip." January, 1949.

———. "Myron H. Avery." September, 1952.

———. "Letters from our readers." November–December, 1998.

———. "1999 Annual Report." September–October, 2000.

Associated Press. "Jim Taylor, State C. Of C. Secretary, Believed Drowned." September 7, 1949.

Avery, Myron. "The Appalachian Trail." *Scientific American* 153 (July 1935): 5–7.

Avery, Myron, Collection. Maine State Library Special Collections, Augusta.

Avery, Myron, and Kenneth S. Boardman. "Arnold Guyot's Notes on the Geography of the Mountain District of Western North Carolina." *North Carolina Historical Review* 15 (July 1938): 251–318.

Batteau, Joel. *The Invention of Appalachia.* Tucson: University of Arizona Press, 1990.

Birmingham, David. "The 1848 Unification of Switzerland." *History Today* 45 (Sept. 1995): 37–43.

Bramwell, Lincoln, and James G. Lewis. "The Law that Nationalized the U.S. Forest Service." *Forest History Today* (Spring/Fall 2011): 8–16.

Brown, Andrew. "Skyline Trail from Maine to Georgia." *National Geographic Magazine* (Aug. 1949): 219–251.

Brown, Dona. *Inventing New England: Regional Tourism in the Nineteenth Century.* Washington, DC: Smithsonian Institution Press, 1995.

Brown, Margaret Lynn. *The Wild East: A Biography of the Great Smoky Mountains.* Gainsville: University Press of Florida, 2000.

Bryant, Paul. "The Quality of the Day: The Achievement of Benton MacKaye." PhD diss., University of Illinois, 1965.

Bryson, Bill. "St. Patrick: Man of Multiple Myths." *Detroit Free Press,* March 17, 1978.

———. "These Are Heady Times, and His Head Is Splitting." *Los Angeles Times,* July 24, 1979.

———. "Fat Girls in Des Moines." *Granta* 23 (Spring 1988): 23–43.

———. *The Lost Continent: Travels in Small-Town America.* New York: Harper Perennial, 1989.

———. *Neither Here Nor There: Travels in Europe.* New York: Morrow, 1991.

———. *Notes from a Small Island.* New York: Doubleday, 1995.

———. *A Walk in the Woods: Rediscovering America on the Appalachian Trail.* New York: Broadway Books, 1998.

———. *In a Sunburned Country.* New York: Broadway Books, 2001.

———. *A Short History of Nearly Everything.* New York: Broadway Books, 2003.

———. *The Life and Times of the Thunderbolt Kid.* New York: Broadway Books, 2007.

———. Personal interview by Philip D'Anieri, October 20, 2019.

Bureau of Outdoor Recreation. "Trails for America: Report on the Nationwide Trails Study." Washington, DC: U.S. Department of the Interior, 1966.

Carson, Rachel. *Silent Spring.* Boston: Houghton Mifflin, 1962.

Casada Collection of Horace Kephart and George Masa. University of Tennessee, Knoxville, Special Collections Library.

Chamberlin, Silas. *On the Trail: A History of American Hiking.* New Haven, CT: Yale University Press, 2016.

Chappell, George. "Hearing on Trail Protection Disrupted." *Bangor Daily News,* August 5, 1999.

Christofferson, Bill. *The Man from Clear Lake: Earth Day Founder Senator Gaylord Nelson.* Madison: University of Wisconsin Press, 2004.

Churcher, Sharon. "How a Drunken Drug Addict Took a Walk in the Woods with Bill Bryson . . . and Came Out as Paul Newman." *Mail on Sunday,* May 15, 2005.

Colgate University Board of Trustees Records. Colgate University Special Collections and University Archives, Hamilton, NY.

Confino, Alon. *The Nation as a Local Metaphor: Wurttemberg, Imperial Germany, and National Memory, 1871–1918.* Chapel Hill: University of North Carolina Press, 1997.

Cornell University Libraries. "The Passionate Collector: Willard Fiske and His Libraries." Online exhibit, available at https://rmc.library.cornell.edu/collector/index.html; accessed May 28, 2020.

Cowles, John T. "Green Mountain Chronicles." Oral History Transcriptions. Vermont Historical Society, Barre.

Cronon, William. "The Trouble with Wilderness; or, Getting Back to the Wrong Nature," in *Uncommon Ground: Toward Reinventing Nature*, ed. William Cronon. New York: W. W. Norton, 2004.

Curtis, Jane, Will Curtis, and Frank Lieberman. *Green Mountain Adventure: Vermont's Long Trail.* Waterbury Center, VT: Green Mountain Club, 1985.

Dana Family Papers. Yale University Library Manuscripts and Archives, New Haven, CT.

Dana, James D. *Memoir of Arnold Guyot 1807–1884.* Washington, DC: Judd and Detweiler, 1886.

Darwin, Charles. *On the Origin of Species by Natural Selection.* London: John Murray, 1859.

Davis, Teresa. "Women of the Long Trail 1910–1940." Undergraduate paper, Dartmouth College, 1993.

DeGagne, Julia. "Hiking Benton MacKaye's Hike: Expanding the Appalachian Trail Experience." Master's thesis, University of Pennsylvania, 2007.

Deutscher Wanderverband. *125 Jahre Wandern und mehr.* Petersberg, Germany: Michael Imhof Verlag, 2008.

Dillard, Annie. *Pilgrim at Tinker Creek.* New York: Bantam Books, 1975.

Donaldson, David, and Maurice Forrester. *A Grip on the Mane of Life: An Authorized Biography of Earl V. Shaffer.* Gardners, PA: Appalachian Trail Museum, 2014.

Donegan, Lawrence. "Bill Bryson: Lost in the Woods." *The Guardian*, October 27, 1997.

Eissler, Frederick. "The National Trail System Proposal." *Sierra Club Bulletin*, June 1966.

Ellement, John. "Appalachian Trail: 50 years, 2,099 Miles." *Boston Globe*, August 16, 1987.

Ellis, George. "The Path Not Taken." Master's thesis, Shippensburg University, 1993.

Ellison, George. Introduction to *Our Southern Highlanders*, by Horace Kephart. Gatlinburg, TN: Great Smoky Mountains Association, 2014.

Ellison, George, and Janet McCue. *Back of Beyond: A Horace Kephart Biography*. Gatlinburg, TN: Great Smoky Mountains Association, 2019.

———. Introduction to *Camping and Woodcraft*, by Horace Kephart. Gatlinburg, TN: Great Smoky Mountains Association, 2011.

Fairfax, Sally. "Federal-State Cooperation in Outdoor Recreation Policy Formation: The Case of the Appalachian Trail." PhD diss., Duke University, 1974.

Ferrell, Edith. "Arnold Henry Guyot 1807–1884." *Geographers Biobibliographical Studies* 5 (1981): 63–76.

Field, David. *Along Maine's Appalachian Trail*. Charleston, SC: Arcadia Publishing, 2011.

Foster, Charles. *The Appalachian National Scenic Trail: A Time to Be Bold*. Harpers Ferry, WV: Appalachian Trail Conference, 1987.

Frost, William Goodell. "Our Contemporary Ancestors in the Southern Mountains." *Atlantic Monthly* 83 (Jan. 1899): 311–319.

Gajewski, Ryan. "'A Walk in the Woods' Director on Why Robert Redford Put Film on Shelf After Paul Newman's Death." *Hollywood Reporter*, September 2, 2015.

Garner, Dwight. "Thinking on His Feet." *New York Times Book Review*, May 31, 1998.

Gettell, Oliver. "Ken Kwapis is Directing 'A Walk in the Woods.'" *Los Angeles Times*, May 5, 2014.

Goldman, Hal. "James Taylor's Progressive Vision: The Green Mountain Parkway." *Vermont History* 63 (Summer 1995): 158–179.

Grant, S. Hastings. "With Professor Guyot on Mounts Washington and Carrigain in 1857." *Appalachia* 11 (June 1907): 229–239.

Green Mountain Club Records. Vermont Historical Society, Barre.

Guyot, Arnold. Letter to the Editor of the *Asheville News*, July 18, 1860. Reprinted in Thomas L. Clingman, *Selections from the Speeches and Writings of Hon. Thomas L. Clingman, of North Carolina*. Raleigh, NC: John Nichols, 1877.

———. "On the Appalachian Mountain System." *American Journal of Science and Arts* 31 (1861): 157–187.

———. *The Earth and Man*. Boston: Gould and Lincoln, 1869. (Original work published 1849.)

———. *Memoir of Louis Agassiz 1807–1873*. Princeton, NJ: Robinson and Co., 1883.

————. *Creation, or the Biblical Cosmogony in the Light of Modern Science.* New York: Charles Scribner's Sons, 1884.

Hakola, John. *Legacy of a Lifetime: The Story of Baxter State Park.* Woolwich, ME: TBW Books, 1981.

Harrison, Blake. *The View from Vermont: Tourism and the Making of an American Rural Landscape.* Burlington: University of Vermont Press, 2006.

Hays, Samuel P. *Conservation and the Gospel of Efficiency: The Progressive Conservation Movement, 1890–1920.* Cambridge, MA: Harvard University Press, 1959.

————. *Beauty, Health, and Permanence: Environmental Politics in the United States, 1955–1985.* New York: Cambridge University Press, 1987.

Hill, Gladwin. "Environment May Eclipse Vietnam as College Issue." *New York Times,* November 30, 1969.

Hodge, Paul. "Bike Path to Extend South of Alexandria." *Washington Post,* November 11, 1971.

Holmstrom, David. "Path With a View Is Center Of Maine Ski Resort Dispute." *Christian Science Monitor,* June 6, 1997.

Irmscher, Christoph. *Louis Agassiz: Creator of American Science.* New York: Houghton Mifflin Harcourt, 2013.

Isserman, Maurice. *Continental Divide: A History of American Mountaineering.* New York: W. W. Norton, 2016.

Johnson, Lyndon. Remarks at the University of Michigan, May 22, 1964. Available online at the American Presidency Project, www.presidency.ucsb.edu/documents/remarks-the-university-michigan.

————. Special Message to the Congress on Conservation and Restoration of Natural Beauty, February 8, 1965. Available online at the American Presidency Project, www.presidency.ucsb.edu/documents/special-message-the-congress-conservation-and-restoration-natural-beauty.

Jones, Leonard. "Arnold Henry Guyot." *Union College Bulletin* 23 (Jan. 1930): 31–57.

Kephart, Horace. "Continuity." *Harper's Weekly* 34 (Aug. 20, 1890): 686.

————. "Notes from Camp Nessmuk." *Forest and Stream* 44 (1895): 343, 408, 440, 460.

————. *Our Southern Highlanders.* New York: Outing Publishing Co., 1913.

————. "Horace Kephart." *North Carolina Library Bulletin* 5 (June 1922): 49–53.

————. *A National Park in the Great Smokies.* Raleigh: North Carolina Park Commission, 1925.

————. "Then and Now." *National Sportsman* (April 1931): 52–57.

————. *Camping and Woodcraft*. Gatlinburg, TN: Great Smoky Mountains Association, 2011. (Original work published 1916.)

Kephart, Horace, Papers. Western Carolina University Library Special Collections, Cullowhee, NC.

Kermode, Mark. "'A Walk in the Woods' Review: Undemanding Hiking Comedy." *The Observer*, September 20, 2015.

Kilen, Mike. "The Real Life of Bill Bryson's 'Stephen Katz.'" *Des Moines Register*, August 31, 2015.

Kilgannon, Corey. "Friars Locked in Dispute Over Land." *New York Times*, August 1, 2000.

King, Brian. "Book Reviews." *Appalachian Trailway News* (July/Aug. 1998): 30.

————. *The Appalachian Trail: Celebrating America's Hiking Trail*. New York: Rizzoli, 2012.

————. "The A.T. Bill of 1978: 'Protection Necessary to Preserve.'" A.T. Footpath Blog, Appalachian Trail Conservancy, March 18, 2018.

King, Don. Phone interview by Philip D'Anieri, March 12, 2019.

Kohlstedt, Sally Gregory. *The Formation of the American Scientific Community: The American Association for the Advancement of Science, 1848–1860*. Champaign: University of Illinois Press, 1976.

Larsen, Kristin. *Community Architect: The Life and Vision of Clarence S. Stein*. Ithaca, NY: Cornell University Press, 2016.

Lehmann-Haupt, Christopher. "On the Trail, with Wit and Insights." *New York Times*, May 21, 1998.

Library Journal 29 (May 1904): 270. "Librarians."

Longden, Tom. "Famous Iowans: Bill Bryson." *Des Moines Register*, April 27, 2003.

Luxenberg, Larry. *Walking the Appalachian Trail*. Mechanicsburg, PA: Stackpole Books, 1994.

MacKaye, Benton. "The Recreational Possibilities of Public Forests." *Journal of the New York State Forestry Association* 3 (Oct. 1916): 4–10, 29–31.

————. "Employment and Natural Resources." Washington, DC: U.S. Government Printing Office, 1919.

————. "An Appalachian Trail: A Project in Regional Planning." *Journal of the American Institute of Architects* 9 (Oct. 1921): 325–330.

————. *The New Exploration: A Philosophy of Regional Planning*. Champaign: University of Illinois Press, 1962. (Originally published 1928.)

————. *From Geography to Geotechnics.* Edited by Paul Bryant. Champaign: University of Illinois Press, 1968.

MacKaye, James. *The Economy of Happiness.* Boston: Little, Brown and Co., 1906.

MacKaye Family Papers. Rauner Special Collections Library, Dartmouth College, Hanover, NH.

Maine Land Use Regulation Commission. "Public Hearing, Zoning Petition ZP 702, Maine Mountain Power, LLC." September 2007.

Malloy, Jerry. "Buffalo's Steele MacKaye, the 'Father of Modern Acting.'" *Buffalo History Gazette.* www.buffalohistorygazette.net/2011/06/buffalo-steele -mackaye-of-modern-acting.html, accessed June 14, 2020.

Martin, Geoffrey J. *All Possible Worlds: A History of Geographical Ideas,* 4th ed. New York: Oxford University Press, 2005.

Marx, Leo. *The Machine in the Garden: Technology and the Pastoral Ideal in America.* New York: Oxford University Press, 1964.

McNeely, James. "Report on a Study of the Record as to the Actual Route of the 1948 Appalachian Trail Hike of Earl V. Shaffer from Mt. Oglethorpe, GA to Rockfish Gap, VA (April 3, 1948–May 19, 1948)." Available at www.atmuseum .org/uploads/5/5/8/1/55813761/shaf-report-509.pdf.

McPhee, John. *Annals of the Former World.* New York: Farrar, Straus and Giroux, 1998.

Melosi, Martin. "Lyndon Johnson and Environmental Policy," in *The Johnson Years, Volume Two: Vietnam, the Environment, and Science,* ed. Robert Divine. Lawrence: University Press of Kansas, 1987.

Miller, Clarence. "Horace Kephart, A Personal Glimpse." *Missouri Historical Society Bulletin* 15 (June 1959): 304–310.

Mittlefehldt, Sarah. *Tangled Roots: The Appalachian Trail and American Environmental Politics.* Seattle: University of Washington Press, 2013.

Montgomery, Ben. *Grandma Gatewood's Walk: The Inspiring Story of the Woman Who Saved the Appalachian Trail.* Chicago, IL: Chicago Review Press, 2014.

The Mystery of George Masa. Documentary film. Asheville, NC: Bonesteel Films, 2002.

Nash, Roderick. *Wilderness and the American Mind,* 4th ed. New Haven, CT: Yale University Press, 2001.

National Park Service. "Comprehensive Plan for the Protection, Management, Development and Use of the Appalachian National Scenic Trail." September 1981. Harpers Ferry, WV: Appalachian Trail Project Office.

————. "Appalachian National Scenic Trail Protection Progress Report." July 31, 2019.

Nelson, Gaylord, Papers. Wisconsin Historical Society, Madison.

————. "An End to Detergent Pollution." *Congressional Record* 109, part 4 (March 15 to April 3, 1963): 4834–4837.

New York Times. "Body of J.P. Taylor of Vermont is Found." September 11, 1949.

Niedzaliek, Carol, ed. *A Footpath in the Wilderness: The Early Days of PATC.* Vienna, VA: Potomac Appalachian Trail Club, 2003.

Nuquist, Reidun. "The Founding of the Green Mountain Club, 1910." *Vermont History News* 36 (May–June 1985).

Olson, Brent. "Paper Trails: The Outdoor Recreation Resource Review Commission and the Rationalization of Recreational Resources." *Geoforum* 41 (May 2010): 447–456.

Paris, Louis. "The Green Mountain Club." *The Vermonter* 16 (May 1911): 151–170.

Pierce, Daniel. *The Great Smokies: From Natural Habitat to National Park.* Knoxville: University of Tennessee Press, 2000.

Post, Bruce. "The National Park That Got Away." *Burlington Free Press,* March 4, 2016.

Raitz, Karl, and Richard Ulack. *Appalachia: A Regional Geography.* Boulder, CO: Westview Press, 1984.

Richie, Marina. Phone interview by Philip D'Anieri, February 27, 2019.

Risinit, Michael. "Friars, Feds Find Path to Common Ground." *Journal News* [White Plains, NY], March 9, 2001.

Rome, Adam. *The Bulldozer in the Countryside: Suburban Sprawl and the Rise of American Environmentalism.* New York: Cambridge University Press, 2001.

————. *The Genius of Earth Day: How a 1970 Teach-In Unexpectedly Made the First Green Generation.* New York: Farrar, Straus and Giroux, 2013.

Rubin, Robert. "The Short, Brilliant Life of Myron Avery," in *Trail Years: A History of the Appalachian Trail Conference,* special commemorative issue of *Appalachian Trailway News,* July 2000: 22–29.

Rutland Herald. "Jim Taylor." September 14, 1949.

Ryan, Jeffrey. *Blazing Ahead: Benton MacKaye, Myron Avery, and the Rivalry That Built the Appalachian Trail.* Boston: Appalachian Mountain Club Books, 2017.

Schama, Simon. *Landscape and Memory.* New York: Knopf, 1995.

Scherer, Glenn. *Vistas and Vision: A History of the New York-New Jersey Trail Conference.* New York: New York-New Jersey Trail Conference, 1995.

Schmitt, Peter. *Back to Nature: The Arcadian Myth in Urban America.* New York: Oxford University Press, 1969.

Schulten, Susan. "Mapping Appalachia." *New York Times,* June 6, 2013.

Schultz, Jaime. "The Physical is Political: Women's Suffrage, Pilgrim Hikes and the Public Sphere." *International Journal of the History of Sport* 27, no. 2 (Apr. 2010): 1133–1153.

Sellers, Christopher. *Crabgrass Crucible: Suburban Nature and the Rise of Environmentalism in Twentieth-Century America.* Chapel Hill: University of North Carolina Press, 2012.

Shaffer, Earl. "Earl Shaffer's Appalachian Trail Hike Diary, 1948." Washington, DC: Smithsonian Institution Transcription Center. Available online at https://amhistory.si.edu/media/NMAH-Ac0828-0000025.pdf.

———. *Walking with Spring.* Harpers Ferry, WV: Appalachian Trail Conference, 1983.

———. *The Appalachian Trail: Calling Me Back to the Hills.* Englewood, CO: Westcliffe Publishers, 2001.

Shaffer, Earl, Papers. Archives Center, National Museum of American History, Washington, DC.

Shales, Tom. "Glen Echo Coming to Life." *Washington Post,* March 13, 1972.

Shankman, David, and L. Allan James. "Appalachia and the Eastern Cordillera," in *The Physical Geography of North America,* ed. Anthony Orme. New York: Oxford University Press, 2002.

Simmons, Daniel. "The Creation of Shenandoah National Park and the Skyline Drive, 1924–1936." PhD diss., University of Virginia, 1978.

Snow, Mary. "The Girls at Ponca City." *Sports Illustrated,* July 4, 1955: 17.

———. "Pat on the Back: Mrs. Emma Gatewood." *Sports Illustrated,* August 15, 1955: 84.

———. "Pioneer Grandmother." *Sports Illustrated,* October 10, 1955: 12.

Spann, Edward. *Designing Modern America: The Regional Planning Association of America and Its Members.* Columbus: Ohio State University Press, 1996.

Sports Illustrated. "Memo from the Publisher." November 12, 1956.

Stallings, Constance. "The Last Interview with Benton MacKaye." *Backpacker,* April 1976: 54–57, 81–85.

Startzell, Dave. "The Long Journey of Dave Richie, 1932–2002." *Appalachian Trailway News,* March–April 2003.

———. Personal interview by Philip D'Anieri, February 15, 2019.

Stephens, Dennis. "Librarian as Barbarian: Horace Kephart, 1862–1931." *PNLA Quarterly* 67 (Fall 2002): 28–31.

Streyckmans, Felix. "Wisconsin Governor Outlines Broad and Progressive Recreation Program." Izaak Walton League newsletter, July 1962. Madison: Wisconsin Historical Society. Available online at nelsonearthday.net.

Sutter, Paul. *Driven Wild: How the Fight Against Automobiles Launched the Modern Wilderness Movement.* Seattle: University of Washington Press, 2002.

Taylor, James P. "The Blazing," in *Footpath in the Wilderness: The Long Trail in the Green Mountains of Vermont.* Middlebury, VT: Middlebury College Press, 1941.

———. "Green Mountain Glimpses: Winter." In Green Mountain Club Records. Vermont Historical Society, Barre.

Taylor, James P., Biographical File. Colgate University Special Collections and University Archives, Hamilton, NY.

Taylor, James P., Collection. Vermont Historical Society, Barre.

Thoreau, Henry David. "Ktaadn," in *A Week on the Concord and Merrimack Rivers; Walden, or, Life in the Woods; The Maine Woods; Cape Cod.* New York: Library of America, 1985.

Turner, Frederick Jackson. "The Significance of the Frontier in American History," in *Report of the American Historical Association for the Year 1893.* Washington, DC: American Historical Association, 1894, pp. 199–227.

Turner, James Morton. *The Promise of Wilderness: American Environmental Politics since 1964.* Seattle: University of Washington Press, 2012.

Udall, Stewart. *The Quiet Crisis.* New York: Holt, Rinehart and Winston, 1963.

Underhill, Pam. Personal interview by Philip D'Anieri, February 15, 2019.

U.S. Department of Interior vs. 16.03 Acres of Land, 26 F. 3d 349 (1994).

Walls, David. "On the Naming of Appalachia," in *An Appalachian Symposium: Essays Written in Honor of Cratis D. Williams,* ed. J. W. Williamson. Boone, NC: Appalachian State University Press, 1977.

Waterman, Laura, and Guy Waterman. *Forest and Crag: A History of Hiking, Trail Blazing, and Adventure in the Northeast Mountains.* Boston: Appalachian Mountain Club, 1989.

Washington Post. "Jean Stephenson, Retired Editor, Dies." January 26, 1979.

Watson, Elgiva. "Mitchell, Elisha," in *Dictionary of North Carolina Biography,* 6 vols., ed. William S. Powell. Chapel Hill: University of North Carolina Press, 1979–1996.

Watson, Rose. "A Woman's 'Hike' in Vermont; How She Tramped Over the New Mountain Highway Constructed by the Green Mountain Club." *New York Times*, August 22, 1915.

Williams, John Alexander. *Appalachia: A History*. Chapel Hill: University of North Carolina Press, 2002.

Wilson, Jeffrey. *The German Forest: Nature, Identity, and the Contestation of a National Symbol, 1871–1914*. Toronto: University of Toronto Press, 2012.

Wulf, Andrea. *The Invention of Nature: Alexander von Humboldt's New World*. New York: Knopf, 2015.

Yardley, Jonathan. "The Trashing of America." *Washington Post*, September 3, 1989.

INDEX